ArtScroll Mesorah Series®

Rabbi Nosson Scherman / Rabbi Meir Zlotowitz

General Editors

simchas torah

SHEMINI ATZERES/SIMCHAS TORAH — ITS
SIGNIFICANCE, LAWS, AND PRAYERS / A PRESENTATION
BASED ON TALMUDIC AND TRADITIONAL SOURCES.

Published by
Mesorah Publications, ltd

שְׁמִינִי עֲצֶרֶת־
שִׂמְחַת תּוֹרָה

by
Rabbi Moshe Lieber

Overview by
Rabbi Nosson Scherman

FIRST EDITION
First Impression . . . August 1996

Published and Distributed by
MESORAH PUBLICATIONS, Ltd.
4401 Second Avenue
Brooklyn, New York 11232

Distributed in Europe by
J. LEHMANN HEBREW BOOKSELLERS
20 Cambridge Terrace
Gateshead, Tyne and Wear
England NE8 1RP

Distributed in Israel by
SIFRIATI / A. GITLER — BOOKS
4 Bilu Street
P.O.B. 14075
Tel Aviv 61140

Distributed in Australia & New Zealand by
GOLDS BOOK & GIFT CO.
36 William Street
Balaclava 3183, Vic., Australia

Distributed in South Africa by
KOLLEL BOOKSHOP
22 Muller Street
Yeoville 2198, Johannesburg, South Africa

ARTSCROLL MESORAH SERIES ®
"SHEMINI ATZERES / SIMCHAS TORAH" — Its Significance, Laws, and Prayers
© Copyright 1996, by MESORAH PUBLICATIONS, Ltd.
4401 Second Avenue / Brooklyn, N.Y. 11232 / (718) 921-9000

ISBN
0-89906-317-9 (hard cover)
0-89906-318-7 (paperback)

Typography by Compuscribe at ArtScroll Studios, Ltd.

Printed in the United States of America by Noble Book Press
Bound by Sefercraft, Quality Bookbinders, Ltd. Brooklyn, N.Y.

Table of Contents

⊰ Selected Laws and Customs

⊰ Observance

⊸§ Preface

Yamim Tovim are not days of joy, they are days for joy. As wellsprings of joy, we draw inspiration from them throughout the year (Chidushei HaRim).

As humdrum as our everyday existence may become, we all are able to experience moments of greatness when we are elevated beyond our "natural" limitations and spiritually come in contact with our true selves.

Every *Yom Tov* serves as a spiritual way-station. We finish a *Yom Tov*, but we never leave it. We look back to it and desperately try to hold on to the heightened perspective we enjoyed during that special time. It is the *Yom Tov* that we anxiously await, focusing our spiritual telescope on it, hoping that it serve as the safe port to which we will steer the battered ship of our mundane existence.

In the words of R' Yitzchok Hutner זצ״ל, "Never say a *Yom Tov* is gone. Say instead, 'I have experienced another *Yom Tov.'"

Shemini Atzeres imbues us with the realization of how much our Father loves us; Simchas Torah joyously uplifts us making us cognizant of how much we love Him. It is my heartfelt hope that this *sefer* afford others a taste of these unique *Yamim Tovim* as I have experienced them.

My father ז״ל, R' Aharon ב״ר Moshe Mordechai, was the quintessential *Simchas Torah Yid* — every day of the year. Hundreds of young people were brought to Torah and *Yiddishkeit* through being exposed to his infectious joy. Even those who never were able to make the full trek back were moved and uplifted by his penetrating love of life and *Yiddishkeit*.

My Rebbe זצ״ל, HaRav Shlomo Freifeld, sought all his life to teach the secret of סַלְסְלֶהָ וּתְרוֹמְמֶךָ, *Lovingly caress it and it will uplift you* (Proverbs 4:8). Torah must not merely be studied; it must infiltrate our minds, hearts and emotions and force us to engage with our מְאֹד, the great treasure trove of "veryness" which can help us propel ourselves to be bigger than the midget-like dimensions to which our spiritual narrowness might otherwise confine us.

I dedicate this *sefer* לעלוי נשמתם, with a prayer that their teachings penetrate my heart and the hearts of my dear family.

I wish to acknowledge the editorial assistance of R' Shimon and Tova Finkelman, Mrs. Judi Dick and Ms. Faygie Silverman. R' Moshe Weinberger graciously provided unlimited access to his library. My *chavrusah*, R' Mattis Friedman, served as a constructive sounding board for much of what I wrote. *Yiyasher kochachem*!

To R' Meir Zlotowitz, R' Nosson Scherman and R' Sheah Brander, I humbly offer my thanks for the *zechus* to be a foot soldier in the ArtScroll Revolution.

May the *Ribbono Shel Olam* grant me, my wife Batsheva תחי׳ and our children עמו״ש opportunities to serve as sources of pride and joy for Him so that we, along with all of His children, may become יִשְׂרָאֵל אֲשֶׁר בְּךָ אֶתְפָּאָר.

Moshe Mordechai Lieber

Rosh Chodesh Av, 5756

❧ An Overview —
Climax of Joy

Nature of the Festival
Its Special Message
The Festival's Uniqueness

⊰ An Overview —
Climax of Joy

בַּיּוֹם הַשְּׁמִינִי עֲצֶרֶת תִּהְיֶה לָכֶם

The eighth day [from the beginning of Succos] *shall be a restriction for you* (*Numbers* 29:35).

לְפִי שֶׁכָּל יְמוֹת הָרֶגֶל הִקְרִיבוּ כְּנֶגֶד שִׁבְעִים אוּמוֹת וּבָאִים לָלֶכֶת אָמַר לָהֶם הַמָּקוֹם "בְּבַקָּשָׁה מִכֶּם עֲשׂוּ לִי סְעוּדָה קְטַנָּה כְּדֵי שֶׁאֵהֲנֶה מִכֶּם"

Since all the days of the festival [the Jewish people had brought] offerings for the benefit of the seventy nations, and then came to depart [for their homes], the Omnipresent One said, "I beg of you, make for Me a small feast so that I can enjoy your company" (*Rashi* ibid. *Succah* 55b).

I: Nature of the Festival

Wisdom **S**hemini Atzeres and Simchas Torah are singular
Is Step among Jewish holy days in that they are one festival
One with two names. According to the Torah's commandment, there is only one day — the eighth day from the beginning of Succos — but since, in the Diaspora, a day is added to festivals, Shemini Atzeres, like the other festivals, became two days. In *Eretz Yisrael*, however, it is still one day — and a busy day it is! In addition to the regular festival ritual, there is *Geshem*, or the Prayer for Rain, and *Yizkor* — and the celebration that Diaspora Jews know as Simchas Torah, with the delirious singing and dancing that are part of the Seven *Hakafos*, the

circuits around the synagogue with the Torah scrolls. In Israel, which observes a single day, all the observances are compressed into one day, and it is generally known as Simchas Torah.

There are two reasons for the special joy of Shemini Atzeres/Simchas Torah: It is ordained by the Torah itself (see below), and, secondly, the completion of the year's Torah reading is in itself cause to rejoice. The Sages derive this from the experience of King Solomon. After God blessed the young king with unprecedented wisdom, Solomon came to Jerusalem and offered many sacrifices in gratitude and joy. This example teaches that עוֹשִׂין סְעוּדָה וּשְׂמֵחִין לְגָמְרָהּ שֶׁל תּוֹרָה, *we arrange a feast and rejoice upon the completion of the Torah (Koheles Rabbah* 1).

Solomon's precedent is the basis for the celebrations that are made upon completion of tractates and other significant accomplishments in Torah study. It is noteworthy that he expressed his gratitude to God for the blessing that put him on the threshold of knowledge, not its conclusion. The blessing of wisdom was only a beginning, for it enabled Solomon to go further and utilize his newly granted potential toward ever greater accomplishments in Torah scholarship and leadership of the people. For that, he rejoiced. Had he been content to close his books and rely only on the new blessing, it would have been a hollow festivity. So too, the ceremony accompanying the completion of a tractate includes the declaration that the scholar will go on to study and complete more and more tractates.

Scholarship is worthy of the greatest respect if it is accompanied by the resolution to grow. So it is that when we conclude the Torah reading on Simchas Torah, we immediately turn to the Book of Genesis and begin the reading anew, always striving for more knowledge and new insights into God's wisdom. This would be enough to explain the happiness of Simchas Torah, but even before the Sages instituted the current schedule of the Torah reading, Shemini Atzeres was Scripturally ordained as a day of rejoicing.

The Only Thing Left

In describing Succos, *the Torah says* וְהָיִיתָ אַךְ שָׂמֵחַ, *you shall be completely* [lit. *only*] *joyous* (Deuteronomy 17:15). From the apparently superfluous word אַךְ, the Sages derive that the commandment to be joyous extends beyond Succos, and extends to Shemini Atzeres also. The commentators raise a difficulty, however. The word אַךְ, *only*, is always an exclusionary word, meaning that it indicates that something is exempted from the category under discussion. Since the above verse refers specifically to Succos, it would seem only logical that the word *only* should indicate that other days are *excluded* from the commandment of joy, not added to it. How, therefore, can the Sages derive from that word that Shemini Atzeres is to be *added* — not excluded — from the commandment of joy?

The Sages derive that the commandment to be joyous on Succos extends to Shemini Atzeres also.

The *Vilna Gaon* explains. The festival of Succos includes the commandments of the Four Species, *succah, and* joy, but on Shemini Atzeres all the tangible observances are excluded — there are no Four Species and no *succah* —only the celebration remains. Thus the exegesis of the Sages: On Shemini Atzeres, you shall be *only, completely* joyous.

On Shemini Atzeres all the tangible observances are excluded — only the celebration remains.

This status of Shemini Atzeres as a festival dedicated to joy is in itself a powerful reason to combine its celebration with Simchas Torah — our celebration with the Torah and the privilege that God chose Israel to receive His Torah and be the bearer of its teachings to all of mankind. Just as someone who has suddenly enjoyed some great good fortune will immediately want to share it with those he loves the most — his spouse, his children, his parents — so the God-intoxicated Jewish people dedicate their every blessing to God. When such a person has a great business success, his first instinct is to contribute to charity; when he feels an upsurge of love, he shares it with God Who gave him success.

When such a person feels an upsurge of love, he shares it with God Who gave him success.

When Jacob finally saw Joseph after twenty-two years of separation, the Patriarch recited the *Shema* (*Rashi, Genesis* 46:25). Why just then? Shouldn't Jacob have rushed to embrace and kiss his beloved son? Couldn't he have recited the *Shema* earlier or later? *Gur*

Aryeh explains that righteous people utilize every opportunity and resource to serve God. Now, as Jacob felt a surge of joy and love at the sight of Joseph after such a long and painful separation, he submerged his personal feelings and offered all his love to God. The recitation of *Shema* represents acceptance of God's sovereignty and acknowledgment that He is the Source of all blessing. That is what Jacob wanted to do at this moment of overpowering emotion.

As Jacob felt a surge of joy and love at the sight of Joseph, he submerged his personal feelings and offered all his love to God.

A Family Gathering

The seven days of the Succos festival were unique in that part of the Temple service consisted of seventy offerings that were specifically meant to call down Heavenly blessings upon the seventy primary nation groups of the world. In fact, the Sages declare that if only the nations of the world had realized how much they benefited from the Temple service, they would have dispatched troops to protect it from attack (*Bamidbar Rabbah* 1:3).

This seven-day Succos festival was climaxed by Shemini Atzeres/Simchas Torah, which is both a separate festival and is linked to Succos. In the metaphor of the Sages, after the seven days when Israel had lavished offerings for the sake of the nations of the world, God longs for the intimate company of His own children. With Succos over and the people of Israel packing their bags, as it were, to return to their towns and farms, God appeals to them to tarry for one more day, a new one-day festival that would be dedicated exclusively to the closeness between the Heavenly Father and His earthly children, His Chosen People.

With Succos over and the people of Israel packing their bags God appeals to them to tarry for one more day.

The Sages used a parable of a small, informal feast between the king and his closest courtiers, after the week of public festivities was over. It is as if the king says, "Enough of the pomp and ceremony of the multitudes. True, they are part of my kingdom and I owe them health and prosperity — but now I long for the company of my dearest ones. The celebration of a father and his children does not require lavish feasts and expensive trappings; our joy requires nothing more than

our closeness. Let us make a small, simple feast, one whose major ingredient is our companionship."

This was the climax of the Succos joy, a celebration that belonged exclusively to God and Israel — so it was only natural that the Sages would dedicate this gladness to Israel's greatest exultation, Simchas Torah, so that Israel would express its joy that the nation's life and destiny, are inextricably united with the Torah, as expressed by the cycle of the Torah reading. We complete the annual reading on Simchas Torah, and begin the new cycle without delay, for Israel cannot live without the constant intellectual and spiritual renewal it derives from the Torah.

Israel cannot live without the constant intellectual and spiritual renewal it derives from the Torah.

II: Its Special Message

Blessing for the Nations What is the special significance of Shemini Atzeres? If it is indeed a separate festival, then why does the Torah speak of *Three* Pilgrimage Festivals, instead of four? Why must Shemini Atzeres come immediately after Succos, instead of several weeks later, following the example of Shavuos after Pesach? How does the extra day, with its "small feast," ease the pain of the "children" parting from their "Father"? And why should the feast be "small"?

Rabbi Moshe Feinstein (Darash Moshe) discussed the symbolism of the weekful of offerings for all the nations of the world, and why it was that the "small feast" of Shemini Atzeres had to follow immediately upon the Succos festival, in contrast to Shavuos, which comes seven weeks after Pesach.

It was God's wish to create a world in which people would have to depend on one another. From such mundane needs as food and clothing to lofty concerns with intellectual advancement to international coexistence, sensible people must recognize that they cannot survive without the efforts of their fellows. In such a world, logic would dictate that there should be peace, because no man or country can stand alone without the help and cooperation of others. Indeed, if people were to be at

Sensible people must recognize that they cannot survive without the efforts of their fellows.

selfish cross-purposes to one another, life would be brutish and contentious, without happiness or security.

As a result, common sense — indeed, simple sanity — would dictate that people cannot afford the luxury of conflict. Compromise and forbearance would be small prices to pay for serenity and friendship.

Compromise and forbearance would be small prices to pay for serenity and friendship.

The adage "the customer is always right" is hardly an objective judgment. Experience shows that the customer is wrong at least as often as he is right, but simple business sense convinces the merchant that his success depends on the good will of his customers, on their confidence in him and his product, and on their willingness to part with hard-earned coin to purchase his product. And if the way to gain their trade is by smiling and agreeing to an occasional unreasonable demand, it is a small price to pay for healthier profits.

The Blessing of Peace

One of the great *roshei yeshivah* of the last generation used to counsel his disciples that when two families are becoming united through the marriage of their children, the most important thing is to avoid unnecessary arguments. Differences of opinion are inevitable, but no one should make an issue of them unless the matter is truly important; otherwise it is better to give in than to risk igniting animosity. The profits of peace are worth far more than the corrosive thrill of prevailing in a dispute.

The Succos offerings in the Holy Temple taught this universal lesson. God does not want blessings to flow exclusively to any one nation — not even the nation of Torah. Not only are all nations precious before their Creator, but the blessing of each should accrue to the benefit of all. By bringing offerings on Succos for all the nations, Israel signified that the needs of all nations are important to God, and that Israel's Season of Gladness is complete only if all other peoples share in His beneficence.

Not only are all nations precious before their Creator, but the blessing of each should accrue to the benefit of all.

Blessing is an empty boon, however, if it becomes a cause of envy and strife. The merchant who smiles at his customers may be far from a saint, but self-interest refines his behavior. Why is it, therefore, that individuals, corporations, and countries let their desire for gain

and glory lead them to destructive and disastrous competitions that can end in ruin and war? How common it is for dispassionate observers to shake their heads in wonderment and dismay at how otherwise sensible leaders could have plunged their companies or countries into corporate battles and bloody conflicts over issues that had more to do with ego than substance.

Dispassionate observers shake their heads at how sensible leaders could have plunged their companies or countries into battles and conflicts over issues that had more to do with ego than substance.

This is why God commanded that Succos be climaxed with Shemini Atzeres/Simchas Torah, without delay. By uniting God and Israel in a spiritual, moral intimacy, Shemini Atzeres provides a focus for Succos and its blessings of prosperity. Shemini Atzeres declares that the world must seek direction in the moral teachings of the Torah; the alternative is disaster. This lesson could not wait for seven weeks; it had to be taught immediately after Succos, before the blandishments of success could blind its beneficiaries to their higher responsibilities.

Shemini Atzeres declares that the world must seek direction in the moral teachings of the Torah; the alternative is disaster.

It is poignant that Rabbi Feinstein gave this homily during Succos of 1940, when, as he noted sadly, the world had plunged into World War II, as if to prove how foolish man can be when he lets pettiness, greed, and ambition misdirect his wealth and power.

The Atzeres Lesson

HaK'sav V'haKabbalah notes that the Torah applies the name *Atzeres* to only two festival days: the last day of Pesach (*Deuteronomy* 16:8) and Shemini Atzeres. This indicates that there is something unique about the conclusion of a festival, something that teaches a lesson all its own, a lesson that is implied by the word *atzeres*. The word can have several meaning: to refrain from work, to gather together, to press out the essence, to retain. Which one is implied by the fact that the Torah uses *Atzeres* just for these two festive days?

It is natural for people to strive for material comforts and acquisitions; if they did not, commercial activity would come to a standstill.

It is natural for people to strive for material comforts and acquisitions; if they did not, commercial activity would come to a standstill. True, the potential ruthlessness of the profit motive must be regulated, but it cannot be ignored. To satisfy the perceived need for more and more "things" takes a heavy toll on most

people — not only in hard work and long hours, but also in the sacrifice of spiritual goals. There is a cost associated with the "good life" in a "better" neighborhood, with keeping up with affluent friends and relatives, with being stylishly clad and groomed, with having enough of the right model cars in the driveway, with vacationing in the prestigious places and sending children to the right schools and summer camps. And the cost is measured not merely in dollars, but in time and concentration robbed from study and prayer, in time taken away from raising children, in failure to contemplate the *meaning* of life, not just its cost.

The more one feels compelled to acquire temporal wealth, the more one discards eternal values. In order to free people from this sort of yoke and replace it with the yoke of Heaven, God ordained the festivals as Israel's rendezvous in time with the Divine. The festivals are an anchor to true reality, and an antidote to the poison of greed and desire.

The Torah refers to the festivals as מוֹעֲדֵי ה, *appointed festivals of HASHEM (Leviticus* 23:4), because they are days when Jews can "meet" with God, as it were. In the words of *Rabbi Samson R. Hirsch (Horeb* ch.23):

> *Moadim,* appointed seasons, summon us to submit ourselves entirely to the contemplation and inner realization of those ideals which lie at their foundation. Just as *Moed* in space refers to the locality which men have as their appointed place of assembly for an appointed purpose [such as the *Ohel Moed,* the Tent of Meeting, where God communicated with Moses], so *Moed* in time is a point in time which summons us continually to an appointed activity — in this case an inner activity. Thus *Moadim* are the days which stand out from the other days of the year. They summon us from our everyday life to halt and to dedicate all our spiritual activities to them . . .

The *Moadim* interrupt the ordinary activities of our life and give us the spirit, power, and consecration for the future by revivifying those ideas upon which our whole life is based, or they eradicate such evil consequences of past activity as are deadly to body and spirit, and thus restore to us lost purity and the hope of blessing.

Holding On

The festivals arouse people to nobler goals. They are days of Divine service, free from the encumbrances of regular labor and the values of the marketplace. Even the preparation of food, which is permitted on festivals, is elevated, because the day conveys the message that one does not live to eat, but one eats to have peace of mind and health of body to serve God. During these exalted days, Jews come to realize that the rest of the year, too, should have a higher goal; that there are more important pursuits at all times than sheer profit and pleasure. Or, better said, that the most enduring profits and the most meaningful pleasures are those that make one a better person, rather than a richer one.

During these exalted days, Jews come to realize that the rest of the year, too, should have a higher goal.

But what will happen tomorrow, *after* the festival? Will it be back to business as usual, or will the lesson of the *Moadim* remain?

The word *Atzeres* has the connotation of *retention*, of *holding back* the inspiration of the festival, so that it will not dissipate when the calendar says that it is time to return to the regular routines of life. The last day of Pesach and Shemini Atzeres have the same message: "Make yourself an *atzeres*, find a way to retain the inspiration of the festival. Don't store it in your closet with your holiday clothing. It must remain with you to ennoble the rest of your year, to make yourself better and your time holier" (*HaK'sav V'HaKabbalah; R' Hirsch* to *Leviticus* 23:36).

Make yourself an atzeres, find a way to retain the inspiration of the festival. Don't store it in your closet with your holiday clothing.

III: The Festival's Uniqueness*

The Nation's Joy

The Three Pilgrimage Festivals are in the merit of the three Patriarchs: Pesach in the merit of Abraham, Shavuos in the merit of Isaac, and Succos in the merit of Jacob (see *Tur Orach Chaim* 417). In whose merit is Shemini Atzeres? This fourth festival is in the merit of the Jewish people as a whole, and it represents Israel's inseparable unity with God and the Torah, as the *Zohar* states, אוֹרַיְתָא וְקוּדְשָׁא בְּרִיךְ הוּא וְיִשְׂרָאֵל כּוּלְהוּ חַד, *The Torah, the Holy One, Blessed is He, and Israel are all one*.

The Torah and its commandments are the means to bring Jews together as one.

This is the deeper significance of Hillel's famous teaching that the primary commandment of the Torah is *Love your fellow as yourself* — the rest is commentary; go and study! (*Shabbos* 32a). Hillel meant to say that the Torah and its commandments are the means to bring Jews together as one, and when there is the proper kind of unity among Jews, then the Torah can achieve its purpose of bringing about unity between Israel and God. So it was that the Torah could be given at Sinai only when Israel had banished strife from itself and gathered at Sinai כְּאִישׁ אֶחָד בְּלֵב אֶחָד, *like one person with one heart* (*Rashi, Exodus* 19:2).

Unity among people has a tremendous spiritual force when it is exercised for good, and even when it is employed for evil.

Unity among people has a tremendous spiritual force — when it is exercised for good, and even when it is employed for evil. So it was that when mankind, shortly after the Flood of Noah's time, had the audacity to build a tower with the delusion that they could storm Heaven; as it were, their extraordinary unity of purpose would have had such cosmic repercussions that God intervened and caused them to turn against one another (see *Genesis* ch. 11, with *Rashi*). As several of the great Torah leaders in the period between the two world wars commented, when asked why the enemies of Torah life enjoyed such success, "It is true they are fighting for an evil cause, but they are doing so with conviction and unity!"

This part of the Overview is based on the *Sfas Emes*.

Shemini Atzeres represents this national perfection achieved through a united effort. The cycle of the Three Pilgrimage Festivals had given Jews, each in his own way, the opportunity to perfect themselves — and as a result they had earned the Heavenly gift of a new, independent festival. Shemini Atzeres also comes as the climax of the three festivals of the month of Tishrei, Rosh Hashanah, Yom Kippur, and Succos, the month and the occasions when the Jewish people face God's judgment and elevate themselves through repentance and joy.

The cycle of the Three Pilgrimage Festivals had given Jews the opportunity to perfect themselves.

There is an allusion to this in the previously noted verse from which the Sages derive the commandment to be joyous on Shemini Atzeres: וְהָיִיתָ אַךְ שָׂמֵחַ, *you shall only be joyous (Deuteronomy 16:15).* See above for an explanation of the Sages' exegesis. The word אַךְ has the numerical value of twenty-one, alluding to Tishrei's twenty-one days up to Shemini Atzeres, as if to suggest that those days and the performance of their commandments prepare the nation for the explosion of joy that takes place on Shemini Atzeres.

Those days prepare the nation for the explosion of joy that takes place on Shemini Atzeres.

Moses' Role

The one who brought about this unity was Moses, who was God's agent to present the Torah to Israel. *Midrash Tanchuma* expounds on the Torah's description of Moses as אִישׁ הָאֱלֹהִים, *the man of God (Deuteronomy 33:1)* — Moses was part man and part angel [i.e, a Godly creature], for he was the one who bridged heaven and earth, among other things, by bringing God's Torah from the province of the angels and presenting it to human beings. Whatever Moses did, however, he did for the sake of Israel, as implied by the very last words of the Torah, that all his miraculous deeds were performed before the eyes of the people.

Whatever Moses did, he did for the sake of Israel.

It is noteworthy that as soon as we conclude the Torah by praising Moses' accomplishments, we begin once again to read the Torah, reciting the words בְּרֵאשִׁית בָּרָא אֱלֹהִים, *in the beginning of God's creation* ... As *Rashi* explains on the first verse of Genesis, the word *bereishis, beginning,* refers to the Torah itself, for it is the beginning, the *source* of everything. Thus by connecting the final words of the Torah with its first

words, we declare, in effect, that whatever Moses did was accomplished only through the power of the Torah.

Separate, Yet One

It is axiomatic in Jewish thought that, although each of the Patriarchs had his own unique form of combined service, each built on the teachings and spiritual legacy he had inherited. Thus, Isaac absorbed Abraham's heritage of kindness [חֶסֶד], and to it he added his own strength and introspection [גְּבוּרָה]. Jacob absorbed the teachings of Abraham and Isaac, and to them he added his attribute of truth and Torah [אֱמֶת]. Because Jacob combined all three attributes, he represented a level of spiritual refinement that surpassed those of his predecessors. That is why he is referred to as the possessor of the attribute of "splendor" [תִּפְאֶרֶת], and why the Sages refer to him as בְּחִיר שֶׁבָּאָבוֹת, *the select of the Patriarchs* (*Bereishis Rabbah* 76:1).

Because Jacob combined all three attributes, he surpassed his predecessors.

Abraham, Isaac, and Jacob are called the "fathers" of the nation because all our spiritual characteristics derive from them. There are infinite blends of their attributes — one individual may stress Abraham's attribute of kindness, another may emphasize Isaac's attribute of service, and a third may concentrate on Jacob's attribute of Torah study — but in whatever blends of these attributes various people choose, the Patriarchs are the source of all the essential ingredients of Jewish existence.

Shemini Atzeres/ Simchas Torah is the natural outgrowth of the Three Pilgrimage Festivals.

This explains the anomaly of Shemini Atzeres/Simchas Torah: It is a *separate* festival, yet it is not a *fourth* festival. Rather, it is the natural outgrowth of the Three Pilgrimage Festivals, just as only Abraham, Isaac, and Jacob are Patriarchs, while Moses, for all his greatness, is their successor, not their equal. Thus, Shemini Atzeres/ Simchas Torah is the amalgam of them all, rather than a fourth and unrelated one (*Sfas Emes*).

Anchored in the Tangible

In a sense, Shemini Atzeres surpasses all the festivals. *Sefer HaChinuch* explains why Succos has several commandments associated with it, while Shemini Atzeres has none.

> *Since the days of the Succos festival are a time of great rejoicing for Israel — for it is*

*the time when the crops are harvested
and fruits are brought into the house, and
then people rejoice with great gladness,
and therefore [Succos] is called the harvest
festival — that is why God commanded
His people Israel to declare a [religious]
festival before Him at that time, in order
that the primary celebration be dedicated
to Him [i.e., God decreed that the harvest
days be sanctified through the observance
of Succos, so that the nation would realize
that their prosperity resulted from His
blessing and should be dedicated to His
service.*

*Since celebration has a powerful appeal to
the body and such a time can easily cause
people to forget their fear of God, He
commanded us that at that time we should
take something tangible in our hands, something that will remind us that all the joy in
our hearts should be for His sake and for His
glory.*

*Celebration has a
powerful appeal
to the body and
such a time can
easily cause peo-
ple to forget their
fear of God.*

The *Chinuch's* point is very simple. People can easily
be carried away by joy, as our everyday experience
shows very clearly. Celebrations of family and national
victories often turn ugly. Few things frighten police
forces as much as the crowds careening through the
streets to celebrate the home team's win in a champi-
onship final. On the other hand, joy can be a valuable tool to bring one closer to God. As the Sages teach,
prophecy rests only on a joyous person, and during
the years when Jacob grieved for his missing son
Joseph, God did not reveal himself to him. But
happiness can be dangerous. All too often the Evil
Inclination seizes upon it to remove all inhibitions and
unleash people's most animalistic passions. Therefore
the Torah channeled the joy of the harvest into the
commandments of Succos, the Four Species and the
commandment to surround oneself with God's Presence
by dwelling in a *succah.*

*On the other
hand, joy can be
a valuable tool
to bring one
closer to God.*

*Therefore the
Torah channeled
the joy of the
harvest into
the command-
ments of Succos.*

What of Shemini Atzeres? The *Chinuch* continues:

And if you ask: Since Shemini Atzeres contains great joy for Israel, why are the [Four Species] not taken on it? The answer is that Shemini Atzeres in its entirety is devoted to God. As the Sages say, it is like a king who made a huge feast [for all his subjects, and then, when the mass festivities were over, said to his children], "Stay behind with me for one more day, for it is hard for me to part from you." Therefore it is called Atzeres [staying behind], and consequently it does not need any [tangible] remembrance.

It is called Atzeres [staying behind], and consequently it does not need any [tangible] remembrance.

So unlike Succos, the joy of Shemini Atzeres/Simchas Torah does not need a tangible *mitzvah*-performance to channel it away from harmful influences. What is the key to this?

The difference is simply in the nature of the event that causes one to celebrate. For example, if someone experiences a great victory in a business competition, it is natural that he will celebrate with his colleagues; if the cause of the joy was a family event — a birth, a marriage, the completion of a tractate of the Talmud — one will celebrate with the family and close friends. It is inevitable, as well, that the nature of the celebration will depend on the likes and dislikes of the people involved.

When an Orthodox Jew feels uncomfortable about the antics in an office party, it speaks well of him, but it is not a reflection on his colleagues; he is reflecting his upbringing and beliefs and they are reflecting theirs.

For example, when an Orthodox Jew feels uncomfortable about the antics in an office party, it speaks well of him, but it is not necessarily a reflection on his gentile colleagues; he is reflecting his upbringing and beliefs and they are reflecting theirs.

Since Succos is a festival that revolves around the happy harvest season — a material event — there would be an understandable tendency to descend to a carnival atmosphere. But what of the God Who gave the rain and held the plant blight at bay? What of the One Who blesses commerce and gives the health without which prosperity cannot be enjoyed? When the Jew enters his *succah* and nestles in the shelter of faith,

when he holds his *lulav* and *esrog*, his *hadassim* and *aravos*, and waves them in all directions to show that God is the Master of the winds and rain, and of everything above and below, there comes upon him a recognition that the festival is not a "Mardi gras" but a sublime reminder that HASHEM, *He is God, it is He Who made us and we are His, His people and the sheep of His pasture* (*Psalms* 100:3).

The festival is not a "Mardi gras" but a sublime reminder that Hashem, He is God.

The Joy of Being Together

There is another sort of joy, one that derives entirely from closeness to God. The Jew who exults in the elevation of prayer, the performance of a *mitzvah*, the thrill of Torah study will celebrate by drawing closer to his Maker. Like the king and his children when the madding crowd is gone and they can hasten to enjoy one another's company, the Jew on Shemini Atzeres/Simchas Torah has only one primary thought — to rejoice with God!

For seven days he has expressed his gratitude for God's material blessings and — whether through the actual offerings in the Temple or the recitation of the offerings as part of the daily *Mussaf* prayer — he has beseeched God to spread His blessings upon the nations of the world. Now, there is a day that belongs only to him and God.

Now, there is a day that belongs only to him and God.

After retelling the parable of the king inviting his children for an intimate feast, the *Zohar* gives the "menu" for the feast, the "program" that will bring out the joy of their intimacy: "Israel makes a celebration called Simchas Torah, and beautifies the Torah scroll with its crown." The primary delicacy of Israel's feast with its Father, the King is the joy of having been given His Torah and enjoying the exciting privilege of studying and absorbing His wisdom, the joy of declaring that, in the words of the daily *Maariv* service, *With an eternal love have You loved the House of Israel, Your nation. Torah and commandments, decrees and ordinances have You taught us . . . for they are our life and the length of our days . . . may You not remove Your love from us forever.*

The primary delicacy of Israel's feast with its Father is the joy of having been given His Torah.

As noted above, there is an intrinsic unity between

the Torah, Israel, and God. The Torah is the means, the
glue, as it were, that binds the other two. The Torah is
the soul, the life-giving force of Israel, the basis of our
undying attachment to God. It is the conduit through
which God's spiritual bounty flows to Israel.

The Torah is the conduit through which God's spiritual bounty flows to Israel.

That is why the celebration of Shemini Atzeres
became Simchas Torah, because there is no better
expression of the intimate love between the King and
Israel than the Torah.

Sfas Emes comments homiletically that Simchas
Torah can be translated as the *Torah's celebration*, i.e.,
the Torah itself rejoices in its relationship with Israel.
One might suggest that, whereas during the Hoshana
ritual of Succos, the Torah scroll was held at the
bimah-table of the synagogue and Jews circled *it*, on
Simchas Torah the scrolls themselves join in the circuits.
It is as if the Torah scrolls were symbolizing that they
are part of the celebration, that they are glad to join the
people holding them in the happy ceremony of the
festival.

On Simchas Torah the scrolls themselves join in the circuits as if symbolizing that they are part of the celebration.

Exhilaration and Constancy

One of the popular refrains in the Simchas Torah
liturgy is שִׂישׂוּ וְשִׂמְחוּ בְּשִׂמְחַת תּוֹרָה, *Rejoice and be glad on
Simchas Torah*. What is the difference between these
two expressions of joy? *Malbim* explains that שִׂישׂוּ,
rejoice, from the root שָׂשׂוֹן, refers to a sudden outpouring of joy, an emotional surge; שִׂמְחָה, *gladness*,
refers to a constant feeling of happy contentment, one
that is consistent and unchanging.

On Simchas Torah, we need both. On the one hand,
there is the exultant joy that is the highlight of the
Hakafos, the dancing with the Torah. On the other
hand, it is a day of *Atzeres*, a day that urges us to *retain*
the lessons of the festival and carry them with us into
the fall and winter, when there will be no festival, but
which need the legacy of the month of Tishrei and its
Shemini Atzeres/Simchas Torah climax.

On the one hand, there is exultant joy; on the other, it urges us to retain the lessons of the festival.

When Jews customarily wish one another "a healthy
winter" at the end of Simchas Torah, they mean
spiritual, as well as physical health. They mean that the
exhilaration of Simchas Torah should be carried into the

rest of the year, that the oneness of Torah, God, and Israel remain healthy and enduring always.

May we all merit this blessing, always!

Rabbi Nosson Scherman

Menachim Av 5756 / July 1996

► Insights — Shemini Atzeres

Epitome of Love

A Multifaceted Jewel

A Portent of Things to Come

Rain — Key to Prosperity

Farewell to the Succah

Shemini Atzeres:
Epitome of Love

A Nation Apart

⟨⟨ The day following the seventh day of Succos is called Shemini Atzeres. The source for this festival is a verse in *Numbers* (29:35): *The eighth day shall be one of assembly for you.*

Shemini Atzeres is a time when God showers the nation of Israel with a great outpouring of love, bonding them to Himself as the festival departs. It is a day which is reserved exclusively for Israel, in contrast to the preceding days of Succos during which the nations of the world also have a role. In Temple times, seventy bulls were offered on the Altar during the seven days of Succos, corresponding to the number of primary nations enumerated in *Genesis,* Chapter 10 (*Succah* 55b).

These offerings had two purposes. One was to safeguard the gentile nations from affliction and to serve as a prayer for their physical sustenance. The Midrash declares that had the nations realized how much they benefited from these sacrifices, they would have sent legions to surround Jerusalem and guard it from attack.

The second purpose was to symbolize the gradually diminishing power of the nations over the course of time. Thirteen bulls were offered on the first day, and the number decreased by one each succeeding day, showing that the power of those who oppose God's teachings will grow progressively weaker, until, in Messianic times, the nations will accept His dominion, under the spiritual leadership of Israel.

On Shemini Atzeres, a single bull was offered, representing the Jewish people. In granting us this holiday, God says to Israel, as it were, "Make a small banquet for Me so that I can enjoy your [exclusive] company." This can be likened to a king who ordered his servants to make a great banquet for all his subjects. When it was over, he asked his children to arrange a small meal where he could enjoy their company intimately, without the presence of outsiders. So too, following the offerings for the nations, God longs for the exclusive company of His beloved, chosen people. Thus, the single

bull offered on Shemini Atzeres was symbolic of Israel's unique relationship with God.

While all people are created בְּצֶלֶם אֱלֹהִים, *in God's image* (see *Avos* 3:18 and *Tiferes Yisrael* ad loc.), only the Jewish people are considered His children (ibid.). God does not want to part with His beloved children. As the pilgrims in Temple times prepared to return home from Jerusalem at the end of Succos, the holiday of Shemini Atzeres was God's way of declaring: "קָשָׁה עָלַי פְּרֵידַתְכֶם, *It is too hard for me to bear the separation*. Please stay just one more day; please remain with Me just a bit longer." Even in exile, this remains the message of Shemini Atzeres.

Too Great a Separation

◆§ Why is it that Succos is granted this extension? Neither Pesach nor Shavuos has an additional day. Another puzzling matter is the fact that even though God always finds separation from His children painful, He asked us to stay only one extra day following Succos. How can one day make a difference?

Chizkuni explains with a parable. The children of the king came to visit their father. Before they were ready to leave, he asked them, "When will you return?" "In fifty days we will be back," they replied, and he sent them on their way. When they returned he was overjoyed. The time came for them to leave again, and again he asked, "When shall we see each other again?" This time they would be gone for longer. "In four months we shall come to visit once again," they told their father. "Fine," he replied. "Go in peace."

When they returned for a third time, the emotional intensity of this joyous reunion was almost tangible. "And when you leave me at the end of this visit, how long will I have to wait until I see you again?" he asked his children.

"This time it will be many months — six or seven — and then we will be together again," answered the children.

"No, no," he said, "that is too long. The pain of such an extended parting is too much for me to bear. Please stay another day so that I may be sated with your company."

After Pesach we return to God's courtyard only seven weeks later, for Shavuos. God has to wait only four months more before we come once again to Jerusalem, on Succos. The four-month wait, while straining, is not unbearable. However, the thought of a long, six- or seven-month winter without a visit from His children causes God to

say, "קָשָׁה עָלַי פְּרֵידַתְכֶם, *It is too hard for Me to bear the separation.* Remain here just one day and let us enjoy each other's company." God wants, so to speak, to hold on to the memory.

A Lasting Impression

◆§ The question still remains, however: What is gained by this one day of Shemini Atzeres? The pain of parting will be just as great on the following day.

Toras Emes explains: While on all the other days of Succos we perform practical *mitzvos* which relate to the festival, on Shemini Atzeres we achieve a unique closeness to God without any intermediary activity. The closeness achieved through a practical *mitzvah* can dissipate after we have completed its performance, but this is not the case with the bonding that occurs between God and His people on Shemini Atzeres. It is only a single day, but the pure and heightened love that develops during that short time is everlasting.

Shem MiShmuel offers another perspective: Seven is a number which represents the limitations of nature (the week has seven days and then begins again), while the number eight is symbolic of that which is not bound by the strictures of nature. (See p. 51.)

We human beings are very forgetful. In fact, we often forget even those events and impressions which have been very meaningful to us. However, if an event or idea were to be conveyed to us in a supernatural way, surely it would remain indelibly etched in our minds and hearts. Thus, the impression of our seven-day meeting with God on Succos is liable to be worn down by the sands of time during the weeks and months ahead as we fall back into the humdrum routines of our daily lives. By remaining "alone with God" for an *eighth* — i.e., supernatural — day, we are able to capture that special closeness to Him and retain it forever.

Atzeres, according to this interpretation, may be translated as *retention.* "*The eighth day shall be for you a [day of] retention.*" It is on this day that we are able to "freeze the moment in time" and thus preserve the love between ourselves and God, long after the festival has ended.

A Time to Beseech

◆§ Shemini Atzeres is not only a time of special closeness between God and His people, it is also a time when He looks favorably upon requests.

When a pauper knocks on the door to request alms, it is he who asks the wealthy householder to give him some time. Once the donation is given, however, and the poor man is ready to leave, the householder may call him back in order to talk with him and get to know him. Similarly, God, like the wealthy householder, gives us His undivided attention during Succos, as we pray that He bestow His blessings upon us — the equivalent of the poor man's request for alms. On Shemini Atzeres, as we prepare to take leave of Him, He holds us back and, in a gesture of love, asks us to remain with Him just a little bit longer (*HaYashar VeHatov*).

Yalkut (*Pinchas* 782) elaborates: Rav compared this idea to groups of people who came to a royal banquet and offered tribute to the king. The queen, who was looking on, signaled to the members of the king's household, "Remember to ask the king for your own needs." They ignored her and spent all their time at the feast making requests on behalf of others. Left with no choice, the queen finally sent everyone else home and kept the king's children for an extra day in order to be sure that they would beseech the king for their own necessities. This is the meaning of the verse: "בַּיּוֹם הַשְּׁמִינִי עֲצֶרֶת תִּהְיֶה לָכֶם, *On the eighth day shall be a restriction for you*" (*Numbers* 29:35). During the seven days of Succos we asked God, by means of the seventy bulls, to provide for the needs of the nations. On the eighth day — Shemini Atzeres — the Torah, which is symbolized by the queen, restricts us from leaving God's presence. We are then alone with the King and may ask לָכֶם, *for you* — for our own personal needs.

Zohar teaches: "On Shemini Atzeres we are invited to enjoy a visit with the King and receive His blessings for the entire year. No one shares in this joyous celebration with the King other than His people, Israel. When one has a private audience with the King, he may ask for his heart's desires and they will be granted." [See p. 61 for more on this theme.]

The Wisest Request of All

◆§ What should one ask for on so auspicious a day? *Nesivos Shalom* suggests that rather than asking for one's particular needs of the day, whether physical or even spiritual, one would do better to request he always be allowed access to the King in order to speak to Him.

Most needs are temporary and subject to change. Even if today's wish is granted, tomorrow may bring new desires and necessities.

However, when one asks God to grant him the closeness to Him that will enable him to turn to Him in prayer at all times, this wish will be granted. This is a request which, in essence, encompasses all others, for he now has the key of prayer which can unlock all gates. Close to God everything is always good.

King David had the emotional depth and clarity of perspective to make this request of God: "אַחַת שָׁאַלְתִּי מֵאֵת ה׳ אוֹתָהּ אֲבַקֵּשׁ שִׁבְתִּי בְּבֵית־ ה׳, כָּל יְמֵי חַיַּי לַחֲזוֹת בְּנֹעַם ה׳ וּלְבַקֵּר בְּהֵיכָלוֹ, *One thing I asked of Hashem, that shall I seek: That I dwell in the House of Hashem all the days of my life; to behold the sweetness of Hashem and to contemplate in His Sanctuary*" (*Psalms* 27:4). King David, the prototypical master of personal repentance (*Avodah Zarah* 4b), said: "I have only one desire ... and אוֹתָהּ אֲבַקֵּשׁ, *that shall I* [continue to] *seek*, because this request — to dwell in the House of Hashem all the days of my life — embodies all of my desires. May God grant that every moment of my life be an intimate encounter with Him and thus I will receive the innermost desires of my heart."

Unadorned Love

∾ The Midrash refers to the single bull and ram offered on Shemini Atzeres as a small meal (סְעוּדָה קְטַנָּה), in contrast to the large banquet of the seventy bulls offered during the seven days of Succos. Why do we bring such a paltry offering compared to that which is offered on behalf of the seventy nations?

R' Azariah Figo (author of *Binah L'Itim*) offers an insightful thought: When one senses that a loyal friend may soon leave, one goes to great lengths to delay his departure. In an attempt to enjoy the pleasure of his company just one more time, he will prepare a meal and ask his friend to join him. However, if the host prepares a lavish feast with a multicourse menu, the banquet will be counter-productive, for instead of enjoying each other's company, the two will become preoccupied with sampling all the delectable dishes. In order to assure that the time they spend together will be dedicated to the enjoyment of each other's company, it is necessary that the meal be kept simple and small.

God's love for us is so intense and passionate that our parting at the end of Succos is, so to speak, a terribly painful experience for Him. In order to delay our departure from His courtyard, He asks us to remain yet one more day — Shemini Atzeres — so that He can enjoy our company. Thus, He commanded His children in His Torah to

arrange only a *small* meal — one bull, one ram — to demonstrate that the meal is incidental to the true agenda — that of taking pleasure in their company.

The *Dubno Maggid* offered this penetrating parable: A man once journeyed to a faraway land on business. At home, his family anxiously waited for him to return. His wife, his children, and his stepchildren (born to his wife from a previous marriage) all counted the days until the master of the house arrived.

Before he came home, the man made sure to buy presents for everyone. For his stepchildren he purchased lavish gifts, sparing no expense, while for his own children he bought simple, inexpensive trinkets.

Onlookers wondered and asked the man an obvious question: "Are your stepchildren more precious to you than your own flesh and blood? Why do you differentiate between your wife's offspring and your own?"

Replied the man: "I want everybody to be happy upon my return. For my stepchildren, to whom my mere presence is no reason for special happiness, I bought beautiful presents in order to gladden their hearts. My own children, however, are ecstatic over my return and don't need presents to put them in a joyous frame of mind. It would be almost insulting were I to ply them with lavish gifts, as if I doubt that my presence itself gives them cause to rejoice."

Similarly Israel, God's chosen people, makes only a token offering on this day of spiritual intimacy, for the feeling of love is so intense that a gift of offerings is almost superfluous.

Permanent Gains

◄§ The pain of separation from God that we seek to redress during Shemini Atzeres has another dimension as well: It is our *teshuvah* which we seek to solidify. During the Days of Awe, we are purified from the sins that separated us from God, and we are then reunited with our beloved Father during Succos. *Atzeres* means to *retain*; it is through the festival of Shemini Atzeres that we seek to reinforce our newly cemented relationship with God so that its intensity never wanes.

Binah L'Itim notes that only three times a year does the *mussaf* offering consist of one bull and one ram; Rosh Hashanah, Yom Kippur, and Shemini Atzeres. On Rosh Hashanah the *shofar* urges us to arise from our spiritual slumber; on Yom Kippur, God forgives our sins and

grants us purity of spirit so that we can thrive and grow. Shemini Atzeres is the time when, in an atmosphere of unqualified love, we are able to internalize the gains of the *teshuvah* (repentance) process.

King David declared: "בִּי עִמְּךָ הַסְּלִיחָה לְמַעַן תִּוָּרֵא, *For with You is forgiveness, that You may be feared*" (*Psalms* 130:4). God in His mercy grants us forgiveness so that we may rid ourselves of the albatross of sin and once again revere Him properly, enjoying the pleasure of His closeness.

This three-part process is succinctly described in the words of *Joel* (2:15): *Sound the shofar in Zion,* thereby awakening us to our purpose in life (referring to Rosh Hashanah); *sanctify the day as a fast,* and through the purifying process of Yom Kippur bring sanctity to even the mundane details of life; and *call for a day of retention* (Shemini Atzeres), when one gathers the penitential harvest of these sacred days into the storehouse of his mind and heart.

A Sign of Forgiveness

≈§ Shemini Atzeres is a time when God lets us know that He has forgiven us for our sins — that the process of *teshuvah* begun in Elul is now complete. King David provides the precedent for this concept.

The Talmud (*Moed Kattan* 9a) relates that King David asked God for a sign that he had been forgiven for the incident with Bathsheba, the wife of Uriah the Hittite. God replied that such an omen would be shown to his son, King Solomon.

This promise was fulfilled at the dedication of the Temple, when King Solomon sought to bring the Holy Ark inside. The gates of the Temple remained firmly in place and could not be opened. King Solomon offered many prayers to God that the gates open, but to no avail. Finally, he called out to God, "HASHEM, turn not away the face of Your anointed; remember the devout deeds of David, Your servant" (*II Chronicles* 6:42), and the gates opened up. King David's enemies felt ashamed of having belittled him over the incident, for they realized that God had forgiven him. This is alluded to in *I Kings* (8:66): "On the eighth day, he released the people and they blessed the King; they went to their tents, joyous and good hearted over all the good that HASHEM did for His servant David and His people Israel." The "eighth day" was Shemini Atzeres. It was then that everyone recognized all the good which God had done for King David. They understood that He had forgiven him his sin and that he was still beloved to God.

Shemini Atzeres and its special joy serves in this capacity for the entire Jewish nation, signifying that God has accepted our repentance and loves us with the same intensity as He loved us before we sinned (see *Shaarei Teshuvah* 1:42).

Zeved Tov notes in addition that King David prayed for recognition of true forgiveness of his sin with the words, "עֲשֵׂה עִמִּי אוֹת לְטוֹבָה וְיִרְאוּ שֹׂנְאַי וְיֵבֹשׁוּ, *Display for me a sign for good so that my enemies may see it and be ashamed*" (*Psalms* 86:17). The word לְטוֹבָה numerically equals 52, an allusion that on Shemini Atzeres, the fifty-second day since the beginning of Elul (when the period of repentance began), God showed David this sign. The Jewish people as well are granted the ability to rejoice on Shemini Atzeres and it is this joy which is an omen of God's forgiveness (*Imrei Moshe*).

The Mitzvah of Pure Joy

◁§ The month of Tishrei is referred to as *Yerech Ha'eisanim,* the Month of the Mighty (*I Kings* 8:2). The Talmud (*Rosh Hashanah* 11a) interprets this term as referring to the vast number of festival-related *mitzvos* that are performed during this month. There is the *shofar* on Rosh Hashanah; the fast of Yom Kippur; the *succah,* the four species, the water libations in the Temple, and the *aravah* on Succos. Only on Shemini Atzeres is there no specific *mitzvah* to perform. However, there is one *mitzvah* which involves our emotions.

The obligation to rejoice on Succos is stated explicitly in the Torah: "וְשָׂמַחְתָּ בְּחַגֶּךָ, *You shall rejoice in your festival*" (16:14). This *mitzvah* applies to Shemini Atzeres as well. The call for special joy on Shemini Atzeres, however, is derived from the words, "וְהָיִיתָ אַךְ שָׂמֵחַ, *And you shall be purely joyous*" (*Deuteronomy* 16:15).

Homiletically, the meaning of this phrase can be derived from the *gematria,* numerical value, of the word אַךְ, which is twenty-one. The first twenty-one days of the month of Tishrei are colored both by the awe of the judgment period, which actually concludes on Hoshanah Rabbah, and by the joy of Succos. The conclusion of this period ushers in the holiday of Shemini Atzeres. Thus, after twenty-one days, the element of awe recedes and we celebrate a time of unadulterated joy.

There is another reason for rejoicing on this day. The word עֲצֶרֶת can also mean *assembly,* alluding to the merits of the myriad *mitzvos* of the holiday period, which come together and bear witness to the intrinsic righteousness and spiritual grandeur of God's chosen people (*Sfas Emes*).

Shemini Atzeres and the Yamim Noraim

◄§ *Pachad Yitzchak* (*Rosh Hashanah* 10) discusses the two series of Scriptural festivals which Jews celebrate, the *Yamim Noraim* (Days of Awe) and the *Shalosh Regalim* (Three Pilgrimage Festivals of Pesach, Shavuos and Succos).

The *Yamim Noraim* begin with the *selichos* prayers, when we ask for God's assistance as we seek to restructure our lives and cleanse ourselves of past misdeeds. The wake-up call of the *shofar* on Rosh Hashanah rouses us from our spiritual slumber and is also, in a sense, a clarion call to crown God as our King, Whose commandments we will faithfully observe. The therapeutic repentance of Yom Kippur, with its awe-inspiring prayer in an atmosphere that is totally removed from the physical, allows man to redefine his relationships with both God and man.

Succos, and even more so Shemini Atzeres, serve as the climactic events of this transformational period and are permeated with undiluted joy.

The secret of this joy is taught to us by *Rabbeinu Yonah* (*Shaarei Teshuvah* 1:42): "It is possible that a person can be forgiven for his transgressions and yet not reattain the degree of closeness that had existed previously in his relationship with God. It is the return of this love that the true penitent passionately seeks. This is what King David meant when he asked God to *'Restore me to the joy of Your salvation and let a generous spirit support me'* (*Psalms* 51:14). In heartrending tones he begged of God, 'Let me be as beloved to You as in days gone by.' " It is this reaffirmed closeness to God that is granted us on Shemini Atzeres, and which is cause for an outpouring of joy (*Bnei Yissachar*).

King David alludes to this exalted day when he speaks of Rosh Hashanah and the succeeding days as "בַּכֶּסֶה לְיוֹם חַגֵּנוּ, *the time appointed for our festive day"* (*Psalms* 81:4). The word כֶּסֶה is related to כְּסוּי, *covering*. Homiletically, this teaches that the hidden intent of the Days of Awe and Succos is to bring us to the most festive of days, Shemini Atzeres (*Sfas Emes*).

Shemini Atzeres and the Shalosh Regalim

◄§ As we have seen, Shemini Atzeres in relation to the Days of Awe is a celebration of the acceptance of our *teshuvah*. In relation to the *Shalosh Regalim,* it is the completion of a mission.

The *Shalosh Regalim,* the three pilgrimage festivals, coincide with the agricultural cycle. Springtime planting (Pesach) is followed by summer reaping (Shavuos), which in turn reaches its culmination in the fall (Succos) with the ingathering of the harvest into one's home and granary.[1] According to *Maharal,* this cycle finds a parallel in the three points of contact between a dispatcher and his agent. The first point of contact is when the dispatcher appoints the agent to fulfill his task, investing him with the power to act on his behalf. Having established the agent's power to act, it is then necessary for the dispatcher to instruct the agent regarding his plans and how they should be fulfilled. The third and final meeting is when the agent returns to the dispatcher to report that he has performed his mission and successfully completed his charge.

Similarly, on Pesach, we became Divine agents when we were freed from the spiritual and physical oppression of the Egyptian exile. The Nation of Israel was born, and the ambassadors of the Heavenly Kingdom were empowered with the mission of fulfilling God's will and bringing His message to all of mankind. On Shavuos, when God gave us His Torah, we received detailed instructions on how to imbue every aspect of our lives with this spirit. The תּוֹרַת חַיִּים, *Torah of Life,* is the blueprint which conveys, down to the most minute detail, the method by which our mission in this world should be fulfilled. On Succos, when the festival is completed, the Jew is able to come before his Master and declare, "I have done my duty and fulfilled my mission."

The three pilgrimage festivals thus form a progression: from the birth of the nation on Pesach and the assumption of its mission, to the instructions for its mission on Shavuos, to the successful completion of its task on Succos. This ascending order of achievement is reflected in the Torah's description of the observance of the respective festivals. Nowhere is the term שִׂמְחָה, *gladness,* applied explicitly to Pesach (although Pesach is included in the *general* commandment to rejoice on the festivals). Only once does the Torah command Israel to rejoice on Shavuos (*Deuteronomy* 16:11) — but no less than three times is Israel enjoined to celebrate with joy on Succos (*Leviticus* 23:40 and *Deuteronomy* 16:14,15). The implication is clear.

The greatest cause for celebration is the attainment of a goal. Succos symbolizes the successful fulfillment of the spiritual goals

---

1. [See "Overview: Succos and the Festival Cycle" in the ArtScroll *Succos Machzor* for a brilliant treatment of this theme.]

inherent in the festival cycle; surely, this is ample reason for the Torah to stress three times, and for the Sages to incorporate into the prayers of the day, that Succos and Shemini Atzeres are "זְמַן שִׂמְחָתֵנוּ, *the season of our gladness*" (*Sfas Emes*). The pinnacle of this joy is Shemini Atzeres, which has no other *mitzvah* beside joy: "וְהָיִיתָ אַךְ שָׂמֵחַ, *and you shall be purely joyous.*"

A Mirror of Affection

◈ The *Baal Shem Tov* adds another dimension to the fulfillment of our spiritual goals on Shemini Atzeres. He interprets the phrase ה' צִלְּךָ, *God is your shadow* (*Psalms* 121:5), as indicative of the mirror-image relationship that man shares with God. Just as a person's shadow reflects his image, so does God act toward man as a shadow, behaving toward him in whatever fashion he relates to God or to his fellow man. On Shemini Atzeres, the mirror image is perfect: *God rejoices in His creations* (see ibid. 104:3), namely, His people Israel, for their role in the fulfillment of creation's purpose, while the Jewish people *exult in their Maker* (see ibid. 149:2).

Joyous Acceptance

The joy of Shemini Atzeres also complements the acceptance of the Torah which occurred on Shavuos. When God saw fit to place the mountain of Sinai over the heads of the Jewish people and "coerce" them to accept the Torah (see *Shabbos* 88a, *Tosafos*, and *Maharal* in *Tiferes Yisrael*),[1] the joy in accepting it was somewhat diminished. The unrestrained joy of Shemini Atzeres, which reaches its peak as we celebrate Simchas Torah, is comparable to a renewed acceptance of the Torah with unadulterated joy (*Eizor Eliyahu*).

Without Intermediaries

◈ As the last holiday of the festival cycle, Shemini Atzeres showers us with spiritual and physical blessings to last us the entire year. It is on this day that a Jew comes in touch with his innermost feelings of heartfelt attachment and closeness to God. With no festival-related *mitzvos* serving as intermediaries between himself and God on this day, the Jew experiences the full intensity of his Heavenly roots.

_____

1. This teaching is discussed in the ArtScroll *Shavuos*, p. 108.

Nesivos Shalom offers this perspective as to why Shemini Atzeres has no unique *mitzvah*. During their courtship period and even after they are engaged, a bride and groom always take care to dress well and keep themselves well groomed in order to find favor in each other's eyes. They exchange gifts which they hope will strengthen their developing relationship. However, once they are married, their relationship is so close and so firmly implanted in their hearts that it can flourish without any external manifestations. Just to be together, even when they are engaged in no particular activity, is a source of endless joy for the two lovers.

God and His people are like a groom and bride. As the New Year unfolds, the romance between them is rekindled. Rosh Hashanah and Yom Kippur are times when we seek, through the *mitzvos* of the day, to put our best foot forward spiritually and make ourselves "attractive" to God. Even on Succos, when God symbolically brings us into His home, we still offer gifts in the form of the *mitzvos* of *succah* and *arbah minim*. Only on Shemini Atzeres, when the undying love between us reaches its zenith, is there no need for the performance of a specific *mitzvah,* no need for a symbolic communication of the sentiments of love that exist between God and His people. Rather, they merely spend time together to rejoice in their mutual affection: וְהָיִיתָ אַךְ שָׂמֵחַ, *And you shall be purely joyous* (*Deuteronomy* 16:15).

A Sublime Connection

◈§ Why in fact does the sanctity of Shemini Atzeres find no concrete expression except in joy?

Shemini Atzeres expresses the most sublime level of connection between God and His people. This relationship functions on two levels. God is joyously proud of us because of our actions — *what we do*; on a more basic level, He loves us simply for *who we are*. A Jew, even if he sins, still remains a child of God (see *Rashba, Responsa* 1:194 and 242). His love for us is not only the conditional love of a father, but the unconditional love of a mother.

The days leading up to Shemini Atzeres are filled with *mitzvos*, which causes God to be happy with us. On Shemini Atzeres we celebrate together with God the passionate noncontingent love that exists between us. On this day, no intermediaries are necessary to forge the link between God and His nation (*Toras Emes*).

[This reflects yet another dimension to the unity among Jews which finds expression in Shemini Atzeres. While God's "joy" in

regard to our actions is of varying degrees according to the intensity of each person's commitment and performance, His unconditional love for the essence of His people is granted equally to all Jews. Thus, it is Shemini Atzeres, the day of God's exclusive spiritual communion with His people, which melds together all Jews in a bond of love.]

A Multifaceted Jewel

Shemini Atzeres — A Microcosm of the Festivals

•§ The term עֲצֶרֶת bears many shades of meaning. *Nesivos Shalom* suggests that it means *retaining within* (see *Deuteronomy* 11:17, וְעָצַר אֶת הַשָּׁמַיִם), for it contains the major spiritual elements of all three festivals. [It is for this reason that it is an independent holiday and yet is not considered a fourth pilgrimage festival.]

On Pesach, God showered Jews with unqualified love and kindness by redeeming them from the Egyptian bondage, though they were mired in spiritual impurity (see ArtScroll *Pesach*, p. 26). The Jews responded with unrestrained love for God by following Him out to the barren wilderness (see *Jeremiah* 2:2).

This mirror of reciprocal love is reflected in Shemini Atzeres, when God, as it were, secludes Himself with His beloved people for a final day of Festival celebration.

The special quality of Succos is also one of the components of Shemini Atzeres. Like Succos, it is a time when a mitigated atmosphere of Divine judgment hangs over us, for the *Zohar* teaches that Shemini Atzeres is the final day of judgment that began with Rosh Hashanah. We pray for rain and, by extension, for physical sustenance on this day.

Even the defining feature of Shavuos, the receiving of the Torah, plays a crucial role in the aura of Shemini Atzeres. It is on this day (on the next day in the Diaspora) that we celebrate Simchas Torah, joyously recommitting ourselves to more intense study and practice of Torah.

Thus, Shemini Atzeres is an independent holiday which encapsulates the three festivals and serves as their crowning glory. *Heichal Berachah* notes that the *gematria* of שָׁלוֹשׁ פְּעָמִים בַּשָּׁנָה, *Three times a*

year all your males should appear before HASHEM *(Deuteronomy* 16:16), equals that of בַּיוֹם הַשְּׁמִינִי עֲצֶרֶת, *on the eighth day shall be a restriction* [for you]. This alludes to the fact that the sanctity of all three pilgrimage festivals is incorporated in this special day.

Shemini Atzeres —
Unity Under the Banner of God

ᴥ§ *Onkelos* renders the word *atzeres* as כְּנִישִׁין, *assembly.* According to this translation, the festival is an auspicious time for unity among the Jewish people. In truth, the entire festival of Succos celebrates the theme of unity.

According to the Midrash, the four species collectively represent the many kinds of people in the community of Israel. The *esrog* is a food containing both טַעַם וְרֵיחַ, *taste and pleasant aroma;* it symbolizes righteous people, who possess both Torah knowledge and good deeds. The *lulav,* branch of a date palm, is odorless, but it produces sweet, nourishing food; it symbolizes the scholar who possesses Torah knowledge but is deficient in good deeds. The fragrant, tasteless myrtle leaf represents common people who possess good deeds but lack Torah scholarship. Finally, the odorless, tasteless willow leaf symbolizes those who lack both Torah and good deeds. God wishes the Jewish nation to unite into a *community,* and the Jew, by gathering the four species together, expresses this sense of Jewish unity.

Furthermore, the Talmud (*Succah* 27b) discusses the possibility of all Jews residing in one *succah.* We may understand this allegorically as an allusion to the idea that Succos is a time well suited for Jews to learn to live together in peace. The Torah calls Succos חַג הָאָסִיף, *the Festival of Gathering (Exodus* 34:22), a reference not only to the ingathering of produce of the harvest season, but also to the unification of Jewish souls in pursuit of a common purpose — to perform the will of Hashem.

If Succos is a time of unity in pursuit of Godly service, how may we be assured that the effects of this time of gathering will last beyond the festival itself? How can the Jew ensure that when he leaves his *succah,* he will take with him into his home and heart the dream of Jewish unification?

Shemini Atzeres is the guarantor that the unity achieved during Succos will endure. The Torah's very brief description of the festival, *On the eighth day an atzeres shall be for you,* can be understood as

follows: "On the eighth day, the spirit of gathering (i.e., unity) achieved on Succos will become yours." Shemini Atzeres helps a Jew assimilate the feeling of unity attained on Succos into his thoughts and emotions (*Imrei Emes*).

On One Foot

◄§ The Talmud (*Shabbos* 31a) tells us the famous story of a non-Jew who asked Hillel to teach him the entire Torah while he stood עַל רֶגֶל אַחַת, *on one foot*. Hillel replied, "Whatever is hateful to you do not do to your friend." R' Yisrael of Rizhin explained the proselyte's question as a reference to Shemini Atzeres.

The underlying theme of every Jewish holiday is specified in the Torah: Pesach is the season of our freedom, Shavuos is the time for accepting the Torah, Rosh Hashanah signifies the crowning of God as King, Yom Kippur calls for introspection and repentance, and Succos teaches us to recognize our dependence on God. But what is the lesson of Shemini Atzeres, which is a רֶגֶל בִּפְנֵי עַצְמוֹ, *an independent festival*?[1]

The Rizhiner explained that Hillel's reply to the proselyte was an answer to this question as well: All Jews are one. The oneness of the Jewish people demands that we unite in joy and brotherhood to pool our resources and efforts in the service of God. "Do unto your brother as you would have done unto yourself," for in truth we are all complementary parts of one great nation.

Homiletically, this is God's plea to us on Shemini Atzeres: "קָשֶׁה עָלַי פְּרֵידַתְכֶם. The פירוד, *divisiveness,* among you is very painful to Me, so to speak; My greatest joy is when all My children are united" (*R' Avraham of Slonim*).

This is the message of Shemini Atzeres. God calls upon us to dissolve whatever friction and disharmony that exists among us so that brotherly love and friendship will dwell in our midst.

Retaining the Spiritual Yield

◄§ The term *assembly* has other connotations as well. Often one is able to achieve spiritual attainments, yet finds great difficulty in sustaining

---

1. The word רֶגֶל can mean *foot* or *festival* — specifically, one of the three pilgrimage festivals when Jewish males are commanded to make a pilgrimage to Jerusalem. In this homiletic interpretation of the proselyte's question to Hillel, the word רגל is rendered as *festival.*

his gains. The great *Mussar* masters saw a homiletic allusion to this problem in the words of King David, מִי יַעֲלֶה בְהַר ה' וּמִי יָקוּם בִּמְקוֹם קָדְשׁוֹ, *Who may ascend the mountain of Hashem and who may stand in the place of His sanctity (Psalms 24:3)?* Firstly, asks King David, who will rise to great spiritual heights and ascend the Godly mountain? Secondly, who will be able to *maintain* that spiritual plateau and remain standing in the place of God's sanctity?

It is in this light that *R' Samson Raphael Hirsch* comments that the last day of a festival is the time when one should "assemble" the lessons he has derived from the festival, in order that he be able to "take them home with him" and keep them long after the days of sanctity have passed. One should take great care not to let his spiritual growth and accomplishments slide away.

Shemini Atzeres and Shavuos

ـⱥ§ The name *Atzeres* is also the name by which the Sages refer to Shavuos.[1] This, says *Rabbeinu Bachya*, teaches that Shemini Atzeres is a day as exalted as Shavuos, when we received the Torah and were imbued with our national destiny.

However, unlike Shavuos, which is preceded by the seven-week preparatory period of *Sefiras HaOmer*, Shemini Atzeres is preceded only by the seven days of Succos. The many *mitzvos* that we perform in the course of the Days of Awe and Succos provide us with the preparation we need for Shemini Atzeres, when we merit a very special closeness to God. Uplifted by these *mitzvos*, we can achieve in seven days the spiritual plateau which takes us seven *weeks* to attain after Pesach (*Sfas Emes*). In addition, just as on Shavuos God revealed His Divine Presence on Mount Sinai and affirmed our status as His chosen people, so too on Shemini Atzeres He restrains us from departing as He delights in the company of His beloved nation alone.

Times of Restraint

ـⱥ§ Shemini Atzeres and Shavuos are also united by a powerful theme which they share — that of self-restraint, one of the most basic foundations of Torah living. It is for this reason that Shavuos, the day on which God gave us the Torah, is called *Atzeres,* meaning restraint;

---

1. See ArtScroll *Shavuos — Its Observance, Laws and Significance.*

for in Torah study and observance lie the key to self-control, the ability to channel one's energies and passions toward the service of God.

Shemini Atzeres, too, represents our freedom from the negative influences of the gentile world as we achieve full *dveikus,* spiritual attachment, to our beloved Maker. According to *Yismach Moshe,* God alludes to this idea when He declares: "קָשָׁה עָלַי פְּרֵידַתְכֶם, *It is too hard for Me to bear the separation"* (see pp. 30, 31, 48). Unfortunately, when the festival season passes, people often slip back into their old habits and lose the sensivity to wrongdoing that they so carefully built up during the previous weeks. God therefore calls out to us, "Restrain yourselves. Muster all your spiritual strength to retain the freedom from sin that you achieved during the Holy Days. After we have grown so close to one another, it is difficult for Me to see you leave and grow distant again."

Beis Avraham (Slonim) views this as the homiletic message of the Torah's instruction regarding Shemini Atzeres, בַּיּוֹם הַשְּׁמִינִי עֲצֶרֶת תִּהְיֶה לָכֶם, *On the eighth day there shall be restraint for you.* The Talmud often interprets לָכֶם, *for you,* as a reference to man's physical needs. Thus, the Torah is instructing us to make the final day of the festival season one in which we will *restrain* ourselves and harness our physical desires. This is the very reason, in fact, that God is able to grant us a full share of prosperity on this day; He is confident that we will exercise proper caution and not abuse His blessings by using them for anything else besides His service.

An Infusion of Spirituality

◆§ The idea of *restraint,* indicated by the word *Atzeres,* is also connected to the function of Shemini Atzeres as a day to consolidate spiritual gains. It implies that the Jew should restrain himself for one day after the festival of Succos before returning to his mundane life, in order to absorb the festival's teachings and dedicate himself to the service of God and the study of His word. He must undergo a day-long sojourn in God's Sanctuary before returning to everyday life (*Sforno*).

The *Netziv of Volozhin* elaborates: A primary purpose of ascending to Jerusalem and the Temple on the three pilgrimage festivals was in order to absorb the enlightening words of instruction offered by the *Kohanim* and other scholars. Jerusalem was the spiritual nerve-center of the nation, from which Torah and spiritual guidance emanated to the entire Jewish people. Spiritually refreshed by this period of

inspiration, Jews returned home with a sense of purpose and direction which would guide them throughout the year.

During the days of Succos, the people were preoccupied with the myriad obligatory offerings of the holiday (*olas re'iyah, shalmei chagigah,* holiday *mussaf* and daily *tamid*), in addition to many vow offerings that individuals had promised in the course of the year. However, on Shemini Atzeres, only one communal bull and ram were offered. This gave the people a respite from activity and the peace of mind necessary to fully absorb the teachings they had heard, which would provide their souls with sustenance for the long winter ahead. Even today Shemini Atzeres is a day of introspection to charge our spiritual "batteries" for the days ahead.

Restraint Born of Love

⋖§ The continued practice of restraint on our part is very precious to God and enables us to draw closer to Him, a process which increases in intensity during the days of Succos. The words וִימִינוֹ תְּחַבְּקֵנִי, *His right arm embraces me* (Song of Songs 2:6), is symbolic of the *succah,* whose (minimum) two-and-a-fraction walls appear like the outstretched right arm of a mother who embraces her children warmly and welcomes them back home (see pp. 63-64).

The climax of this intense expression of God's love is Shemini Atzeres, when our uplifted state strengthens our bond with Him. This is alluded to in the verse יְמִינְךָ ה׳ תִּרְעַץ אוֹיֵב, *Your right hand, HASHEM, smashes the enemy* (Exodus 15:6); meaning that Hashem's right hand, which draws us close on Succos, smashes the ultimate enemy — the Evil Inclination. The letters of תרעץ can be rearranged to spell עצרת, for it is on this day when we are able to subdue our inappropriate desires and scale the heights of spirituality (*Beis Avraham*).

Holding Back the Decree

⋖§ A final interpretation of the concept of restraint is related to the judgment we undergo during the Days of Awe. According to *Zohar,* the Heavenly sentence for each individual for the coming year is not delivered to the angels who carry out the decree until Shemini Atzeres. This day is one when God, as it were, "restrains" delivery of the decree, giving man a last chance to repent so that the decree may be rescinded altogether (*Be'er Moshe*).

Shemini Atzeres and Pesach

◆§ In addition to Shavuos, both the seventh day of Pesach (see *Deuteronomy* 16:8) and the eighth day of Succos are called *Atzeres*. On the seventh day of Pesach, the Jewish nation passed through the Sea of Reeds while the Egyptians drowned in it. On that day, they were freed from the fear of physical danger as the enemies who had persecuted them for so long were destroyed.

On the eighth day of Succos we also achieve a respite — from the fear of *spiritual* danger. Freed on Yom Kippur from the grip of sin, we spend the days of Succos sheltered in God's abode, protected from the wiles of the Evil Persuader. On Shemini Atzeres, having symbolically diminished the power of the nations by offering seventy bulls in a descending progression, we enjoy a release from the other insidious source of spiritual ruination — the influence of a non-Jewish culture. Alone with God, we enjoy a respite from the war that is waged for our souls (*Sfas Emes*).

Bringing the Succah Inside

◆§ According to *Targum Yonasan ben Uziel,* the word *atzeres* indicates *ingathering.* Thus, בַּיּוֹם הַשְּׁמִינִי עֲצֶרֶת תִּהְיֶה לָכֶם (*Numbers* 29:35), is interpreted as *On the eighth day you shall joyfully return from your succos to your homes. Rambam* views this return as a continuation of the joy of Succos. Those opportunities for experiencing the joy of the festival which could not be accommodated in the fragile conditions of the *succah* may now be conducted inside in the comfort of one's home (*Moreh Nevuchim* 3:43).

This return to the home occurs while the festival is still in progress so that we are still in the *Yom Tov* spirit. This alleviates the trauma of making a sudden transition from the spiritual haven of the *succah* to our permanent abodes, whose sanctity is less intense. Therefore, God, in His love, provided us with Shemini Atzeres, a sanctified day which acts as a buffer to enable us to bring the atmosphere of the *succah* into our homes and make them spiritually habitable.

This is the thrust of our recitation in the holiday prayers and *Kiddush*: וַתִּתֶּן לָנוּ ה' אֱלֹהֵינוּ בְּאַהֲבָה אֶת יוֹם חַג שְׁמִינִי הָעֲצֶרֶת הַזֶּה, *God, in an expression of love, gave us the day of Shemini Atzeres to ease our transition from the sanctity of the *succah* to the more spiritually meager confines of the home (*R' Uri of Strelisk*).

Unity — the Greatest Mitzvah

~§ As we have seen, there are three festival days called *Atzeres*. The seventh day of Pesach and the eighth day of Succos are referred to in Scripture as *Atzeres* (see *Deuteronomy* 29:35 and 16:5), and the Sages apply this term to the festival of Shavuos as well. Unlike Pesach, Succos, Rosh Hashanah, and Yom Kippur, which all have their own festival-related *mitzvos*, these three festival days have no specific *mitzvah*;[1] rather, their sanctity is purely the result of Jews gathering together to rejoice with one another and with God. There is no greater expression of sanctity than when Jews unite in brotherly love. No specific *mitzvah* is needed on these days, for the love between Jews transcends all else (*R' Leibel Eiger*).

R' Mendel of Kossov offers the following parable to shed light on the unifying power of this holiday:

A father had many sons, all of whom were a source of pride and joy. The sons lived in peace and harmony, which added to their father's happiness. One day, an argument broke out among the brothers and soon turned into a heated dispute. Word of the dissension among the brothers reached the father, who was heartbroken.

"Nothing is more painful to me than strife among my children. I must do something," thought the father. He finally devised a plan. He invited all of his sons to a festive banquet in order that they enjoy each other's company, but instead they all sought to avoid one another.

Finally, the father gathered them all around the table and began speaking softly. "Strife among brothers is dangerous. When brothers are united, there is almost nothing they cannot accomplish. Isn't it a shame that your love for each other cannot overcome whatever petty reasons caused you to fight among yourselves? And last but not least, don't you realize how pained I am by the strife and division among you?" In this way, the father succeeded in renewing within his children a spirit of brotherly love.

The Jewish people are considered God's children, and nothing gives Him more joy than when we live together in peace and harmony. "קָשָׁה עָלַי פְּרֵידַתְכֶם, *The strife and separation among you causes Me undue hardship,*" says God. On Shemini Atzeres, God makes a special banquet only for Israel, His children, in order to engender a spirit of solidarity and mutual support among them.

---

1. While *chametz* is forbidden on the seventh day of Pesach, the only time when one is Scripturally commanded to eat matzah is the first night of the festival.

A Portent of Things to Come

A Private Celebration

⋐ *Yalkut Shimoni* (*Pinchas* 782) describes the special quality of joy experienced on Shemini Atzeres with the following simile:

A king celebrated a seven-day feast. During the entire period of the festivities, his son the prince was busy tending to the needs of the guests. At the end of the seven days, the king summoned the prince and said to him, "Now that the festivities are over and you no longer need to tend to the guests, let us celebrate together. Don't bother to prepare anything lavish; whatever is left over will do just fine."

During the seven-day holiday of Succos, the Divine feast is attended by many guests. The nations of the world benefit from the seventy bulls offered on their behalf. Only on Shemini Atzeres, when the guests depart laden with the blessings of the holiday, can God and His prince, Israel, join in a small, private feast celebrating their connection.

Israel, excited by the prospect of such an intimate rendezvous with God, begins to praise Him with the words of King David: זֶה הַיּוֹם עָשָׂה ה׳, נָגִילָה וְנִשְׂמְחָה בּוֹ, *This is the day HASHEM has made; let us rejoice and be glad on it* (*Psalms* 118:24). R' Avin inquires about the meaning of the word בּוֹ. Does it refer in this case to joy in the day, or in God Himself? The words of King Solomon offer the answer: *You brought me into Your innermost chambers,* נָגִילָה וְנִשְׂמְחָה בָּךְ, *let us rejoice and be glad in You* (*Song of Songs* 1:4) — in You and Your Torah, in You and Your salvation. While on all other festivals we rejoice over our experiences of God's manifestation in history, on Shemini Atzeres we rejoice in *God Himself*. As the *Baal HaTanya* said, "God, I don't want Your *Gehinnom,* I don't even want Your *Gan Eden;* I want You alone."

On Shemini Atzeres this prayer is answered. נָגִילָה וְנִשְׂמְחָה בָּךְ, *We will rejoice and be glad in You.* The word בָּךְ itself alludes to *Shemini Atzeres* on the 22nd day of Tishrei (בך = 22), since on this day, a microcosm of the World to Come, we experience God without any intermediary.

A Taste of the Ultimate Triumph

⋐ On Shemini Atzeres, as God and His people rejoice in each other's company, we partake of a taste of that ultimate victory when the

forces of evil will be vanquished forever — the days of the coming redemption. At that time, Israel will achieve ascendance over the other nations in fulfillment of the verse וַיִּוָּתֵר יַעֲקֹב לְבַדּוֹ, *And Jacob remained alone (Genesis* 32:25). It is this verse which introduces the confrontation between good and evil, personified by Jacob and the guardian angel of Esau, in the guise of a human being.

This confrontation was one of the cosmic events of Jewish history. The Sages teach that every nation has a Heavenly agent, an angel who guides its destiny on earth and acts as its "intermediary" with God. Two nations, however, are unique — Israel and Esau. Israel needs no intermediary; it is God's own people. Esau's guardian angel is different from all the others; his angel is the prime force of evil — Satan himself.

"Satan descends and seduces man [to sin]; then he ascends to incite [God, by prosecuting man for his sinfulness], and then he receives permission to take man's life . . . Satan, the Evil Inclination, and the Angel of Death are one and the same" *(Bava Basra* 16a). The angel of Esau *had* to attack Jacob in fulfillment of his role, because Jacob, as the Patriarch who represented the power of Torah, symbolized man's spiritual struggle to raise himself and the rest of the world with him — and Satan exists for the very purpose of crippling that effort. Thus, the battle between Jacob and the angel represented the eternal struggle between good and evil, between man's capacity to perfect himself and Satan's determination to destroy him. This struggle will continue throughout history until the dawn of salvation, when Jacob will remain triumphantly "alone," having finally vanquished the forces of evil. At that time, the oneness of God will be perceived by all mankind, in fulfillment of the prophetic promise, *on that day* HASHEM *will be One and His Name will be One (Zechariah* 14:9).

The Midrash *(Bereishis Rabbah* 77:1) draws a parallel between God and His people on that great day of Redemption. The prophecy of וְנִשְׂגַּב ה' לְבַדּוֹ בַּיּוֹם הַהוּא, *and God alone will be exalted on that day (Isaiah* 2:11), will be mirrored by the prophecy of וַיִּוָּתֵר יַעֲקֹב לְבַדּוֹ, indicating Israel's spiritual and physical supremacy over the nations. Shemini Atzeres is a glimpse into that glorious time when God and Israel's oneness will infuse the world.

Taste of Another World

◆§ According to *Arizal*, the reason why Shemini Atzeres is not clearly defined in Scripture as an independent festival is because, unlike all other festivals, which find worldly expression through their practical *mitzvos*, Shemini Atzeres is a portent of the World to Come. The sanctity of the day is a taste of the ultimate redemption, when all of creation will achieve fulfillment. That time is so awesome that it is really incomprehensible to us. In the words of the *Arizal*, "God will then rejoice over us as a bridegroom with his beloved bride."

This other-worldly quality of Shemini Atzeres is reflected in the fact that it is the *eighth* day of Succos, a number which represents transcendence of the physical world. *Maharal* explains that the number seven is indicative of natural phenomena; a week, for example, lasts for seven days and then repeats itself. Likewise, any given center point can be extended in six directions (north, south, east, west, up, and down), with the center itself the seventh point. Eight, however, is symbolic of things which transcend nature. It was on the eighth day of the dedication ceremonies of the *Mishkan* (Tabernacle) that the Presence of God manifested itself; and it is on the eighth day of life that a Jewish male enters into the covenant of circumcision, which sanctifies the soul and empowers man to rise above the confinements of the mundane world and cleave to God and His commandments. Similarly, on Shemini Atzeres, the eighth day, every Jew can rise above his "natural" limitations and attach himself to God and His Torah.

Seven represents the greatest degree of achievement attainable in this world (just as the Sabbath, the seventh day, was the culmination of Creation), while eight alludes to the World to Come. Shemini Atzeres symbolizes the spiritual pleasures of the World to Come, where the soul, unfettered by physical constraints cleaves to God with unadulterated joy *(Nesivos Shalom)*.

A Taste of Homecoming

◆§ Shemini Atzeres is also an allusion to Messianic times in terms of our return to the Land of Israel.

Rabbeinu Bachaya views the *succah*, a temporary abode, as symbolic of the sojourn of the Children of Israel in the Wilderness. The desert served as a training ground where the Jews, totally

dependent on God, developed a healthy sense of faith and trust which was to serve them in good stead when they entered *Eretz Yisrael,* their permanent home.

We are commanded to repeat this exercise in faith yearly when we give up our homes for a temporary sojourn in the makeshift shelter of the *succah.* There we demonstrate our dependence on God, and on Shemini Atzeres we reenter our homes with a bolstered sense of trust in Him. We may therefore suggest that this day is symbolic of Messianic times, when all Jews will finally leave the temporary existence of the exile and return home again to an authentic Jewish homeland.

Triumph Over the Nations

◆§ The *Vilna Gaon,* in examining the wording of the text, offers a fascinating insight into the listing of the seventy bulls that are offered on Succos on behalf of the nations. On the first, second, and fourth days, the goat brought as a sin offering (חַטָּאת) is referred to as שְׂעִיר עִזִּים, *one male of goats,* while on the third, fifth, sixth, and seventh days of Succos the same offering is called שְׂעִיר (חַטָּאת) אֶחָד, *one he-goat* (see *Numbers* 29:12-34). The *Gaon* (based on *Zohar*) suggests that שְׂעִיר עִזִּים refers to Ishmael, while שְׂעִיר refers to Esau. Ishmael symbolizes the Arab nations, while the Sages equate Esau with Rome and Christian anti-Semitism. Thus, Ishmael and Esau represent the primary antagonists and oppressors of the Jewish people in the current exile.

The numbers of the offerings support this idea. On the first day of Succos we offer thirteen bulls, on the second day we offer twelve, and on the fourth day ten, for a total of thirty-five. On these days we bring sin offerings of שְׂעִיר עִזִּים, corresponding to the thirty-five nations who descend from Ishmael. On the third day we offer eleven bulls, on the fifth day nine, on the sixth day eight, and on the seventh day seven, again for a total of thirty-five. On these days the Torah calls the sin offering שְׂעִיר, for these bulls are representative of the thirty-five nations whose progenitor is Esau.

R' Zalman Sorotzkin views this allusion as a reflection of our own times, when the oppression of Jews comes from two sources — east and west. The hatred of Jews incited by Moslem fundamentalists from the East, along with the more insidious destruction inherent in the lure of Western values, both jeopardize Jewish integrity and survival.

We must remain "one bull and one ram" and maintain our distinctiveness as a nation apart. As Balaam prophetically described the people of Israel, *Behold! It is a nation that will dwell in solitude and not be reckoned among the nations* (Numbers 23:9). The mission of the Jewish people is to remain separate and distinct from the nations of the world, both Eastern and Western, and to resist assimilation.

Shemini Atzeres is a portrait of the future, when we will be rid of the threats and influences of foreign nations. At that time, the Jewish people will experience unparalled preeminence as it leads the world toward recognition and service of the one and only God.

Peace Among the Nations

&s *R' Moshe Feinstein* offered the following deep insight on Shemini Atzeres of 5702 (1942), explaining the celebration of Simchas Torah in conjunction with Shemini Atzeres.

God created the world in such a way that no man, and no nation, can survive alone. Each country is blessed with varying natural resources but must rely on others for those it lacks. Likewise, no individual is completely self-sufficient; he must depend on others to provide for many of his needs. Dissent among nations and among people can totally undermine the continued existence of the world, since without cooperation everyone will lack some necessities basic to survival. It is for this reason that over the course of Succos, we offer seventy bulls on behalf of the community of nations in order that peace reign among them. This is ultimately to our benefit, for it is through the cooperative efforts of all humanity that man is able to obtain what he needs to survive and prosper.

The necessity for peace is therefore self-evident, and yet the world is filled with strife, both nationally and individually. This self-destructive path is the result of a narrow vision which sees life as nothing more than a means for achieving power, pleasure, or prestige. To the self-seeking opportunist, hatred, jealousy and the like are all justified, since they all serve to help him achieve his wicked goals.

Thus, after we pray for the peace and welfare of the gentile nations during Succos, we celebrate Shemini Atzeres in recognition that the *purpose* of peace in a functional society is in order to provide us with the conditions to serve God and rejoice in His Torah.

Festivals — Mirrors of Redemption

≈§ The Sages teach that the four cups of wine that we drink at the Pesach *Seder* symbolize the four expressions of redemption used in the Torah to describe the progressive stages of the Exodus (see *Pesachim* 99b and *Rashi* ad loc.). A fifth expression, וְהֵבֵאתִי, *and I shall bring,* refers to the ultimate redemption, when God will bring His people back to the Land promised to our forefathers.

Homiletically, these expressions allude to the unique message and impact of each of the festivals. וְהוֹצֵאתִי, *and I will remove you* [from under the burdens of Egypt] (*Exodus* 6:6), refers to the festival of Pesach, the first in the yearly cycle, when Jews were freed from the Egyptian bondage. It is during this time every year that Jews can experience spiritual freedom.

This is followed by Shavuos, when God gave us the Torah and thereby rescued us from the decadent lifestyle of the foreign nations. This is alluded to by the term וְהִצַּלְתִּי, *I shall rescue you* [from their service] (ibid.).

On Rosh Hashanah and Yom Kippur we undergo a spiritual redemption through the process of *teshuvah,* and are freed from the tentacles of sin. The expression וְגָאַלְתִּי אֶתְכֶם, *and I shall redeem you* [with an outstretched arm], alludes to the way in which God stands with outstretched arms, as it were, waiting to accept penitents who respond to His call: ''שׁוּבָה אֵלַי כִּי גְאַלְתִּיךָ, *Return to Me, for I have redeemed you*'' (*Isaiah* 44:22).

The fourth term, וְלָקַחְתִּי, *and I shall take you* [to Me] (ibid. 6:7), alludes to Succos, the time when God welcomes us back from the distance imposed by our sins and lovingly embraces us in the *succah.* Finally, the fifth term, וְהֵבֵאתִי, *and I shall bring you to the Land* (*Exodus* 6:8), symbolizes Shemini Atzeres, when we return from the temporary dwelling of the *succah* to our permanent homes. This process is a metaphoric expression of the great ingathering of the exiles which will occur at the time of the Final Redemption.

Purifying Waters

≈§ The *Vilna Gaon* writes (*Even Shleimah* 11:10) that the month of Tishrei mirrors the World to Come. Rosh Hashanah is a yearly day of judgment, followed by Yom Kippur, which cleanses us of sin. Similarly, in Days to Come we will undergo a great and awesome day of judgment (see *Malachi* 3:23) and a purification process which is

described by the prophets. Ezekiel (36:25) prophesied that in the future *God will sprinkle pure water upon us and we will be cleansed of sin,* and Jeremiah (50:20) speaks of God forgiving all remaining sins in the End of Days.

Succos alludes to the future time when God will envelop His people in a cloud which will act as a *succah* to protect them from all enemies and evil (see *Isaiah* 4:6).

Shemini Atzeres therefore epitomizes Messianic times, when God will eradicate all iniquity from this earth and rejoice exclusively with His people.

Rain — Key to Prosperity

Rain on Succos

◆§ One of the hallmarks of Shemini Atzeres is the prayer for rain. On this day we begin to add the phrase, מַשִּׁיב הָרוּחַ וּמוֹרִיד הַגֶּשֶׁם, *He makes the wind blow and the rain descend,* to the second blessing of the *Shemoneh Esrei* prayer.[1] According to *Yonasan ben Uziel,* the name *Atzeres,* in its translation of *assembly,* indicates that on this day Jews should *assemble* together in order to pray for rain (see *Leviticus* 23:36). As the Midrash (*Koheles Rabbah* 7:3) states, "God says, 'I made no better intercessor for the rains than the day of Shemini Atzeres.' "

This facet of the day is also mentioned in another Midrash, this time emphasizing the translation of *Atzeres* as *restraint*: On Pesach, when we *cease* to pray for rain, God curbs the rain and winds so that we may be involved in agricultural activities during the summer. On Shemini Atzeres, we place restraints on ourselves by remaining with God, as it were, for one more day, in order to pray that He open His storehouse and bring wind, rain, and prosperity (*Yalkut, Pinchas* 782).

The Talmud (*Rosh Hashanah* 2a) teaches that there are different types of judgment at various times of the year. On Succos we are judged with regard to water and rainfall. Since the fall and winter are the rainy season in *Eretz Yisrael,* a land that is dependent on rainfall for the success of its crops, the Sages ordained that the prayer for rain

---

1. The text of the Prayer for Rain, with commentary, appears on p. 144.

be recited on Succos, the pilgrimage festival in closest proximity to the rainy season. This poses a problem, however: Since the festival is celebrated primarily in the *succah*, and it is regarded as a symbol of Divine displeasure for rain to prevent people from eating and living there, it would be incongruous to pray for rain at a time when we do not want it to fall. Therefore, we begin to recite the prayer for rain on Shemini Atzeres, when there is no Scriptural commandment to eat in the *succah*.

Mateh Moshe suggests that this is the reason many people limit the extent of their dwelling in the *succah* on Shemini Atzeres, even though it is not prohibited (see Laws pp. 115-117). Since rain impedes dwelling in the *succah* and might be regarded as a negative sign from Above, people might be unable to pray wholeheartedly for it. By staying out of the *succah*, they are able to pray for rain without such concerns.

The Diluted Wine

෴ The Sages compare rainfall on Succos to a servant who brought a decanter of water in order to mix it with wine and pour a cup for his master. The master poured the decanter out into his face, showing that the servant's action was unacceptable and not desired. Similarly, rain on Succos is an indication that G-d is dissatisfied with our service, as expressed in our fulfillment of the *mitzvah* of *succah*, and is desirous that we leave (*Succah* 29a and *Rashi* ad loc.).

The *Vilna Gaon* offers a deep explanation of this Talmudic parable. He questions why the Mishnah did not simply state that a slave was coming to hand over a cup to his master and that the master poured it into his face. Instead it speaks specifically of a decanter of water used to dilute the wine.

The *Gaon* explains that Rosh Hashanah and Yom Kippur are days of judgment when many harsh decrees are issued. They are followed by the festival of Succos, with its abundance of *mitzvos: lulav, esrog, hadassim, aravos,* and dwelling in the *succah*. All of these are aimed at eliciting the Almighty's mercy (רַחֲמִים). By not allowing us to fulfill the *mitzvah* of *succah* the Almighty is telling us that He does not wish to temper His justice with mercy.

In the allegorical terminology of *Kabbalah*, wine represents harsh justice and water represents mercy. The Mishnah uses the term לִמְזוֹג, *to mix,* to indicate that the slave is coming to dilute the cup of wine held by his master. This represents Israel, who seeks to dilute the

severe judgment of the High Holy Days with mercy. But if the master takes the jug of water held by the slave — the tempering agent itself — and pours it into the slave's face, no dilution will take place. The Almighty, by not allowing the Jews to fulfill the *mitzvah* of succah, indicates that He is not yet ready to temper justice with mercy (*Divrei Eliyahu*).

Based on this profound idea of the *Vilna Gaon,* we might suggest homiletically that it is particularly appropriate to offer prayers for rain on Shemini Atzeres. This day is one of unabashed love between God and His people, and in the words of King Solomon, וְעַל כָּל פְּשָׁעִים תְּכַסֶּה אַהֲבָה, *Love covers all sins* (*Proverbs* 10:12). Thus, the mitigation of Divine justice which could not be accomplished during Succos is now possible because of God's unrestrained love for His people at this time. Now, only goodness and blessing will result from our prayers for rain.

Silent Prayers

◄§ Though we refrain on Succos from petitioning directly for rain, we are nonetheless involved in many *mitzvos* which allude to rain and serve as a silent prayer for it. The taking of the four species, all of which require an abundance of water for their growth, serves as a form of prayer that God have mercy upon His people and provide its land with timely and beneficial rainfall.

This is analogous to a king who informed his servant that for the next week he would be attending the gala celebration of a friend's marriage. "For the next week, take care of your own needs, and when I return I will continue to support you from my table." The servant was discomfited and wondered what to do. Finally, he decided to go with his family to the location of the wedding celebration so that the king would notice him and remember his commitment to provide for the servant's family. The unuttered message was clear: "I understand that here, where the food is not your own, there is nothing you can do for us. But, dear king, please remember us as soon as you return home and provide for our needs once again, for we rely on no one but yourself."

Similarly, we appear before God with our *lulav* and *esrog* and thus convey an unstated plea: We know, dear God, that now is not the proper time for rain. But please take note of our needs, and as soon as we have concluded the *mitzvah* of *succah,* provide us with the rain we so desperately need (*Menoras HaMaor*).

Emulating Adam

◆§ The prayers for rain are offered in the *Mussaf* service on the day of Shemini Atzeres rather than in the *Maariv* prayer on the previous night or in the *Shacharis* prayer. *Tur* (O.C. 114) gives several reasons: In Talmudic times, synagogues were often located on the outskirts of town, and nighttime attendance was dangerous. Since many people were unable to attend services, the Sages feared that no uniform custom would develop and some would begin reciting *Mashiv Haruach* during *Maariv,* while others would not. In addition, to begin the prayer for rain during *Shacharis* might lead people to assume that the recitation had begun the night before, and they might mistakenly recite it at night the following year.

Finally, since one may not begin reciting *Mashiv Haruach* until the public announcement to this effect is made in the synagogue (see Laws Section §17), it is delayed until *Mussaf* in order to avoid an interruption between the blessing of גָּאַל יִשְׂרָאֵל and the beginning of the *Amidah* during *Maariv* and *Shacharis* (see *Shulchan Aruch, Orach Chaim,* 111:1).

R' Yissachar Dov of Belz offered a more homiletic explanation for the delay of the prayer *for rain* until *Mussaf*: Our prayer for rain mirrors the entreaty of the first man, Adam, who also prayed for rain. The Torah teaches that prior to the creation of Adam, all the vegetation that God had created remained just below the surface of the earth since no rain had been provided yet. Man, who is able and expected to appreciate the greatness of the gift of rain, had to be created before rain could fall. On the day of his creation, Adam indeed prayed for rain, and only then did God grant it and cause the vegetation to grow (see *Genesis* 2:5 and *Rashi* ad loc.). When did Adam pray? The *Midrash* (see *Tanchuma, Shemini*) teaches that it was in the seventh hour of the day of his creation — exactly the hour by when the *Mussaf* prayer should (ideally) be recited (see *Shulchan Aruch O.C.* 286:1 *M.B.* §2). Thus we follow the model of Adam and pray for rain during *Mussaf*.

[This may suggest yet another reason for offering prayers for rain on this day. The *teshuvah* process reaches its zenith on this day when Jews experience a heightened love of God and His Torah. Through repentance we are able to regain the purity of heart and commitment to God that was the essence of Adam's life. We therefore seek to emulate him and pray for rain in the seventh hour, as he did.]

Link to the Holy Land

◆§ As mentioned earlier, the prayers for rain are conducted during Shemini Atzeres since it is the festival closest to the rainy season in *Eretz Yisrael,* which begins during fall and continues into winter. Seemingly, however, these prayers should be recited during the festival closest to the rainy season of *each particular* locality. Why do all places pray for rain on the basis of the seasons in *Eretz Yisrael*? R' *Aryeh Tzvi Frommer (Eretz Tzvi)* explains: The Torah refers to *Eretz Yisrael* as "*a land that HASHEM your God seeks out; the eyes of HASHEM, your God, are always upon it from the beginning of the year to year's end"* (*Deuteronomy* 11:12). Though God is omniscient and oversees the entire universe, His principal attention is focused on *Eretz Yisrael,* while the rest of the world enjoys His blessing on a secondary level. *Eretz Yisrael* serves as the conduit for God's beneficence on Earth, and only after attending to it does He bless other lands (see *Rashi* ad loc.). The key to rain and prosperity around the globe lies, therefore, in God's blessing the Land of Israel. We therefore pray that He grant rain in the Holy Land and that through this, Jews the world over will merit the blessing of rain, each person in his own locale.[1]

Rain as a Personal Prayer

◆§ On the Days of Awe we pray for spiritual growth. *Shelah,* in fact, cautions that one's prayers on Rosh Hashanah should be concerned only with the enhancement of God's glory in the world. This focus on the spiritual realm continues through Yom Kippur. Even on Succos, offerings were brought altruistically on behalf of the nations of the world.

It is only on Shemini Atzeres that we focus on our practical concerns — a type of prayer aptly described by the word גֶּשֶׁם, which literally means *rain* but is also related to גַּשְׁמִיּוּת, *the physical.* This

---

1. A secular Jew who rose to prominence in Israeli political circles related that as a child in Czarist Russia, he was once under his father's *tallis* during the *Geshem* prayer when he realized that rain was falling outside the synagogue. "Father, why do we need to pray for rain?" he asked. "Isn't it raining outside?" The father forcefully retorted, "That is not *our* rain!" Only many years later did the child realize the truth of the father's words. Jews reside in all four corners of the earth, but they are aliens in a land not their own. Only *Eretz Yisrael* is truly ours!

idea is homiletically conveyed in the verse describing Shemini Atzeres: בַּיּוֹם הַשְּׁמִינִי עֲצֶרֶת תִּהְיֶה לָכֶם, *On the eighth day shall be an assembly* לָכֶם, *for you* — for all your personal needs (*R' Moshe Leib of Sassov*).

Divrei Shmuel shows us the importance of praying for the right things at the right times. He compares our prayers on the Days of Awe to a prince who was banished from his father's home for behavior unbefitting the son of a king. The young man joined up with a band of ruffians. After a while, the prince lost all vestiges of royalty and became as grossly uncouth as his new friends.

One day, his father discovered his whereabouts and sent a messenger to bring him home. The messenger told the young man, "Ask anything of the king and it will be granted." Were he merely to have asked, the messenger would have taken him home to the palace. Instead, the young prince requested a pair of new boots. He had sunk to such a low level that there was nothing more significant to him now than a shiny pair of boots. The messenger and the king were both distraught.

Likewise, on Rosh Hashanah, God sends us a message giving us the opportunity to return home to Him. All we need to do is ask and God will bring us back. How foolish it would be to ask instead for physical necessities; once we "come home" to God, He will provide us with all our needs! Thus, on Rosh Hashanah we pray only for the restoration of God's glory and that God accept our repentance.

However, once the prince comes home, he may ask his father for even the most mundane item. Likewise, on Shemini Atzeres, having fully returned to God, we may now focus on our material needs.

An Auspicious Hour

∾ The day of Shemini Atzeres, as we have mentioned earlier, is an auspicious time for our prayers to find favor in God's eyes. In fact, all the prayers that one recited without proper concentration or intent throughout the year can be rectified and accepted on Shemini Atzeres along with the prayers of the day itself (*R' Bunim of P'shischa*). *R' Yissachar Dov of Belz* suggests a homiletic allusion to this in the acronym for the six aspects in which Shemini Atzeres is an independent festival rather than merely a continuation of Succos (see p. 113). That acronym, פַּזַ"ר קַשַׁ"ב, may be interpreted as: "May You now hearken (קשב) to our heartfelt pleas, and also accept those

prayers that we prayed while our minds and hearts were distracted and our thoughts were dispersed (פזר)."

The efficacy of prayer on Shemini Atzeres may also be related to the purity of heart achieved through repentance. *Zohar* teaches that "one who has vanquished the snake [a metaphor for the Evil Inclination] is allowed to marry the daughter of the king [a metaphor for prayer]." Thus, after the cathartic experience of *teshuvah* one is granted the gift of effective prayer (*Imrei Moshe*).

The *Rebbe of Ostrovtze* offered a brilliant source based on the Midrash and *Zohar* for the special acceptability of prayer on Shemini Atzeres. The Midrash teaches that Moses, in his entreaties to God that he be allowed to enter the Holy Land, offered 515 prayers. This is derived from the word וָאֶתְחַנַּן, *I implored* [Hashem] (*Deuteronomy* 3:23), which equals 515 (6 + 1 + 400 + 8 + 50 + 50). Moses did not continue to pray any more, for God instructed him to cease: *And God said to me, "It is too much for you. Do not continue to speak to Me further about this matter"* (ibid. 26).

Had Moses offered just one more prayer, God would have acceded to his request. Why? Explained the Ostrovtzer: In ancient times, the righteous would engage in each prayer for one hour (see *Berachos* 32b). Since Moses began his entreaties on the Rosh Hashanah before his death, he prayed 504 prayers in twenty-one days (21 x 24). He continued to pray throughout the night (eleven prayers over eleven hours). Had he offered one more prayer, he would have reached the morning of Shemini Atzeres. That morning, according to the *Zohar*, is the time of the final sealing of man's fate for the coming year (see p. 41). Had Moses prayed at such an auspicious moment, God would have had no choice but to grant his request; but since He did not want to allow Moses to enter the Land, He told him to cease praying.

The morning of Shemini Atzeres is such a proverbial conduit for prayer that even those entreaties which do not merit a response may receive consideration. Thus the *Zohar* teaches about Shemini Atzeres, "When one has a private audience with the King, he may ask for his heart's desires and they will be granted."

Prayer and the Nations

◆§ The efficacy of prayer on Shemini Atzeres may also be related to the diminished power of the nations of the world, which is expressed through the offering of seventy bulls on Succos. The bulls are

brought in descending numerical sequence in order to symbolize the nations' continually diminishing power and eventual disappearance.

As mentioned earlier, the Vilna Gaon divides the seventy nations into two groups: those who trace their beginnings either to Esau or to Ishmael. It is noteworthy that these two forces of spiritual impurity are, according to *Likkutei Halachos,* representative of the two major impediments to heartfelt prayer. Often, God forbid, one tires of praying and becomes disillusioned, believing that his entreaties are powerless and cannot improve his situation. Esau reflects this attitude in his claim, *"Look, I am going to die, so of what use to me is a birthright?* (*Genesis* 25:32). Why should I want the firstborn status and the privilege of performing the sacrificial service since I am going to die anyway? Nothing I may do, including prayer, can affect my life."

The second impediment to effective prayer is the attitude which says, "God doesn't need our prayers; He knows exactly what we need. If He wants to, He will provide it unasked." This approach is personified by Ishmael, whose very name, יִשְׁמָעֵאל, can be translated *"HASHEM has heard your prayer"* (ibid. 16:11). On Shemini Atzeres, having completed the offering of the seventy bulls, we are symbolically free of the power of the nations, and we experience a taste of the ultimate triumph over our adversaries. At this time we are able to pray to our heart's content without fear of either Esau or Ishmael. It is specifically on this day that the *Zohar* teaches that one who is *alone* with the King — free from the influence of all foreign powers and philosophies — may ask for his heart's desires, and they will be granted. Possessing the undiluted power of prayer, we are able successfully to storm the gates of Heaven.

Farewell to the Succah

Taking the Succah Inside

◆§ It is customary to take leave of the *succah* and bid it farewell at the end of the Succos holiday. In the Land of Israel this takes place on *Hoshana Rabbah* (since Scripturally one does not eat in the *succah* on Shemini Atzeres — see Laws, Chapter 1), while in the Diaspora this

occurs on *Shemini Atzeres*. After enjoying a small snack in the *succah* and fulfilling the *mitzvah* for one last time,[1] we recite the appropriate prayers (see Liturgy Section, p. 158).

There are many lessons and ideas which we are to carry with us when we leave the *succah* to come inside. Among these is the realization of the true Source of our sustenance.

The *mitzvah* of *succah* enlightens man as to the temporary nature of this world and all earthly possessions. Particularly at harvest time, man is tempted to think that it is *my strength and the might of my hand [that has] made me all this wealth* (*Deuteronomy* 8:17), seeking a sense of permanence in his daily affairs and accomplishments. The Torah therefore teaches, כָּל הָאֶזְרָח בְּיִשְׂרָאֵל יֵשְׁבוּ בַּסֻּכֹּת, *Every native in Israel shall dwell in booths* (*Leviticus* 23:42). One who feels himself a native rather than a stranger in this world must leave his permanent abode and dwell for seven days in a temporary hut, where he will hopefully come to the realization that his only true protection is in the shadow of God. This world is but an inn on the road, and we are all mere guests passing through (*Kli Yakar, Malbim*).

The construction of the *succah* itself proclaims this message. Its makeshift nature, with a porous cover consisting of discarded vegetation (see *Succah* 12a) such as wood and leaves, is clearly intended as a דִּירַת עֲרַאי, *temporary dwelling*. It tells us to leave behind the seemingly "permanent" possessions which we have accumulated in the physical world, and to migrate to the materially plain, yet unfathomably precious, world of Torah spirituality (*Sfas Emes*).

We bid the *succah* farewell with a prayer in our hearts and on our lips that we have absorbed its lesson and that we will carry it with us. Even when we are back inside the more solid structures of our homes, we must remind ourselves that it is only in the protection of God that we can find true security.

A Motherly Embrace

☙ Another experience which we hope to maintain in our hearts when we return home is the special love Hashem has showered on us during Succos and Shemini Atzeres. *Beis Avraham* homiletically explains that the walls of the *succah* represent the warm, motherly

---

1. See Laws section for a discussion regarding eating in the *succah* on Shemini Atzeres. Even those who do not eat in the *succah* take leave of it on this day by reciting the appropriate prayers.

embrace with which God accepts His people after the purifying experience of Elul and Tishrei. One wall symbolizes the upper arm, one symbolizes the forearm, and the third partial wall [see *Succah* (6a)] represents the hand which holds us tight, conveying to us God's confidence in our ability to make Him, as it were, proud of our accomplishments. When we take leave of the *succah,* it is with the hope that the emotionally uplifting experience of our closeness to God will accompany us into our homes and throughout our lives (*Imrei Moshe*).

A Sense of Unity

~§ A third gift that we take home with us is the sense of unity engendered by Succos. After the nation has been purified of its sins on Yom Kippur, Succos creates a unique spirit of togetherness, coloring our relationships with each other and with Hashem. This togetherness is symbolized by the *succah,* an inviting place for Jews of all stations, where they can join together and be as one with Hashem.

The Talmud (*Succah* 27b) teaches that, unlike *lulav,* one need not own his *succah* in order to fulfill the *mitzvah.* In fact, one can even use his neighbor's *succah.* In the words of the Talmud, ''כָּל יִשְׂרָאֵל רְאוּיִין לֵישֵׁב בְּסוּכָּה אַחַת, (*Succah* 27b) *[In theory], all Jews could sit in one succah.* '' Homiletically, this teaches that every Jew, no matter how far he has strayed from his roots during the year, can rejoin his fellow Jews in the shelter of the *succah* and repose in Hashem's embrace.

As we return to our homes and go our separate ways after the festival, it is our fervent prayer that the unity of heart and purpose which was achieved in the *succah* last throughout the year (*Sfas Emes*).

A Parting Kiss

~§ *Shelah* (quoted in *Mishnah Berurah* 477:5) writes: ''I have seen spiritually sensitive Jews who kissed the walls of the *succah* upon entering and when leaving as an expression of their affection for the *mitzvos.* Praiseworthy are those who joyously serve God.''

Parting Prayers

~§ In the prayer customarily recited as we take leave of the *succah,* we express the hope that by next year the Messiah will have arrived and

we will participate in the grand feast to be held in the "*succah* [made of] the skin of the Leviathan (לִוְיָתָן) (see p. 159). In fact, the *mitzvah* of *succah* may very well ensure us a place at that hallowed banquet.

R' *Levi Yitzchak of Berditchev* went to great pains to entertain guests out in his *succah*. He especially sought out simple, uncultivated Jews to grace his table. When asked to explain his custom, the Berditchever replied: "At the End of Days, when the righteous will feast in the *succah* of the Leviathan, I also want to be allowed to come in and participate in that banquet. However, I'm afraid that the angels and the righteous will ask me, 'Levi Yitzchak, how does a simple Jew like you have the nerve to push your way into such a distinguished group?' Now, however, I will be able to answer, 'In my *succah* I also allowed simple and coarse Jews to enter.' "

In the meantime, the לִוְיָתָן, so to speak, gives us encouragement in another way. R' *Aharon of Karlin* understood the term לִוְיָתָן as related homiletically to the expression לְוָיָה, *accompaniment*. As we reenter our houses, we entreat God to allow the influence of the *succah* to remain with us throughout the year and to accompany us on our path through life.

Chashavah LeTovah provides us yet another window on the continued protection of the *succah*. When the Jewish nation emerged from the decadent culture of Egypt, God surrounded them with the עֲנְנֵי הַכָּבוֹד, *Clouds of Glory*, in order to protect them from sinking once again into a spiritual mire. In commemoration of those clouds, we are enjoined to erect *succos* (see *Succah* 11b). Just as the clouds served to prevent the Jews from regressing into sin, so does the *succah* prevent us from losing the purity of Yom Kippur, when we achieved atonement for our sins. We therefore pray in our farewell to the *succah* that this spiritual protection continue to accompany us throughout the year: *that the holy angels who are affiliated with the mitzvah of succah . . . accompany us when we leave the succah . . . to save us from all sin and iniquity.*

Protection from Pain

◦§ The merit of the *mitzvah* of *succah* also helps to ensure that our material needs are provided for throughout the year. *Tiferes Shlomo* sees a homiletic allusion to this in the Talmudic statement, "He who sits with his head and most of his body in the *succah* and his table on the outside has fulfilled the *mitzvah* of *succah*" (*Succah* 28a). One who is physically, intellectually and emotionally involved in the

mitzvah of *succah* will find his table blessed during the rest of the year when he dwells in his house.

Likewise, the *succah* has the protective power to save us from pain and sickness. The Talmud teaches: מִצְטָעֵר פָּטוּר מִן הַסּוּכָּה, *One who finds it painful to dwell in the succah is absolved* [of the obligation] (*Succah* 26a). The great Chassidic masters interpreted this homiletically: "One who is in pain will be absolved and relieved [of that pain] by the *succah*. It is for this that we beseech God as we depart the *succah*, '*May the merit of the succah stand by us . . . may we merit both tables* [i.e., both spiritual and temporal blessings] *with neither pain nor grief.*'"

Total Involvement

◆§ Another prayer is alluded to by the fact that we perform the *mitzvah* of *succah* with our entire bodies. In the words of *R' Bunim of P'shischa*, "One goes in even with his boots," meaning that one performs the commandment with his entire physical being. When we take leave of this all-encompassing experience, we pray that all the *mitzvos* we perform throughout the year will also be executed with every fiber of our beings.

A Prayer for the End of Exile

◆§ Finally, and not least of all, we pray as we leave the *succah* for the blessing of the final redemption.

Yaaros Devash explains why the *mitzvah* of *succah* comes immediately after Yom Kippur. "As the time of repentance comes to a close, we are commanded by the Torah to exile ourselves from our homes: *Leave your permanent abode and go out to a temporary dwelling* (*Succah* 2a). Realize you are a sojourner in this world, rooted in nothing else but your soul's connection to God. Let your eyes look up through the covering of the *succah* and see in the [distant] stars how far you are from your Maker. Pray that God, in His infinite kindness, have mercy upon you, [viewing you] as one who realizes the extent of his spiritual poverty."

As we come in from the *succah*, returning symbolically from exile, we pray that we *may all dwell placid and serene, vigorous and fresh, serving HASHEM in utmost truthfulness* (see p. 161) and that we may merit speedily, in our days, both personal and communal redemption.

‌‌‌Insights — Simchas Torah:

A Joyous Finale / A Joyous Beginning

Celebration of Completion

◆§ The last day of the festival (in the Diaspora) is called Simchas Torah, *Joy of the Torah*. This is the day when we read the final portion of the Torah, *VeZos HaBerachah*, and celebrate the completion of the annual cycle of public Torah reading of the *Chumash* (Pentateuch). We then immediately begin the new cycle of Torah reading with the opening of *Parashas Bereishis.*[1] The custom of celebrating Simchas Torah is mentioned in the *Zohar* and codified in *Shulchan Aruch* (*Rema* O.C. 669).

Why does the completion of the Torah call for a celebration? *Levush* explains by citing the story of King Solomon's ascendance to the throne at the age of twelve. God came to him in a dream and asked him to request whatever he wished. Solomon replied that he wanted "an understanding heart with which to judge Your people, to discern between good and evil."

God was pleased with Solomon's request. He said:

> *Because you requested this and you did not request long life for yourself and you did not request the life of your enemies — but you requested discernment to understand judgment: behold, I have fulfilled your words; behold, I have given you a wise and discerning heart, so that there has never been your equal before you, nor will your equal arise after you. And I have even given you what you did not request, even wealth and even glory, so that no man will be your equal among kings all your days* (I Kings 3:9-13).

When Solomon awoke, he went to the Tabernacle in Giveon, brought offerings of gratitude, and made a feast for all his subjects (ibid. 3:15). Commenting on this incident, the Midrash notes, מִכָּאן שֶׁעוֹשִׂין סְעֻדָּה לִגְמָרָה שֶׁל תּוֹרָה, *From here we derive that we should make a banquet upon completion of the Torah* (*Koheles Rabbah* 1:1 and *Shir HaShirim Rabbah* 1:1).

---

1. In *Eretz Yisrael*, the conclusion and new beginning of the Torah reading, along with dancing and celebration, is held on Shemini Atzeres.

Solomon was taught an important principle in addition to receiving the gift of wisdom. With a wise and discerning heart, steeped in the wisdom of God, come all other human gifts, including wealth and glory, for knowledge of the Torah is the primary good. Solomon had hardly had a chance to use his newly granted wisdom, but the mere fact that he had it was sufficient cause for a celebration, for he had been granted the springboard to greater knowledge of the Torah and the opportunity to use this gift in the service of God and Israel. On Simchas Torah, too, when we reflect that another cycle of Torah reading has led us into a new year of study and knowledge, we respond as Solomon did — with rejoicing and celebration.

Celebrating a New Beginning

◆§ *Matteh Moshe* (976) offers another Midrashic source for the name *Simchas Torah*. On Succos, Satan comes before God to condemn the Jewish people, saying, "They study the Torah, but will not complete it [i.e., they will be caught up in the festivities of Succos and will neglect the study of Torah]." When we do indeed complete the reading of the Torah, God responds to Satan, "But they *have* completed it."

Satan answers, "Even though they have completed it, they will not begin it anew!" As soon as Israel begins its new cycle of reading, God responds, "But they *have* begun it!" — and Satan retires in defeat. Because our devotion to the Torah provides God with grounds to defend us, it is cause for special joy. Therefore, this day is known as Simchas Torah.

Finishing Touch

◆§ Simchas Torah is the culmination of the Torah reading of the past year and the lessons gleaned from it. It is through the joy of Simchas Torah that we are able to internalize the lessons which the Torah has imparted to us throughout the year.

God transmitted the Torah in segments rather than as a unit in order to enable the Jewish people to absorb it in manageable doses. Today too, our exposure to the lessons of the Written Torah does not occur all at once. Instead, we read and examine one portion each week throughout the year. Moreover, each annual Torah cycle has its own messages and its own lessons, since every generation, each

year, finds new meaning in the weekly reading. On Simchas Torah we celebrate not only the completion of the Torah cycle, but also the cumulative lessons gleaned from all of the previous year's weekly Torah readings. The phrase לְגָמְרָהּ שֶׁל תּוֹרָה, *upon the completion of the Torah,* implies that Simchas Torah provides the "finishing touches" to a year of Torah and imprints its messages on our lives (*Sfas Emes*).

Completion of the Days of Awe

◆§ *Sfas Emes* offers some more beautiful insights into the idea of making a banquet for the completion of the Torah.

Simchas Torah is not an isolated festival that happens to follow the High Holy Days and Succos. On the contrary, it is the final destination of the spiritual journey that began on Rosh Hashanah. Just as the commemoration of the physical Exodus every spring is only a prelude to reliving the acceptance of the Torah on Shavuos, so too the spiritual exodus celebrated during the High Holy Days — i.e., the freedom from the stifling albatross of sin — is only a preparation for Simchas Torah. Simchas Torah is the completion of the entire festival cycle, the goal toward which all other holidays pave the way, since in a sense, the purpose of the entire process of spiritual purification during Rosh Hashanah and Yom Kippur is to prepare us to accept the Torah joyfully on Simchas Torah.

The association between Simchas Torah and the High Holy Days is hinted at in the *Shema,* where it is written, וְאָהַבְתָּ אֵת ה' אֱלֹהֶיךָ בְּכָל לְבָבְךָ וּבְכָל נַפְשְׁךָ וּבְכָל מְאֹדֶךָ, *You shall love HASHEM, your God, with all your heart, with all your soul, and with all your resources (Deuteronomy 6:5).* The first part of this commandment, to love Hashem *with all your heart,* is most relevant on Rosh Hashanah, when we attempt to channel all our thoughts, even the negative passions of our hearts, toward spiritual ends. *With all your soul* refers to Yom Kippur, when we afflict our souls through fasting (see *Leviticus* 16:31). *With all your resources* alludes to Succos, when the Jew, despite his successful harvest, abandons the material comforts of his home in favor of the simple *succah.*

The next verse speaks of the ensuing reward: וְהָיוּ הַדְּבָרִים הָאֵלֶּה . . . . עַל לְבָבֶךָ, *Let these matters . . . be upon your heart.* The reward for observing the holidays is that Torah will be implanted in every Jewish heart, and that reward is given on Simchas Torah. The term *completion of the Torah* aptly describes this pinnacle; the fitting

completion of the holiday cycle is the reward of Torah, granted to those who have invested properly during the preceding festival days.

The Effect of Atonement

◆§ The true *baal teshuvah* is not one who only seeks to rectify his sins. True repentance entails a vigorous effort to plumb the depths of Torah in search of God's will. Such a person seeks to come back to God not merely to avoid punishment for his sins or even to achieve atonement for his own soul, but rather in order to be a pure vessel for the service of God. Simchas Torah, therefore, constitutes a rededication to Torah study that is the result of a most pristine *teshuvah*. Jews are happy on this day that they are able to begin anew their service of God with a rediscovered wholeness of heart.

Sfas Emes adds that while Shavuos celebrates the giving and acceptance of the first Tablets, Simchas Torah is the time when we joyously accept the second Tablets given on Yom Kippur. We are able to do this with the special purity of heart that is the lot of the truly penitent.

Baal HaTanya notes that Simchas Torah is thirteen days after Yom Kippur since the full purification of the soul which results from the thirteen attributes of God's mercy (see *Exodus* 34:5-7) takes effect then. Hence, Simchas Torah celebrates the joy of atonement.

Back From Afar

◆§ The special joy of Simchas Torah relates to the fact that we now experience a closeness to God born of the distance we felt from Him as a result of our sins. This is similar to the difference between one who always lived in the king's palace and one who was taken into captivity and was able to find his way back to the king only through heroic efforts. Of course, the joy of being home again is immeasurably greater for the second person. Thus, the Midrash refers to Yom Kippur as יוֹם חֲתֻנָּתוֹ, *the day of nuptials* (*Song of Songs* 3:11), between Israel and her Groom. Yom Kippur is the day when the love between Hashem and Israel is rekinkled after almost having been extinguished by sin. The words בְּיוֹם שִׂמְחַת לִבּוֹ, *the day of gladness of His heart* (ibid.), refers to Shemini Atzeres/Simchas Torah, when God rejoices with His people who have returned to Him, and Israel rejoices with its Maker (*Ohr HaTorah*).

Bearers of God's Banner

◆§ The Torah is referred to as תּוֹרַת חַיִּים, a *living Torah*. In reality it is the Jewish people who give "completion" to the Torah — who "bring it to life," so to speak — by learning its sacred, eternal teachings.

The Talmud relates that when Moses ascended to Heaven to receive the Torah from God, the Heavenly angels protested. "Place Your splendor upon the Heavens," they asked of God, questioning why something so precious was to be given to mere mortals. God then asked Moses to refute the argument of the angels. Moses did so by describing man's vulnerability: "The Torah teaches, *You shall have no gods* of others (*Exodus* 20:3). Do you [angels] live among idolaters [that you need to be taught to avoid their influence]? Do you angels need a Sabbath as a day of rest? Is there jealousy and hatred among you that you need to be commanded not to commit murder? Are you susceptible to the human stirrings of passion that necessitate the prohibition of adultery?"

Torah addresses the human condition, seeking to elevate man and transform him into a spiritual being. Celestial angels have no need for a Torah; therefore, God gave it to man. It is the nation of Israel, God's children, who bear aloft the banner of His sovereignty in this world by living a life of Torah. Simchas Torah reflects the joy *of the Torah itself* over the fact that the Jewish people bring its purpose to fruition (*Zecher Shlomo*).

Blessing of the Torah

◆§ Simchas Torah celebrates not only one's past study and practice of Torah, but even more so, the intrinsic appreciation of Torah that ensures one's accomplishments in the future.

The Talmud (*Nedarim* 81a) teaches that the first Temple was destroyed because the people did not recite the *Bircas HaTorah* (Blessing of the Torah) before engaging in the study of God's word. This blessing thanks God for the priceless opportunity to drink of His wisdom, and *Rabbeinu Yonah* explains that its omission is symptomatic of a lack of reverence for Torah. Only if one appreciates the gift of Torah and is thankful to God for allowing him access to its treasures can he firmly attach himself to it. The joy of Simchas Torah helps one internalize and concretize this appreciation in his heart. The dancing and singing of the day is, in a sense, a monumental

"blessing of the Torah." At the start of the new year, as we commence our reading of the weekly Torah portion, we joyously express our regard and love for God's most precious gift to our people.

Sfas Emes adds: A Jew rejoices in the mere fact that he is privileged to receive the word of God. While the actual knowledge and ideas induce an intellectual satisfaction, the central joy of a Jew is his ability to submit humbly to the Divine Intelligence. Therefore, we are happy on Simchas Torah even before we begin our new cycle of Torah study; like a royal subject anxiously awaiting a missive from the king, we rejoice in the idea that God speaks to us through His Torah and look forward to His word.

Setting the Eternal Compass

◄§ In addition, Simchas Torah is a day which reminds us of our priorities, which tend to become blurred in the daily struggle to earn a living. We tend to forget that earning a livelihood is a means, not an end in itself. עֲשֵׂה תוֹרָתְךָ קֶבַע וּמְלַאכְתְּךָ אַרְעַי, *Make your Torah study permanent and your occupation temporary* (*Rambam, Hilchos Talmud Torah* 3:7). This reminds us not only to give Torah precedence in our schedule, but also to make it the primary focus of our lives.

On Simchas Torah we rejoice in the Torah and set our eternal compasses, charting the course we want our lives to take. Even if we encounter detours along our path during the course of the year, we must always bear in mind our true priorities, and with God's help we will again find the way back to our real purpose in life. Simchas Torah, with its heartfelt joy, ensures that we will always recognize that our roots are in Torah. Even the businessman, preoccupied with his many distractions, will retain his strong ties to Torah if on Simchas Torah he sincerely and joyously makes a commitment to its study (*Simchas Aharon*).

A Vow of Allegiance

◄§ *Kitzur Shulchan Aruch* (138:7) writes that in some communities it is customary to read the beginning of *Parashas Mattos*, which discusses the laws of *nedarim* (vows), on the night of *Simchas Torah*. This is apparently based on *Rema* (669:1), who writes that on the night of Simchas Torah "we read the vows in the Torah."[1]

---

1. See, however, *M.B.* ad loc.

Tirosh VeYitzhar (117) explains the custom. The Talmud is replete with examples of cases when it is advisable to invoke a vow in order to strengthen one's commitment to Torah and *mitzvos*. King David teaches, *I swore and I will fulfill [my oath] to keep Your righteous statutes* (Psalms 119:106). The Talmud (*Nedarim* 8a) explains that although swearing is usually discouraged, it is a laudable practice to swear to fulfill a *mitzvah*. If a person feels that he is growing sluggish in the performance of *mitzvos*, it is advisable for him to intensify his commitment by invoking an oath to accomplish a particular good deed (*Ritva; Nemukei Yosef, Nedarim* 8a).

Maharsha (ad loc.) draws our attention to the Talmudic passage (*Niddah* 30b) that whenever a child is born, an angel comes and makes him swear that he will be a *tzaddik* who will observe *mitzvos* and shun all forms of sin. When a Jew arouses his own yearning for *mitzvos* by taking an oath, his soul is awakened to this earlier oath and is reminded that an irrevocable commitment to *mitzvos* is at the very essence of his being (*R' A. C. Feuer*).

Similarly, at Sinai, the Jewish nation as a whole swore its eternal allegiance to God. On Simchas Torah, the day on which we complete the Torah and then begin it anew, we joyously rededicate ourselves to that original oath. We figuratively give our word to God that we will learn His Torah and keep the *mitzvos*. In order to emphasize the stringency of an oath and help us realize how seriously we must take such a commitment, the custom arose of reading those Torah verses involving vows.

Prerequisite for a Vow

◆§ One year, R' Yitzchak Meir of Gur, author of *Chiddushei HaRim*, hosted one of his relatives for Simchas Torah. The *gabbai* inadvertently neglected to honor the guest with a *hakafah* (circuit), and the slighted relative complained to the *Chiddushei HaRim*. He replied: "Dancing with the Torah on this day is like making a שְׁבוּעָה בִּנְקִיטַת חֵפֶץ, *an oath while holding a sacred object* (see *Rambam, Hilchos Shevuos* 11:8). Are you certain you are prepared for that responsibility?"

On Simchas Torah, we hold the Torah in our hands, in effect pledging our allegiance to it. This is a commitment that can be made only after the holidays of Tishrei have left their impact on us. The Midrash homiletically alludes to this prerequisite by citing the verse *HASHEM, your God, you shall fear; Him you shall serve, to Him shall*

you cleave — and in His Name shall you swear (Deuteronomy 10:20). This verse teaches that only one who has the attributes mentioned — fear and service of God and a strong attachment to Him — has the right to swear, for these qualities assure that he will do so truthfully.

During the Days of Awe, we hopefully acquire this proper sense of reverence for the King of kings. On Succos, we leave our permanent abode and its material comforts to demonstrate our wholehearted service of God. On Shemini Atzeres and Simchas Torah, we are able to cleave to Him and bask in His exclusive love. It is only then that we can joyously vow, without reservation, to learn and keep His Torah every day throughout the year (Imrei Moshe).

Renewed Commitment

ᥱᥴ Simchas Torah is also a reminder of the vital importance of this commitment. Each day when a Jew recites Shema, he accepts upon himself the yoke of the Kingdom of Heaven (עוֹל מַלְכוּת שָׁמַיִם) and the yoke of the mitzvos (עוֹל מִצְוֹת). Torah study, as pleasurable as it is, must also be borne as a yoke, meaning that it must be approached with a sense of obligation.

As with a commitment to any worthwhile undertaking, this acceptance of the yoke of Torah should be made in advance. There is no better day to commit oneself to Torah — and to do so joyously — than Simchas Torah. The Talmud (Shabbos 130a) states that any mitzvah initially assumed with joy will always be performed joyously. One who accepts the Torah gladly on this happiest of festivals will assuredly continue to study Torah joyously throughout the coming year (Sfas Emes).

Gladness is such a powerful tool that it actually effects awesome joy in the Heavenly spheres that can reverberate for generations. Yesod VeShoresh HaAvodah tells us: "Whoever takes pains to rejoice truly with the Torah on this day (Simchas Torah) can rest assured that Torah will never depart from his children."

Personal Valuation

ᥱᥴ The Mishnah Berurah comments on joy as a key ingredient in mitzvah performance. He writes (669 §11) that the Arizal said of himself that the level of achievement in Torah and mitzvos he attained was related to the joy he had experienced while performing the mitzvos.

Why is joy such a potent factor in achieving spiritual success? *R' Yitzchak Hutner* explained: The Talmud (*Kiddushin* 40b) says that if one performs a *mitzvah* and later regrets having done it, he loses all reward for the *mitzvah*. This teaches us that the value of the *mitzvah* is the value that *we* assign to it. If it is worth nothing to us, then in fact it really becomes worthless.

Why are we the ones who established the value of our *mitzvos*? The price of any item is based on supply and demand. If one has a monopoly on a given commodity, he may demand whatever price he wants for the item. Every Jew has a monopoly on his own Torah study and *mitzvos,* since no one but he himself can do the *mitzvos* for him or study Torah on his behalf. Thus, he is the only one who can determine the value of his own Torah study and *mitzvah* performance.

It is through the joy one experiences when doing a *mitzvah* that he truly indicates how valuable he considers it. The *Arizal* felt that all his spiritual achievements were rooted in the joy he experienced while fulfilling *mitzvos,* showing that he accorded them inestimable value. God rewarded him in kind by granting him access to yet greater levels of spirituality and deeper understanding of the profundities of His Torah.

Our dancing on Simchas Torah is our way of showing God how much we cherish the Torah and how important it is to us to be intimately connected to it. God responds by granting us our heart's desire. As King David prayed, *May Your kindness, HASHEM, be upon us just as we yearned for You (Psalms* 33:21).

The Unseen Bride

◦§ Our Sages speak of Shavuos, the day on which we received the Torah, as the "wedding day" of God and Israel (see *Rashi* to *Shir HaShirim* 3:11). Why did the Sages not arrange the schedule of Torah readings in such a fashion that the completion of the cycle coincides with Shavuos? Would not that festival be a most appropriate time for Simchas Torah?

An enchanting parable of the *Dubno Maggid* offers this perspective: A royal duke who was not blessed with children had exhausted all avenues in search of a remedy. Doctors and charlatans alike had been sought out, but to no avail. Finally, his friends suggested that he travel to a renowned Jew who was known for his power to effect miraculous cures. The duke followed their advice and met the

miracle-working Jew. He begged the Jew to entreat God on his behalf and promised him that if he had a child, he would do everything in his power to help the Jews.

The saintly miracle-worker prayed with deep feeling and intent on behalf of the duke, and after a few days reported to him: "Within the year, your wife will give birth to a daughter. However, I must warn you to be careful and not allow the eyes of any man to fall upon her until she marries. If any male gazes upon her beforehand, she will die." Left with no choice, the duke agreed to the condition.

The daughter was born and was promptly ensconced, together with her mother, in a castle that the duke owned on an isolated island far out at sea. Cared for by an attentive staff of female servants, the young girl grew up into a refined and regal princess. From time to time, her mother would return to the duke's palace in order to report to him about his beautiful, charming daughter. And yet, even the duke himself could not see her face, for the saintly miracle-worker had warned him about this.

When the time came to find a suitable mate for the girl, the duke sought out one of his close friends and offered his daughter's hand in marriage to the other's son. "However," he told the father of the prospective suitor, "your son cannot meet my daughter until the wedding." He explained why he must insist on this stipulation, but the other party could not agree to such a condition and negotiations over the match broke off.

This scenario repeated itself again and again as one prospective mate after another, enthralled with the prospect of such a prestigious match, was quickly disappointed when the duke insisted on this condition: No man, not even the groom, could see the bride until the wedding.

After much searching, the duke finally found a young man who was willing to marry his daughter sight unseen. The prospect of a generous dowry, along with the satisfaction of marrying into a family more prestigious than his own, convinced the young man to marry his bride blindly.

After the wedding, the young groom was pleasantly surprised to find that his bride was exquisitely beautiful. Certain, however, that the prenuptial condition had been meant to hide something, he suspected that, despite her beauty, she might be totally devoid of sense and intelligence. After a while, though, it became clear that she was indeed very bright. Only after several months of marriage did he realize what a flawless gem he had been granted

as a wife. At the height of his newfound joy, he went to thank his father-in-law.

The "duke" alludes to God, Who sought to marry off His most precious "daughter," the Torah, to a fitting "groom." However, he had one stipulation — the groom must agree to marry the bride without seeing her first. God went to all the nations of the world and offered them the Torah, but each nation wanted to know what the Torah contained; they wanted to "see the bride first."

God lifted Mount Sinai and held it over the heads of the Jewish nation (see *Shabbos* 88a) and forced them to accept the Torah. Furthermore, the Jews unconditionally accepted the Torah when they proclaimed נַעֲשֶׂה וְנִשְׁמַע, *We will do and we will listen* (*Exodus* 24:7); they willingly accepted the *mitzvos* upon themselves without knowing what the commandments entailed.[1]

When the Jewish people "married" the "bride," they did not fully realize how special a gift their Father in Heaven had given them. Only after studying and keeping the Torah for a period of time could they appreciate the unique blessing of Torah. The parallel now becomes clear: Each year, we renew our "marriage vows" to the Torah on Shavuos. A few months later, after we have tasted the beauty of Torah and *mitzvos,* we convey our profound gratitude to God by rejoicing on Simchas Torah.

Shemini Atzeres and Simchas Torah: A Fitting Combination

Torah — the Focus of Our Joy

◆§ While Shemini Atzeres is a Biblically mandated holiday, the observance of Simchas Torah was instituted in a much later era. In Israel they are observed on one and the same day, for they represent essences which are integrally connected.

R' Mendel of Kotzk viewed Simchas Torah as the natural culmination of Succos; it is a day on which the joy which is the integral

---

1. For an explanation of why it was necessary for God to suspend the mountain above them even though they had willingly accepted the Torah, see ArtScroll *Shavuos,* p. 108.

fabric of Succos is channeled into Torah. Thus, we celebrate our heartfelt bond with the Torah on Shemini Atzeres, a festival which our prayers describe as זְמַן שִׂמְחָתֵנוּ, *the time of our gladness.* In fact, it is precisely because Succos and Shemini Atzeres represent an outpouring of joy that the Sages chose Shemini Atzeres for the celebration of Simchas Torah with its annual completion and beginning of the Torah-reading cycle; Jews utilize their happiness to rejoice over the greatest of all gifts.

Meor VeShamesh sees an allusion to the custom of celebrating Simchas Torah during the Shemini Atzeres Festival in the word עֲצֶרֶת, which is an acronym for עוֹשִׂין צַדִּיקִים רִיקוּדֵי תּוֹרָה, *The righteous make dances for the Torah.*

God's Beloved Children

◄§ An insight of the *Vilna Gaon* sheds another light on the celebration of Simchas Torah as part of Shemini Atzeres. In our daily prayers we beseech God, "Bring us back, our Father, to Your Torah and bring us near, our King, to Your service." In seeking help to return to Torah, we address God as our Father, while in our request to be brought closer to His service, we turn to Him as our King. Why the difference?

The Vilna Gaon explains that while service of God is an opportunity incumbent upon Jews and non-Jews alike (the latter through the seven Noachide laws), the Torah was given to the Jewish people alone. The King allows all his subjects access to Him, but only His children are permitted to enter the inner sanctum of His treasury and enjoy His most prized possession. Thus, it is quite fitting that on Shemini Atzeres, the day when the King celebrates exclusively with His own children (see p. 32), we rejoice with the Torah, the prized possession which He shares only with us (*Imrei Moshe*).

The *Zohar* tells us that when Israel is involved in rejoicing with the Torah, God says to His Heavenly entourage, "Take note of My beloved children, who forget their own troubles and involve themselves in My joy." Our prayer is that this moment will extend itself throughout the year — through the study of Torah. We celebrate Simchas Torah on Shemini Atzeres with the hope that through joy in Torah study, we will always experience the special closeness to God that we feel on this most joyous of days (*Nesivos Shalom*).

The Sages teach, "From the time the Temple was destroyed, all that the Holy One, Blessed is He, has in this world are the four ells of

halachah (Torah study)" (*Berachos* 8a). *Avnei Nezer* explains: God's Presence resides only in places of joy. Depression and destruction are the antithesis of Godliness and do not allow for the manifestation of His Presence. The cataclysmic effect of the Temple's destruction forced the Divine Presence to abandon its earthly abode. Only one place was saved from the ravaging effect of that terrible tragedy — the four ells of Torah study, which pulsate with joy and vibrancy.[1]

Thus, on the festival of Shemini Atzeres, a time of exultation, we celebrate Simchas Torah, for only in Torah can one experience undiminished joy.

Clarity of Vision

◈ When God gave us the Ten Commandments, He opened the heavens above and the nether regions below so that every Jew was able to perceive clearly that there is only one God (see *Rashi* to *Deuteronomy* 4:35). On Shemini Atzeres, in our private audience with the King, we again achieve that pristine clarity. Thus inspired, we revel in the Torah — the key that insures our awareness of the reality of God's Presence in our lives (*Simchas Aharon*).

Rosh Hashanah, Yom Kippur and Succos are all preparatory stages which bring us to the moment at the beginning of the Simchas Torah *hakafos* (circuits), when we can cry out from the depths of our souls, אַתָּה הָרְאֵתָ לָדַעַת כִּי ה' הוּא הָאֱלֹהִים אֵין עוֹד מִלְּבַדּוֹ, *You have been shown [in order] to know that* HASHEM, *He is the God; there is nothing besides Him* [*Deuteronomy* ibid.] (*R' Moshe of Kobrin*).

All Children Equal

◈ Every Jew has his spiritual strengths and weaknesses. As *servants* of God, we each occupy a specific station; however, as *children* of God, we are all equal. Every child is equally beloved by his parent, no matter what his level of achievement.

On Shemini Atzeres we are all God's children, no matter what we have or have not accomplished in Torah and *mitzvos*. It is for this reason that we celebrate Simchas Torah on this same day. Simchas Torah is not solely for scholars. All Jewish males, even young children, receive an *aliyah* to the Torah and the privilege of singing

---

1. It is for this reason that if one celebrates a *siyum* (the completion of a Talmudic tractate) during the nine days before Tishah B'Av, the laws of mourning over the Temple are suspended and one may eat meat and drink wine.

and dancing in its honor. The Torah reading of the morning is repeated numerous times and the *hakafos* extended until everyone has been given a turn to recite the blessings over the Torah and to dance with it, expressing thankfulness for the ability to possess it, study it, and observe it. Our jubilation and security in Torah and its Giver places us all on the same plateau.

The Chassidic master R' Naftali of Ropshitz once said, "Let me tell you about an unlearned wagon driver who got the better of me. He was rejoicing mightily on Simchas Torah. Unable to restrain my cynicism, I said to him, 'Why are you so happy? You have not studied the Torah!' He replied, 'Rebbe, if my brother makes a wedding, shouldn't I rejoice with him? Don't I have a share in his happiness?'

"I said to him, 'You are right, my son. Please forgive me.' "

The Joy of Potential

� Even those who have not yet availed themselves of the opportunity to experience the richness of Torah rejoice in their potential to do so. Much like a simple peasant who feels honored to be invited to the wedding of the royal princess, the Jew who is as yet unlearned is proud to take part in the wedding between Israel and God's Torah.

Thus, the holiday is called *Simchas Torah,* the joy of the Torah itself, rather than the rejoicing of the Jews in the Torah. Were it to be called שִׂמְחַת יִשְׂרָאֵל בַּתּוֹרָה, *the rejoicing of Israel in the Torah,* one could only take part in the festivities if he truly lived up to the exalted title of "Israel." However, since the day celebrates the joy of the Torah itself, all Jews are invited to take part in the celebration (*R' Yaakov of Alexander*).

Closely Related to Torah

⋠⋦ Nonetheless, one should seek to be an integral participant, actively involved in Torah study, rather than merely an involved bystander who is content to limit his involvement to the Simchas Torah celebration. The *Chafetz Chaim* made just this point. After *hakafos* one year, when everyone else had gone home to enjoy the *Yom Tov* meal, the *Chafetz Chaim* remained behind in the synagogue to study for another hour or so. Someone asked him afterward, "Why didn't you go home first, enjoy your meal, and return afterwards to the *shul* to learn?"

The *Chafetz Chaim* offered the following analogy. "If you arrive at a wedding at the height of the festive meal, you'll find everyone dancing. While all are rejoicing, it is almost impossible to tell who is among the immediate family of the bride and groom and who is merely a guest. If you want to find out who belongs to the family, you must wait until the celebration ends, when everyone else leaves. Likewise," said the sage of Radin, "during *hakafos* everybody dances. Now that the festivities are over, I want to show that I am truly a *mechutan* (i.e., close relative) of the Torah."

A Day of Self-Discovery

◦§ One of the primary sources of personal happiness one can experience in life is knowledge of oneself. A person who is able to discover — or rediscover — his own identity has justified cause for celebration. It is for this reason that the celebration of the Torah is the *only* observance of Simchas Torah — because ultimately, the Torah is the key to unlocking the richness of our own souls. Torah is a sourcebook given to man in order to enable him to understand the complexities and depths of his own being. On Simchas Torah we dance and dance until we find ourselves in the Torah (*R' Tzadok HaKohen*).

Looking in the Mirror

◦§ Of course, the self that we discover is hopefully one imbued with spirituality — a self that would make both God and the Torah proud. *Beis HaLevi* notes that the holiday is called *Simchas Torah*, which literally means "the joy of the Torah," because it is not sufficient that we rejoice in the Torah; we must give the Torah cause to rejoice over us. Cradling the Torah scroll in our arms, we promise to be its loyal sons and steadfast bearers of its statutes. Hence, the Torah itself rejoices on this day.

In this vein *Beis Avraham* views Shemini Atzeres/Simchas Torah as a day for introspection. After experiencing the elevating festivals of the month and the sanctity they bring to our lives, we must examine ourselves and take stock of who we are and what we want to be. *Beis Avraham* cites the words of the Sages, שְׁמִינִי עֲצֶרֶת רֶגֶל בִּפְנֵי עַצְמוֹ, which literally means, *Shemini Atzeres is a festival for itself,* and translates them instead as *Shemini Atzeres/Simchas Torah is a festival when one peers into his own [spiritual] face.*

Torah — Our Unbreakable Bond With God

◆§ There is a beautiful parable in the Midrash which offers another explanation for the connection between Shemini Atzeres and Simchas Torah.

The Midrash speaks of the function of the *Mishkan* (Tabernacle). A king had an only daughter, the apple of his eye. When she became of age, he married her off to a royal prince from a faraway land. The prince came to stay in the king's home for awhile and then announced to his father-in-law that it was time for him to return to his country.

The king was beside himself over the thought of being separated from his beloved daughter. "What shall I do?" he said to his son-in-law. "I can't tell you not to leave, and yet the thought of separation is unbearable. Wherever you go, make a small home for me so that I may come along with you wherever you are."

The groom is Israel, the father-in-law is God, and the daughter is the Torah. God instructed His people to construct the *Mishkan* so that He would be able to remain with the Torah no matter where the Jews traveled. The Midrash then concludes that when the Jewish people accepted the Torah, they received God, so to speak, along with it.

Thus, on Shemini Atzeres we joyously accept the Torah, "enabling" God to remain among us and stay close to his beloved Torah. In the process, the Torah forges an unbreakable link between God and us. In the words of the *Zohar,* יִשְׂרָאֵל וְאוֹרַיְיתָא וְקוּדְשָׁא בְּרִיךְ הוּא חַד הוּא, *Israel, Torah and God are one.* It is Torah that unites us with our Father (*Toras Emes*).

Beis Yisrael offers a different perspective on how the joy of Torah can preserve the closeness to God we achieve on Shemini Atzeres.

On Shemini Atzeres we sense the great difficulty of the separation which God and the Jews experience. Aware of the imminent parting, we follow the advice of the Sages that friends only part while discussing words of Torah, for thus they will remember each other (*Berachos* 31a). Therefore, we begin the Torah anew, strengthening our connection to God.

The Torah Rejoices

◆§ The Midrash teaches that before giving the Torah to the Jewish people, God offered it to all the nations of the world, but each one

rejected it. Their refusal was a source of joy for the Torah itself, for had they accepted it, they certainly would not have revered it and treated it with the love that the Jewish people do.

This is analogous to a royal princess who was told that she must marry an uncouth villager. The mere thought of associating with this lowly peasant was appalling. How happy she was when she was rescued from her fate and allowed to marry a refined, sensitive and caring gentleman!

This is the meaning of the Simchas Torah song, שִׂישׂוּ וְשִׂמְחוּ בְּשִׂמְחַת תּוֹרָה, *Rejoice and be glad in the joy of the Torah.* The way in which we exult with the Torah on this day demonstrates our love and reverence of her and is cause for the Torah itself to rejoice (*Divrei Shmuel*).

Restored to Perfection

~§ As mentioned above, it is customary for every male to be called to the Torah for an *aliyah* on this day. This is based on the Aggadic statement that the word יִשְׂרָאֵל, *Israel,* is an acronym for the words יֵשׁ שִׁשִׁים רִבּוֹא אוֹתִיּוֹת לַתּוֹרָה, *There are 600,000 letters in the Torah* — one corresponding to each of the 600,000 souls of the Jewish people.[1] This is a symbolic demonstration of the fact that every one of us is rooted in the Torah.

In the course of the year, as we move away from our roots, our souls become enmeshed in sin and negativity; only after the spiritually redeeming days of Tishrei are we able to uplift ourselves and become reconnected to the Torah scroll of Israel. Thus, it is fitting on this last day of the festival that each of us be honored with an *aliyah* (literally, *rising*) to the Torah and a reconnection to our source (*Meor Einayim*).

The words of King David allude to this sense of participation of the entire people: *The Torah of HASHEM is perfect, it restores the soul* (*Psalms* 19:8). If even a single Jew lacks a connection to Torah, the nation as symbolized by the Torah scroll with its 600,000 letters lacks a letter and is figuratively unfit. Thus, only after the Days of Awe, when every Jew's soul is restored through prayer, repentance and the special *mitzvos* of the season, can the Torah of the Jewish people be considered complete and perfect (*Chesed L'Avraham*).

---

1. According to the Sages, the 600,000 souls who left Egypt during the Exodus are the basic components of the Jewish nation. These souls are implanted (in whole or in part) in all Jews who lived afterward. See *Maharal, Gevuros Hashem* for elaboration of this concept.

Hakafos

The Custom

◄§ Aside from encircling the *bimah* itself on Simchas Torah, the Rishonim mention the separate custom of removing the Torah scrolls from the ark. *Machzor Vitry* (383) writes: "On the seventh day of Succos (*Hoshana Rabbah*) known as the *Yom Aravah* (Day of the Willow Branch), it is customary to remove all the Torah scrolls from the ark. This is not done in order to facilitate the reading of the Torah but rather as a means of honoring God and His Torah. This is also done on Simchas Torah. The prevalent practice is to recite many verses during the removal of the scrolls. Likewise, they recite the liturgical poem which begins אֱלֹהֵי הָרוּחוֹת הוֹשִׁיעָה נָא, *God of the spirits, save now,* and continues with an alphabetical acrostic, concluding with תָּמִים בְּמַעֲשָׂיו עֲנֵנוּ בְּיוֹם קָרְאֵנוּ, *Perfect in His deeds, answer us on the day we call!"*

Zohar (*Pinchas* 256b in *Ra'ayah Mehemna*) writes: "Jews have a custom to rejoice on this day and the day is called Simchas Torah. They adorn the Torah scrolls with their crowns and rejoice with them."

Maharil, who is appropriately known as the father and codifier of the Ashkenazic rite, portrays the scene of Simchas Torah: "Prior to the removal of the scrolls, the reader and congregation read the verses of *Atah Hareisa* responsively. When the reader reaches the verse כִּי מִצִּיּוֹן, *For from Zion,* the scrolls are taken out of the ark."

Rema (669) mentions the custom of making *hakafos* (circuits) around the *bimah.* "They also make *hakafos* around the *bimah* in the synagogue while carrying Torah scrolls, just as is done with the *lulav* [during the *Hoshana* service]." All of these customs are ways through which we rejoice with and show honor for the Torah.

Meanings Behind the Hakafos

◄§ There are different opinions among the commentators regarding the number of *hakafos* to be made on Simchas Torah. The almost universal custom is to make seven *hakafos. Yerushalmi* suggests that the seven *hakafos* parallel the seven times that the Israelites circled

the city of Jericho during their conquest of *Eretz Yisrael* before the seven walls that surrounded that city collapsed (see *Joshua* 6).

Sod Yesharim views the seven *hakafos* as a symbolic way of removing the impediments that surround our hearts, stifling the innate potential of our souls to unite with God's word. Just as the physical walls of Jericho were brought down with seven circuits, so too are the walls of impurity surrounding our souls destroyed through the seven *hakafos*. The *hakafos* plow spiritual furrows in man's heart and mind so that the seed of Godliness in man can take root and flourish. Furthermore, the joy of this day itself can melt the many walls that are erected between man and his fellow and between man and God. *Chida,* in the prayer he composed to be recited prior to *hakafos,* beseeches God: "Through the power of these *hakafos,* all the impenetrable iron curtains between us and our Father in Heaven should fall."

Of Endings and Beginnings

◦§ The word *hakafah* (plural *hakafos*) has many meanings. In its literal sense, it means *circuits,* for on Simchas Torah we circle the *bimah* with the Torah scroll seven times.

The term also indicates that on this day we conclude the yearly reading of the Torah and immediately begin again, thus concluding one *circuit* of reading and embarking on a new one. This is a wonderful metaphor for one of the great processes of life: Often, when we seem to be nearing an end, in truth we are about to begin a new chapter of growth on yet a higher plane. What appears to be a spiritual dead end is sometimes the entranceway to a great new beginning. All of life is a cycle, and if one does not lose sight of this, the new dawn will eventually shine on him in its full brilliance.

This lesson is captured poetically in a mysterious Aggadah taught in the Talmud (*Bava Basra* 74a): "Rabbah bar bar Channah was speaking with an Arab merchant who said to him, 'I will show you the place where heaven and earth touch each other.' Rabbah bar bar Channah went to that spot and saw that heaven was made up of many windows. He took his bread basket, placed it in one of the windows, and went off to the side to pray. When he returned, the basket was gone. He told the Arab, 'There are thieves around here.' The Arab replied, 'The heavenly sphere is rotating, and it took your basket. Wait here until the same time tomorrow and you will find it again.' "

Physical sustenance and, more importantly, spiritual growth, is cyclical. One must be patient, even with himself, and let matters run their full course. His "bread basket" will return. We therefore conduct *hakafos* to strengthen our resolve to approach Torah and *mitzvos* continually with joy, never allowing the perception of a spiritual end to weaken our belief that we are, in fact, at the dawn of a new beginning.

Furthermore, the *hakafos* allude to the humility we must always show toward Torah. We should never think that we have fully plumbed the depths of God's infinite wisdom. Even though we may think we are "at the end" and have learned whatever the Torah has to teach us, in truth we have barely begun to scratch the surface of that endless treasure trove of wisdom, purity and inspiration.

Further Perspectives on the Circuits

◆§ *Maaglei Tzedek* offers an enlightening homiletical perspective on *hakafos,* based on another time-honored custom. Prior to the marriage ceremony, it is customary for the bride to circle the groom seven times. This parallels the seven circuits the Israelites made around Jericho when they wrested the Holy Land from the sinful Canaanites, who contaminated it with their wayward practices. The seven circuits around Jericho, conducted in holiness and purity, destroyed the barriers of evil which enveloped the city. Similarly, the bride's seven circuits around her groom serve as a shield against the forces of impurity which defile the sanctity of a Jewish marriage.

Likewise, on Simchas Torah when we rejoice intensely with God and His Torah, the *hakafos* counteract any negative force that might seek to pierce the barrier and undermine the rarefied sanctity of the moment.

A Symbol of Balance

◆§ Another symbolic message of *hakafos* is moderation. The *hakafos,* along with the cyclical completion and new beginning of the Torah readings, teach us that one should avoid extremes in all areas of life (see *Rambam, Hilchos Deos* 1:4). The uniqueness of an unbroken circle is that one is never at any extreme; rather, he can always see himself as being the middle point of the periphery.

There is an allusion to this idea in the very last and first letters of the *Chumash,* which form the word לֵב, *lev.* While the word means

heart, it also carries the connotation of *center* or *middle* (see *Exodus* 15:8). One's heart and mind must be firmly planted in the center rather than at dangerous extremes (*Zera Kodesh*).

Portraits of Celebration

◆§ The Kabbalists of fifteenth-century Safed embellished upon the customs of earlier generations. *R' Chaim Vital* tells how his master, the sainted *Arizal,* celebrated Simchas Torah: "My master and teacher, of blessed memory, took great care to accompany the Torah scroll on its circuit, dancing either in front of it or behind it. He would dance and sing joyously in front of the Torah and took care to make seven *hakafos* in this manner. Even after he had finished the *hakafos* in his own synagogue, he would join the celebration in any synagogue which he passed on the way home if they were still in the midst of the festivities. He would join in the singing and dancing with full vigor, as if he had not yet celebrated at all. This he did in every synagogue that he chanced upon on his way to his home." *Baal HaTanya* suggests that everyone follow the custom of the *Arizal.*

The great luminaries in all generations would dance and celebrate on Simchas Torah with exultation. *Maaseh Rav* (333) reports that the *Vilna Gaon* would experience joy on Simchas Torah that surpassed even the intense happiness which he displayed throughout Succos. He would sing many liturgical poems and dance with abandon and great strength, clapping vigorously all the while. His countenance took on the radiance of a glowing flame as the wisdom within his heart and mind cast its brilliant light upon his face. He would dance and sing praises to God with all his might in honor of the Torah. Only when the scrolls were returned to the Ark did he return to the tranquilly joyous demeanor that he maintained on all holidays.

R' Shlomo Wolbe paints a word picture of Simchas Torah in the rarefied atmosphere of the prewar Mirrer Yeshivah, with its sainted *mashgiach* R' Yerucham Levovitz:

> While many of the great *Mussar* personalities were concerned lest the joyous celebration and dancing on Simchas Torah lead to boisterousness and lightheadedness, God forbid, R' Yerucham encouraged intense dancing and joy. Simchas Torah with him was an experience never to be forgotten. He would speak words of spiritual encouragement and inspiration with great emotion and end every short

speech with the singing of אַשְׁרֵיכֶם יִשְׂרָאֵל, *praiseworthy are you, Israel*. With his hands raised heavenward and surrounded by his admiring students, he would sing and dance on the *bimah* while we crowded around below, dancing in front of him. Finally, he would descend to the crowd and dance with us as we all cried from the depths of our souls. What a sight it was to see hundreds of his disciples, among them people great in their own right, dancing while simultaneously singing and crying. He himself once cried out in the middle of the festivities, "I don't know which is dearer to God, our Yom Kippur or our Simchas Torah!"

The Behavior of Greatness

⋅§ One should expend great effort and dance on Simchas Torah with all his might in honor of the Torah. He should not say, "It is below my dignity and a dishonor to the Torah for me to dance among the people like an empty-headed simpleton."

This was the sin of Michal, daughter of Saul (see *II Samuel* 6:16-23). When she saw her husband, King David, dancing with wild abandon in front of the Holy Ark as he brought it into its tent, she felt scorn towards him and viewed his behavior as a degradation of his honor and his kingdom's honor. She even went so far as to upbraid him for his unbecoming behavior. King David responded, "Had I lowered myself even more — [even] to be lowly in my own eyes — such actions would be indicative of my true honor, since they were done to honor God and the Holy Ark" (ibid. 22) (see *Mishnah Berurah* 669 §11 and *Shaar HaTziyun* ad loc.).

Rambam poignantly and powerfully captures David's sentiment:

> The joy that one experiences in his fulfillment of *mitzvos* and his love of God, Who commanded him about them, is both a difficult task and an elevated spiritual attainment. One who [fulfills the *mitzvos* yet] refrains from experiencing and expressing such joy deserves to be punished. As the Torah teaches [regarding the cause for all the frightful punishments that would befall the Jewish people if they strayed from God and His Torah], *Because you did not serve HASHEM, your God, amid gladness and goodness of heart (Deuteronomy* 28:47).
>
> One who acts with arrogance and reserves honor for himself in such situations is both a sinner and a fool.

Regarding this did King Solomon teach, *Do not honor yourself in front of the king* (*Proverbs* 25:6). However, one who humbles himself and even treats himself dishonorably in such situations is the truly great and honorable person, who serves God out of genuine love.

True greatness and honor is only to rejoice in front of God (*Hilchos Lulav* 8:15).

An Elevated Moment

ও§ King Solomon teaches: סַלְסְלֶהָ וּתְרוֹמְמֶךָ, *Search for it [the Torah] and it will uplift you* (*Proverbs* 4:8). One who obsessively focuses his energies and interest on Torah, with the rapture of a child totally engrossed in play, will be edified and uplifted. According to *Avnei Nezer* this is the secret of dancing. One who dances attempts, if but for a moment, to rise from the ground, above the earthly and the mundane. As we dance with the Torah, we have in our heart the prayer that it elevate us throughout the year and help us surmount the pull of downward spiritual gravity.

Casting One's Lot With Torah

ও§ Even if one has not learned Torah in the past and has suffered spiritual shortcomings, he may legitimately claim that it is a result of personal weakness, and not, God forbid, of a resistance to Torah. On Simchas Torah, everyone is given a chance to show his sincere essence and to demonstrate that his failures are not the result of an uncaring attitude, God forbid, toward Torah and *mitzvos*.

R' Shlomo Kluger explains how those who have such a negative attitude can be differentiated from those who have simply not been strong enough to maintain a high spiritual standard.

King David declares, *The death blow of the wicked is [the] evil [itself], and the haters of the righteous will be condemned* (*Psalms* 34:22). Why, asks *R' Kluger*, should one who is too weak to combat the forces of evil be liable for his spiritual deficiencies? True, the Sages teach that Torah study is the antidote to the Evil Inclination, but not everyone has the time or opportunity to devote himself with intensity to learning. Why should God punish the spiritually uncultivated person who is unable to fend off the forces of evil through Torah study?

A parable may help us understand. A king sent a platoon of soldiers to fight his enemy, but they were vanquished in battle. The

king was in doubt as to the cause of the defeat. Was it disloyalty to the king which had caused the soldiers to give less than their best effort, or was it simply because they were weaker than the enemy?

In order to ascertain the true cause, the king sent a stronger regiment of soldiers to fight his adversary. The new platoon, in a dazzling display of military prowess, was able to conquer the enemy. The king now looked to see the reaction of the first group to the success of the second group. Were they to rejoice in the victory of their comrades-in-arms, it would be clear that their lack of success and eventual defeat was the result of excusable weakness. However, if they remained dispassionate about the victory, the king would conclude that their own defeat was the result of poor morale — and possibly treasonous sentiment.

Man in this world is a warrior in battle. The enemy is his Evil Inclination, and the stakes of battle are high. If man falls victim to the inner force of evil and is "wounded" in battle, it must be determined whether the defeat is related to his inherent spiritual and emotional frailty or to his lack of regard for the word of God. The way God determines man's intrinsic orientation is by providing the person with exposure to good role models or other spiritually positive experiences. If the individual derives pleasure from the righteousness of others and demonstrates honor and support for those who dedicate themselves to Torah study, it becomes clear that his own defeats at the hand of his spiritual enemy were the result of personal weakness. Thus, he will incur only mitigated punishment. However, if he is disdainful of righteous people and Torah scholars and derives no joy from their spiritual achievements, we must suspect some form of inner corruption.

Rabbeinu Yonah captures this concept in a novel interpretation of King Solomon's words, *The refining pot is for silver and the furnace for gold, and a man is tried according to his praise (Proverbs* 27:21). Just as an oven cleans the silver of impurities and a furnace purifies the gold of its dross, in each case yielding the untainted essence of the metal, so a person's essence becomes revealed when we focus on what he praises. Even if he has not personally maintained a high standard, his value for the standard is a measure of his worth. Through joy on Simchas Torah, one casts his lot with Torah and its Giver. He shows that his sins and omissions are aberrations, and that at heart he is truly connected to Torah.

Wellspring of Joy

◄§ *Chiddushei HaRim* notes that we refer to the pilgrimage festivals as מוֹעֲדִים לְשִׂמְחָה, holidays *for* joy, rather than מוֹעֲדִים שֶׁל שִׂמְחָה, holidays *of* joy. The holidays were given so that a Jew would have a source from which to draw joy throughout the year.

Zohar teaches that Simchas Torah is the wellspring of joy for all the other holidays, which draw their particular form of joyousness from its celebration. This is alluded to in the word שִׂמְחַת, *Simchas,* which, when rearranged, is an acronym for several זְמַנִים, festive *times*: זְמַן שִׂמְחָתֵנוּ, *the season of our joy* (Succos); זְמַן מַתַּן תּוֹרָתֵנוּ, *the season of the giving of the Torah* (Shavuos); and זְמַן חֵרוּתֵנוּ, *the season of our freedom* (Pesach).

Furthermore, each of the holidays of the month of Tishrei serves as the initial source of a specific quality which every Jew needs for his spiritual well-being. This is alluded to in the word תִּשְׁרֵי, *Tishrei,* which can be rearranged to spell רֵאשִׁית, *beginning* (the א is silent). On Rosh Hashanah, our reverence and awe of God are renewed; on Yom Kippur, we are swept by a wave of *teshuvah,* repentance; and on Simchas Torah we receive an infusion of joy which will hopefully invigorate us all year long and help us bring joy to our fellow Jews and to God (*Ohr HaTorah*).

Joyful Repentance

◄§ The joy of this special day serves yet another purpose. *Rambam* (*Hil. Teshuvah* 7:3) teaches that true repentance entails not only the repudiation of the act of sin but also its root causes. Sin is often the product of gloom and despair; true repentance must therefore include a sincere effort to be joyous and develop a positive view of life. As *R' Aharon of Karlin* said: "Nowhere does the Torah forbid despondency, yet it is at the root of all transgression; nowhere does the Torah say that to be happy is a *mitzvah,* yet from a joyous heart emanates the motivation to fulfill all the *mitzvos.*"

After achieving atonement on Yom Kippur, we rejoice in God's Torah, seeking to arouse in ourselves the gladness of heart that is the root of all good.

Thanking the Torah

◄§ The intense joy with which one celebrates Simchas Torah is an expression of his gratitude to the Torah for all it has taught him. The

Sages teach that if one has learned even one word of Torah from someone, he must accord that person special respect and honor (see *Avos* 6:2). *Tanna d'Vei Eliyahu* teaches that God's intense love for the Torah is rooted in the fact that it teaches His children Israel how to improve themselves spiritually. The Torah teaches us about life, how to fulfill ourselves and the will of God, and thus we are bound to cherish it, honor it and express our gratitude toward it. Our joy on Simchas Torah is our way of saying "thank you" for all that the Torah has given us (*Sefas Emes*).

Blessings on Credit

~§ Once on Simchas Torah, the *gabbai* announced that Reb Shalom Ber of Lubavitch was to be given the first *Sefer Torah* during the first of the seven *hakafos*. The *Rebbe,* however, said: "I am not yet ready." He then called upon a certain merchant who traded on a commission basis and asked him to explain the nature of his business and how it operated.

"Simple," he said. "I bring merchandise from the big city and supply it to all the small retailers, and whoever pays up for the previous consignment gets his new batch on credit."

The Hebrew word for "credit" is *hakafah,* the same word for the festive circuits in the synagogue on Simchas Torah.

Said the *Rebbe* to those assembled: "After we have 'paid in cash' by performing the various distinctive rituals of Divine service that characterize the month of Elul, Rosh Hashanah, the Ten Days of Penitence, Yom Kippur, Succos and Shemini Atzeres — only when we have fulfilled these can we take a new consignment of blessings for the year 'on credit' (*behakafah*). Let us now begin the *hakafos* and open our hearts and souls to receive all of God's blessings."

God grants us His beneficence on credit not only because of our cash payments in the past, but also because of His belief in us and His supreme confidence that we will meet our obligations. As mentioned earlier, God is called אֵל אֱמוּנָה, a *God of trust,* since He blesses us with health, sustenance and even wealth, and trusts that we will invest it wisely, using it only for the purpose of enhancing His honor. Even the Torah He enables us to learn is given to us on credit, in the hope that through its study we will be sufficiently elevated to make the Torah our own and thus truly deserve such a priceless treasure.

How does God know that we will not abuse His trust in us? The uninhibited joy we demonstrate in celebrating with the Torah on

Simchas Torah indicates how precious it is in our eyes. God is reassured that His investment in us is one that will reap manifold profits. Thus, our *hakafos* "prompt" God to extend us *hakafah* (credit) (*Simchas Aharon*).

Ateres Yehoshua cites a profound allusion to this idea. The Kabbalists teach that Jacob married Rachel on Shemini Atzeres. While he worked first for Leah for seven years and then received her hand in marriage, the case of Rachel was just the opposite; he was given her "on credit" and only paid Laban after the marriage by working for seven additional years. Similarly, the nation of Israel celebrates its marriage to God through the Torah on Shemini Atzeres/Simchas Torah. We receive everything on credit, as symbolized by the seven *hakafos,* and hope our labor of love in the Torah during the course of the year will redeem our everlasting debt to God. Our *hakafos* are a form of prayer in which we beseech Him to grant us the ability to pay back all our debts and continue to maintain good credit standing with Him.

In Retrospect

ﬠﬦ *Nahor Shalom* offers yet another shade of meaning to the theme of *hakafos.* When Abraham returned to *Eretz Yisrael* from Egypt, he lodged in the same places he had stayed on the way there. *Rashi* (*Genesis* 13:3) comments that he did this in order to pay for that which he had taken on credit in those inns during his trip to Egypt (בַּחֲזָרָתוֹ פָּרַע הַקָּפוֹתָיו).

Homiletically, הַקָּפוֹתָיו, *his credit payments,* may be rendered *his wanderings.* Many of man's wanderings and detours in life are incomprehensible to him. We often wonder why we need to live through certain experiences and often fail to see God's goodness in them. It is only in retrospect, "on the way back," that we begin to acquire a perspective on the deep yet hidden good that God provides for us through the course of sometimes difficult experiences.

Abraham had gone to Egypt to escape famine. Initially, he suffered tribulations there, which later gave way to a vast improvement in his material lot (see ibid. v. 2). Only upon his return from Egypt did he begin to understand the importance of this experience in his own development and in the development of the nation he would found.

Likewise, in the course of the Days of Awe we toil through the process of repentance for our sins. On Simchas Torah, enraptured in the celebration of Torah, we make our *hakafos* symbolic of a return

to the point of embarkment and acquire the retrospective clarity that the Torah provides. We are now able to understand our spiritual gains and why we could only have achieved them through the emotionally trying *teshuvah* process. It is this very sense of clarity that will continue to help us to find joy and good in all of life's episodes.

A Traveling Nation

ك§ The word *hakafah* in its translation of "wandering" can also be considered a metaphor for the entire history of the Jewish people. In our exiles over the centuries, we took the Torah with us from country to country. Following a circuitous route, we went to Babylonia, where the Talmud Bavli developed. Evicted from there, we traveled from Spain to Germany, from Poland and Russia to America, all the while trying our best to carry the Torah proudly aloft. This wandering from place to place will hopefully end soon, when God allows the joy and light of Torah to guide us to a final, tranquil port — *Eretz Yisrael,* from where our circuit began — with the coming of *Mashiach,* speedily in our days (*R' Meir Shapiro*).

Last to First —
Interpretations and Allusions

ك§ It is customary among rabbinic scholars to offer, on Simchas Torah, interpretations that connect the end of the *Chumash* with its beginning, since on this day we end *Parashas VeZos HaBerachah* and immediately begin *Parashas Bereishis.* Just as we dance in a never-ending circle, so we view Torah study as a never-ending process; the end is only the beginning. In this spirit, we offer a sampling of such interpretations; many of them are based on the words that conclude and begin the *Chumash.* The final words of *VeZos HaBerachah* are וּלְכֹל הַיָּד הַחֲזָקָה וּלְכֹל הַמּוֹרָא הַגָּדוֹל אֲשֶׁר עָשָׂה מֹשֶׁה לְעֵינֵי כָּל יִשְׂרָאֵל, *And by the strong hand and awesome power that Moses performed before the eyes of all Israel;* the first words in *Parashas Bereishis* are בְּרֵאשִׁית בָּרָא אֱלֹהִים אֵת הַשָּׁמַיִם וְאֵת הָאָרֶץ, *In the beginning of God's creating the heavens and the earth.*

Moses as Mediator

ℝ The Torah ends with a description of Moses' greatness. *The strong hand* refers to his receiving the Tablets containing the Ten Commandments in his hands from God at Mount Sinai. According to the Midrash, the Tablets were of extraordinary weight, yet Moses was miraculously able to carry them. *The awesome power* relates to the miracles God performed in the Wilderness through the hand of Moses.

By connecting these thoughts to the Torah's beginning, we learn that the only way to carry the heavy burden of Torah is to remember God's great interventions in history, performed (through Moses) on our behalf. If we are able to view these events with the fresh perspective of a new beginning, as if they had just happened, we can make our belief in God as the Creator and our love for His Torah integral and vibrant elements of our lives. This will provide us with the strength and courage to bear the yoke of Torah (*Semuchim La'ad*).

Learning With Heart

ℝ The last letter of the Torah is a ל; the first is a ב. Together, they form the word לֵב, *heart*. This teaches that Torah should be studied with a joyous heart, without excessive worry about one's material needs. One who truly seeks to study Torah for its own sake will be granted everything he needs without overextending himself.

King David compares the man who studies Torah incessantly to a tree replanted by a stream of water, which yields its fruit in season (see *Psalms* 1:3). Like this tree, which needs no artificial irrigation in order to produce fruit, the dedicated scholar will merit to receive his sustenance without inordinate effort. Thus, the key to constant immersion in Torah — which is symbolized by finishing and immediately starting again — is to take to *heart* (לֵב) the reality that *in the beginning, God created the heavens and the earth,* and that he can perform at will the greatest of miracles. He can shatter all natural limitations and provide supernaturally for those who meditate on His Torah day and night (*Chaim Techilah,* see *Rambam, Hilchos Shemittah VeYovel* 13:13).

Eyewitnesses

ℝ When God spoke to His people at Mount Sinai, He introduced Himself as the "God Who has taken you out of the land of Egypt"

Exodus 20:2). Why did God not identify Himself as Creator of the Universe, a title that is more all-embracing than that of Redeemer of the Jewish people? On an elementary level, this description is used because the Exodus was a phenomenon that had been witnessed by the entire Jewish nation. The people *knew* that there had been a Creation, of course, but they had not witnessed it; indeed, one might have contended, ר"ל — as does most of the modern world — that the universe had not been created *ex nihilo*. But no one at Sinai could have questioned the existence of the One Who liberated them from Egypt (*Kuzari; R' Bachya*).

Furthermore, it is the great miracles which God performed during the Exodus that proved beyond the shadow of a doubt that He created all of nature and can do with it as He pleases. As *Ramban* comments:

> The Torah relates the story of the six days of Creation *ex nihilo* to establish that God is the sole Creator and to refute the theories of those who claim that the universe is timeless or that it came into being through some massive coincidence or accident (*Genesis* 1:1).
>
> The open miracles of the Exodus seal into our awareness [the fact] that God created His universe and rules it with unmitigated autonomy. The only difference between nature and miracles is that we are accustomed to the former and awed by the latter (*Exodus* 13:16).

Thus, it was the great miracles that *Moses performed before the eyes of all of Israel* which proved conclusively that בְּרֵאשִׁית בָּרָא אֱלֹהִים, *In the beginning, God created* . . . (*Meloh HaOmer, Yalkut HaGershuni*).

Creation on Condition

◆§ After telling of the Splitting of the Sea, the Torah states, *And toward morning the water went back* לְאֵיתָנוֹ, *to its power* (*Exodus* 14:27). In a homiletic play on words, the Sages interpret the word לְאֵיתָנוֹ as if it read, לִתְנָאוֹ הָרִאשׁוֹן, *to its original stipulation,* meaning that the creation of the sea was originally conditional upon its splitting for the sake of the Jewish people at the time of the Exodus (*Shemos Rabbah* 21:6).

Chasam Sofer suggests that God made such a stipulation with *all* of Creation. Nothing in the universe can stand in the way of the needs of the Jewish people. Thus, all of the *awesome power that Moses performed before the eyes of all Israel* was the result of the contingency which God implanted in the entire universe at the time of Creation (*in the beginning*).

For Those That Are Primary

◄§ Homiletically, the word בְּרֵאשִׁית can be rendered בִּשְׁבִיל רֵאשִׁית, *[the world was created] for the sake of [the things that are called] "beginning"* [i.e., *primary*], meaning that God brought the world into being for the sake of things that are of such basic importance that the Torah calls them רֵאשִׁית. These are the Torah and Israel. Thus, the purpose of Creation was that Israel accept and fulfill the Torah (*Rashi*).

God therefore performed many miracles on behalf of His people throughout history in order that they continue to exist and flourish. All this was done for them so that they would be able to study and perform the Torah, giving meaning to the cosmos that God brought into existence for that very purpose.

We allude to this connection in the words we recite every Sabbath eve in *Lechah Dodi:* סוֹף מַעֲשֶׂה בְּמַחֲשָׁבָה תְּחִלָּה, *Last in deed, but first in thought.* The last word in the Torah, יִשְׂרָאֵל, *Israel,* was first and foremost in thought when God created the heavens and the earth.

Why the Sea Split

◄§ According to *Ramban,* the words *strong hand* at the end of the *Chumash* refer to the splitting of the waters of the Sea of Reeds. The Midrash teaches that when the Jews passed through the sea, the guardian angel of the sea sought permission to drown the Israelites since they carried an idol with them.[1] God Himself replied, "Leave them alone, for eventually they will be rid of their idols when they accept My Torah at Sinai."

Hence, the *strong hand* of the Splitting of the Sea occurred because of בְּרֵאשִׁית, which is an acronym for the words בָּרִאשׁוֹנָה רָאָה אֱלֹהִים שֶׁיְּקַבְּלוּ יִשְׂרָאֵל תּוֹרָה, *In the beginning God saw that [in the future] Israel would accept the Torah* (*Me'am Loez*).

Saying and Knowing

◄§ We often parrot truths that we assimilated at some point in our lives but have never internalized. A famous incident involving R' Levi Yitzchak of Berditchev highlights this phenomenon. Once, when the Berditchever returned home after a visit to his *Rebbe,* R' Shmelke of

---

1. The Talmud (*Sanhedrin* 103b) interprets the verse *Over the sea, affliction passed* (*Zechariah* 10:11) as a reference to this idol, which Micah fashioned and took along when Israel crossed the Sea of Reeds (see *Rashi* ad loc.).

Nikolsburg, his father-in-law asked him, "Tell me, what did you learn from your teacher and mentor?"

"I learned that there is a Creator of the World," he replied.

His father-in-law was dumbfounded and called upon the maid of the house. "Tell me, young lady, is there a God Who created the world?" he asked her.

"Of course!" she declared.

The father-in-law turned to his son-in-law. "You see, even she knows that there is a God. For that you didn't have to go to your *Rebbe*."

Replied R' Levi Yitzchak, "She *says* there is a God, but after being with my *Rebbe*, I *know* there is a God."

After the Days of Awe and Succos we acquire a clarity of perspective on life and reality so that we are able not only to *say* that we believe in God and His Torah, but to *perceive* this truth without distortion. Thus, we begin the *hakafos* with the verse אַתָּה הָרְאֵתָ לָדַעַת, *You have been shown in order to know that HASHEM, He is the God; there is none besides Him* (*Deuteronomy* 4:35). It is this pristine vision which finds an allusion in the connection between the end of the Torah and its beginning. Having completed the Torah, we begin again with a clear awareness of our primary goal — that it become plainly apparent *before the eyes of all Israel* (*VeZos HaBerachah*) that *In the beginning God created the heavens and the earth* (*Bereishis*).

Destruction in the Service of God

§ לְעֵינֵי כָּל יִשְׂרָאֵל, *Before the eyes of all Israel*. Moses took it upon himself to shatter the Tablets before the people's eyes [see *Deuteronomy* 9:17], and God ratified his decision (*Rashi Deuteronomy* 34:12). This shows that it is not sufficient for a leader to be able to make momentous decisions; he must even be willing to destroy his entire life's work if that is what the hour requires. Many people are able to *build* heroically, but few are able to make the decision to *tear down* (*R' Nosson Scherman*). Moses emulated God in his ability to destroy his own accomplishments when the honor of Heaven called for it.

The Midrash (*Bereishis Rabbah* 3:7) teaches that God created many worlds before the present one but destroyed them all, saying, "This world will give Me pleasure, while all the earlier ones gave Me none." Thus Moses learned to shatter the Tablets alluded to in the words *before the eyes of all Israel* by following the cue of God when He created the heavens and earth (*Simchas Aharon*).

The Paradox of Torah

❧ Man's relationship to the Torah is somewhat paradoxical. On one hand, Torah is compared to light because it illuminates man's perception of the will of God; on the other hand, Torah is Divine wisdom, and one can never thoroughly plumb the limits of its profundities. In truth, it is the light of Torah which enables us to perceive that we *cannot* fully perceive God or His Torah.

King David captured this irony when he spoke of his joy over God's Torah. *I rejoice over Your word, like one who finds great treasure* (*Psalms* 119:162). One who finds an enormous treasure has mixed emotions. He is ecstatic over his find, but he is disappointed that no matter how much wealth he can stuff into his bags, it will be insignificant compared to everything he must leave behind. Such mixed emotions were the lot of King David. He rejoiced at the opportunity to fulfill God's commandments, but his joy was tinged with sadness in the knowledge that he could not accomplish nearly as much as he wished. Likewise, one is elated that he can absorb the wisdom of God, yet he is humbled by the knowledge that he can but scratch the surface of His infinite wisdom.

These two aspects of Torah are captured in the name *Atzeres,* which can be translated as *release* [as in the squeezing of oil from olives], and also as *withholding.* Torah is *released* by God so that man may taste of its profundity, but its full understanding is *withheld* from him.

This is the homiletic message which is contained in the connection between the last and first verses of the Torah. Even though everything seems to be clear *before the eyes of Israel,* in truth we have only scratched the surface of the Torah and are still *in the beginning* of our understanding (*Toras Emes*).

Stories

A Dream for Life

❧ מַשִּׁיב הָרוּחַ וּמוֹרִיד הַגֶּשֶׁם, He makes the wind blow and He makes the rain descend.

R' Moshe Schwab zt"l, *mashgiach* of the famed Gateshead Yeshivah, came from a well-known Frankfurt-am-Main family and

was educated with the *Torah-im-Derech Eretz* approach of Rav Samson Raphael Hirsch. While a student of the Mirrer Yeshivah in Poland, he underwent some grave doubts regarding his future. On one hand, his heart and soul impelled him to dedicate his life exclusively to learning and teaching Torah, while on the other hand, his parents were getting on in years and he felt responsibility to assist his father in the family business. It was only a few years earlier that his father had moved to England and started anew, and the effort had sapped his strength, taking a considerable toll. R' Moshe, a spiritually sensitive soul, was torn between two very pure but irreconcilable desires.

The night of Simchas Torah arrived. This night was one of the most inspiring and sublime experiences imaginable for those who had the good fortune to find themselves in the Mirrer Yeshivah. Like a king among his loyal soldiers, the *mashgiach*, R' Yerucham, would dance with the Torah scroll in his arms while all his "cossacks" (close *talmidim*) would dance facing him, their beloved leader. The spiritual elation the students achieved was a result of the yearning of their souls for the Torah they had learned all year and with which they were celebrating on this night.

Caught up in the spirit, R' Moshe danced along with his fellow students, yet his heart was elsewhere. The question of his future allowed him no rest, gnawing on his heart and mind. He felt as if the joy of the Torah, on this night, had not succeeded in penetrating all the barriers and suffusing his essence, until . . .

R' Moshe took a Torah scroll for a *hakafah*, held it tightly to his heart, and swore to himself that he would always learn and teach Torah. He uttered a silent prayer to God that he be granted the strength and courage to battle and conquer any impediment that sought to divert him from this path.

After the holiday he was planning to write his parents to inform them of his decision. While mulling over in his mind exactly how to express himself, he was approached by an elderly man who had just arrived in Mir from Baranovitch. The Jew, a learned gentleman, told R' Moshe of a dream he had had on the night of Simchas Torah.

"An old man told me to go to a young yeshivah student by the name of Moshe Schwab and tell him the following message: מַשִּׁיב הָרוּחַ — the spiritual should acquire permanence; וּמוֹרִיד הַגֶּשֶׁם — the physical (גַּשְׁמִיּוּת) should descend in importance.'[1] The dream repeated itself

---

1. The phrase is from the daily *Shemoneh Esrei,* and it literally means, "[*Hashem*] *makes the wind blow and He makes the rain descend.*" Here, in a play on words, the phrase was interpreted as a comment on רוּחָנִיּוּת (spirituality) and גַּשְׁמִיּוּת (materialism).

again," said the old Baranovitch resident, "so I decided that it must be a serious Heavenly summons. After some inquiries I discovered that you were to be found in the Mirrer Yeshivah, so I followed you here."

R' Moshe immediately understood the import of the dream and realized that it represented an approval of his decision. "Tell me," he asked the old man, "did you recognize the person who appeared to you in the dream?" The man said that he had no idea who it was. R' Moshe began to show him family pictures, and the elderly gentleman recognized R' Moshe's maternal grandfather, R' Avraham Erlanger, as the person who had appeared in the dream.

R' Moshe wrote to his parents describing the entire incident and telling them of his decision. He asked for their consent to remain in the world of Torah. His father sent him an immediate reply, וְאָבִיו שָׁמַר אֶת הַדָּבָר, *And his father waited for the thing* [*to happen*] (*Genesis* 37:11). Apparently, the grandfather in Heaven agreed with R' Moshe's decision to establish himself firmly in the spiritual arena and to allow worldly concerns to play a secondary role.

The Mysterious Baal Tefillah

⊷§ תּוֹרַת ה' תְּמִימָה מְשִׁיבַת נָפֶשׁ, *The Torah of HASHEM is perfect; it restores the soul.*

The Klausenberger *Rebbe zt"l* would often repeat the following story: For the first few years after his marriage, the famed author of the *Yeshuos Yaakov* lived in the home of his father-in-law in the city of Yeroslov. Supported by his in-laws, he spent his days and nights totally immersed in learning and growing in Torah.

One Erev Yom Kippur, as he was standing along with the Jews of Yeroslov in the local synagogue waiting for *Kol Nidrei* to begin, a stranger entered. The man, who looked visibly shaken, immediately walked over to the *amud* and, without asking anyone's permission, began the Yom Kippur prayers. "עַל דַּעַת הַמָּקוֹם," he cried out with a lion-like roar and then began *Kol Nidrei* in an other-worldly voice. Even though he had taken the *amud* without permission and had displaced the regular *baalei tefillah,* none of the congregants protested, wanting at any cost to avoid argument and strife on this holiest of days. Furthermore, the young man prayed with such intensity, excitement and beauty that no one had the slightest desire to stop him.

When he finished *Kol Nidrei* the strange guest remained at the *amud* and continued into *Maariv.* His voice was sweet and powerful

at the same time, and all the people in the synagogue were spellbound. When he finished *Maariv,* he remained in his place and began the traditional recitation of the *Shir HaYichud* prayers, reciting them with overwhelming feeling. This was followed by a slow and heartrending recitation of the entire Book of *Psalms,* which lasted throughout most of the night.

By the time he finished reciting *Tehillim,* the sun had risen and the mysterious visitor immediately began the morning prayers. He rapturously delivered the *Shacharis* prayer, served as the Torah reader, and then offered a powerful and moving *Mussaf* service. The members of the Yeroslov community were in shock over the superhuman effort of their guest, and they started debating quietly among themselves about the guest's identity. "He is certainly an angel," they said. "No human being could perform such feats."

"I myself," the *Yeshuos Yaakov* reported, "couldn't decide if he was a human being or an angel."

To everyone's surprise, upon finishing *Mussaf,* the unknown visitor immediately began *Minchah* and followed it with a stirring rendition of *Ne'ilah,* not once showing any signs of weakness or fatigue. He blew the *shofar* at the end of *Ne'ilah* and led the *Maariv* service. Since he had remained at the *amud* for the entire twenty-five hours of Yom Kippur, everyone was sure now beyond a shadow of a doubt that the *baal tefillah* was nothing less than an angel. When he finished *Maariv,* the guest turned to the congregation and wished everyone a *Gut Yom Tov.*

The *Yeshuos Yaakov* continued: "My father-in-law invited him home to make *havdalah* and break his fast. The guest accepted the offer, and I decided to go with them to see for myself who he really was. My father-in-law asked him to make *havdalah,* which he did with the same energy he had displayed throughout Yom Kippur. Then he drank the wine and immediately collapsed in his chair, complaining that he didn't feel well. He asked that we bring him something to strengthen himself, and we gave him a drink and some cake and cookies. I was sure that the truth was now clear; he was a human being, not an angel. But I was wrong. The mysterious guest cried out, 'No! No! I don't need cake; bring me a *Gemara Succah.*' He immediately began to learn with zest, continuing throughout the night, and only in the morning, when he had finished the tractate, did he go to the synagogue to *daven Shacharis.*"

Later they found out that their mysterious visitor was none other than R' Levi Yitzchak of Berditchev.

The Klausenberger Rebbe concluded: "After the great spiritual exertion of his prayers, R' Levi Yitzchak had indeed felt weak and in need of refreshment. Only *Gemara* and *Tosafos*, and nothing else, could revive him."

God's Torah is perfect; it truly restores the soul.

A Wealth of Promise, A Promise of Wealth

עֵדוּת ה' נֶאֱמָנָה מַחְכִּימַת פֶּתִי ◌◌, *The testimony of HASHEM is trustworthy, making the simple one wise.*

In Europe, many years ago, a man was looking for a *shidduch* (partner in marriage) for his daughter. A certain young man was suggested as a suitable match, but after making some inquiries, the prospective father-in-law had serious doubts about him. The young man in question had a reputation as being very pious and sincere, and was known for his exceptional *hasmadah* (diligence in Torah study). However, he did not possess a very sharp mind, and his comprehension of the Talmud was not as outstanding as the father had been led to believe. The gentleman was in a quandary, for he wanted only the very best *bachur* for his daughter, and this fellow seemed to be lacking in superior abilities. He decided to seek the counsel of Rabbi Yehoshua Leib Diskin, the rabbi of Brisk.

He explained the situation to the *Rav*, who cited a Mishnah in *Avos* (4:11): *Whoever fulfills the Torah despite poverty will ultimately fulfill it in wealth.*

"It is my understanding," he said, "that this refers not only to money but to talent and ability as well. Just as we are guaranteed that those who uphold Torah and *mitzvos*, no matter how poor they are, will eventually uphold the Torah in wealth, those who are diligent in their studies and persevere even though they suffer intellectual 'poverty' are also assured of 'wealth,' meaning that they will attain great heights in Torah. If the young man in question is indeed diligent in his learning and sincere in his performance of *mitzvos*, even though he may presently be 'poor' in comprehension, in time he will surely attain 'wealth' — superior comprehension — and achieve the prominence in Torah that is so important to you. I therefore suggest," concluded the *Rav*, "that you agree to the *shidduch*."

The father consented to the marriage, and the *chassan* eventually became the renowned rabbi of Aishishok, R' Yosef Zundel, and the author of many works on *Shulchan Aruch*, including the noted *Chadrei Deah*.

Torah has the power to expand one's intellectual capabilities. The *testimony of* HASHEM [Torah] *is trustworthy, making the simple one wise* (Psalms 19:8).

The Gift of Sight

✥§ מִצְוַת ה׳ בָּרָה מְאִירַת עֵינָיִם, *The command of* HASHEM *is clear, enlightening the eyes.*

R' Isser Zalman Meltzer told of an elderly *talmid chacham* who visited him one day in Slutzk. R' Isser Zalman saw that the man was unfortunately blind. "He brought me two books that he had published and, after ascertaining which page he had opened to, he pointed to a particular paragraph. 'That is the last original insight in Torah that I developed,' he told me. I asked him to explain.

"He answered, 'All my life I toiled in Torah study, and *baruch Hashem* I was able to develop original insights. As I got older, the regimen of intense Torah study became more and more difficult. When I finished writing the idea I showed you, I thought to myself that the time had come to take it a little easier. Of course I would continue to learn, but not with my regular intensity. Very shortly after that, I suddenly went blind. I sought the best medical help available, but to no avail. After a thorough examination, a world-class eye specialist told me that he couldn't understand how I could have seen *for the last ten years,* as my eyesight was so poor.' "

R' Isser Zalman added the old man's conclusion of the tale: "The doctor couldn't figure it out but I know why this happened. As long as I put my eyesight to good use, God gave me the ability to see. The moment I decided to slacken off, He took His gift back."

Truthfully True

✥§ יִרְאַת ה׳ טְהוֹרָה עוֹמֶדֶת לָעַד, *The fear of* HASHEM *is pure, enduring forever.*

When R' Eliyahu Meir Bloch, the Telzer Rosh Yeshivah, visited *Eretz Yisrael,* he met with all the great people of the time. In his great love for the Land he also traveled to all corners of *Eretz Yisrael,* seeking to experience its many aspects.

One day he hired a taxi to take him up north to visit the Galil. Safed, Tiberias, the Banyas River and all the other panoramic sights were on his itinerary. As they passed by Lake Kinneret in Tiberias, R' Eliyahu Meir asked the driver to stop. "How can I pass by the Kinneret and not go for even a short swim? What will I tell my friends in America

when I return — that I was at the Kinneret but I didn't go in?"

The Rosh Yeshivah got out of the car, went to the back, and opened the baggage compartment in order to find swimming trunks in his valise. After looking around he realized that he had forgotten to pack his swimwear. "*Nu,*" he said to the driver, "I won't be able to tell my friends in America about my swim in the Kinneret."

"Why not?" asked the driver. "Nobody in America will know the difference."

R' Eliyahu Meir insisted that the driver immediately take him back to Jerusalem, canceling the rest of his Galil tour. "I cannot be in the same car with someone who thinks that it is permitted to tell a white lie even if no one will ever know about it."

True fear of Hashem is pure and lasts forever — even if no one will ever know the difference.

Principled Pricing

◆§ מִשְׁפְּטֵי ה׳ אֱמֶת, *The judgments of HASHEM are true.*

R' Shraga Feivel Frank, a close disciple of R' Yisrael Salanter, owned a factory that produced finished hides. A Jewish merchant from another city once came to the factory in order to purchase a sizable number of hides. "What type of discount will you give me on an order of this size?" he asked.

R' Feivel replied, "I set my prices with precision. I take into consideration my cost and add on a reasonable profit margin. My friend, I'm sorry but I cannot bargain, nor can I lower my price. If you want, feel free to buy from one of the other merchants here in Aleksot. In fact, let me give you the names of some of them."

The customer left and went off in search of a better price, but to no avail; R' Feivel's prices were the best. He returned to him and asked if the merchandise he had looked at was still available.

"Yes," replied R' Feivel, "and you can have it at the price you suggested.

"What?" exclaimed the man. "Didn't you say that you don't bargain?"

"Yes," said R' Feivel, "but after you left I began thinking that even if I allow you the discount you asked for, I will still turn a handsome profit. I really should not have been so stubborn and insistent about my business principles. Now that you have come back, I must honor the decision I made in my heart to allow you the consideration you requested."

R' Shraga Feivel Frank, a man who upheld the very highest standards of truth demanded by the Torah, merited sons-in-law who were luminaries in the Torah world: R' Isser Zalman Meltzer, R' Moshe Mordechai Epstein, R' Baruch Horowitz and R' Sheftel Kramer. These great men and their descendants founded most of the major yeshivos in Europe, Israel and the United States.

A Quick Return

8ه הַנֶּחֱמָדִים מִזָּהָב וּמִפַּז רָב 8ه, *They are more desirable than gold, than even much fine gold.*

R' Moshe Shmukler, one of the prized students of the *Chafetz Chaim* in the Yeshivah of Radin, received a very sizable dowry upon his marriage and seriously entertained the idea of entering the world of business after his wedding. The *Chafetz Chaim* told him: "When a young Torah student wants to leave full-time Torah study to pursue financial success, it depends on how much luck he has. If he is very lucky and is truly beloved in Heaven, he will be able to lose his dowry money quickly enough. In this way he will still be able to remember the Torah he learned before he became wrapped up in business. If he has less merit, it will take longer for him to lose his money, and in the interim he will forget the Torah learning of his youth. In such a case he will be left with neither wealth nor knowledge, and will not be able to provide for any of the nation's needs. I therefore want to bless you that you lose your money in a very short time so that you will be able to get back to your studies quickly."

The blessing of the great sage was not long in coming, and R' Moshe lost all of the dowry money on his first investment. Left with no options, he applied himself to his studies in earnest and eventually headed a very successful yeshivah in Lida.

Enlightment Between the Lines

8ه כִּי הוּא לָנוּ עוֹז וְאוֹרָה 8ه, *For to us it* [the Torah] *is strength and light.*

A scholar's ability to determine the Torah's opinion on any matter extends even to cases that are not addressed explicitly in the text. Rabbi Yechezkel Abramsky related a fascinating incident that portrays the ability of Torah scholars to rule on the basis of what is *not* written.

One day a distraught Jew came to Rabbi Chaim Soloveitchik. His father had passed away that morning, and the body was now suffering terrible indignity. A wealthy Jew had died in the early

afternoon, but in violation of the halachah, the chevra kaddisha (burial society) had buried the second deceased person before burying his father. "The Rav must do something," cried the man.

R' Chaim leafed through some pages of his Rambam and told the man, "Go home; I will take care of the problem."

Rav Abramsky, who was present, asked what R' Chaim was looking for, since it is well known that deceased persons must be buried in the order in which they died.

R' Chaim explained, "I was unsure if the basis for this law is due to proper respect for the deceased, or whether it is because of the general rule that 'one may not overlook an opportunity to perform a mitzvah' (Yoma 33a). If it is because of the honor of the dead, then the man's son has a personal interest and a right to protest to the chevra kaddisha about the lack of respect shown his father. But if the basis of the law is that the first mitzvah must be performed first, then it is my responsibility as rav to require the chevra kaddisha to follow the halachah.

"I looked in the Rambam's Laws of Mourning and found no reference to the law that obligates us to bury first whoever died first. I concluded, therefore, that this injustice is not the mourner's obligation, but mine. Therefore, I told him that I would do what is necessary."

Torah provides its loyal sons with enlightenment in all areas of life by casting its rays even where darkness seemingly reigns.

~§ Selected Laws and Customs

Laws of Shemini Atzeres

Laws of Simchas Torah

Appendix: Shemini Atzeres —
　　　　　An Independent Festival

Laws of Shemini Atzeres

1. According to all customs, one must eat in the *succah* on the seventh day of Succos (Hoshana Rabbah). Thus, even those who do not eat in the *succah* on Shemini Atzeres (either those in the Land of Israel or those in the Diaspora who have this custom) should not take their *succah* apart or make it halachically unfit after the morning meal of Hoshana Rabbah, since meals which one might later decide to eat must be eaten in the *succah*. Likewise, if one takes a nap that day, he should do so in the *succah*. Only in late afternoon (after nine and one-half hours)[1] may one begin to remove from the *succah* whatever is needed in the house.[2]

2. One should refrain from eating a full meal on Hoshana Rabbah after nine and a half hours in order to have a hearty appetite for the *Yom Tov* meal at night. Certainly, the practice of those who eat and drink to excess on Hoshana Rabbah until they are unable to make *Kiddush* that night is to be deplored.[3]

3. When Simchas Torah falls out on Friday, it is necessary to make an *eruv tavshilin* on Hoshana Rabbah (Wednesday) to permit cooking and lighting candles on Friday for Shabbos.[4] Preferably, one should not rely on the *eruv tavshilin* he

---

1. The "hour" meant here is the variable hour [שָׁעָה זְמַנִּית], whose length varies with the time of year. A variable hour is $\frac{1}{12}$ of the daylight hours (and is thus shorter than sixty minutes in the winter and longer in the summer). There is disagreement among the authorities about how the day is reckoned with regard to these laws. Some rule that the day is reckoned as beginning with dawn and ending with the emergence of the stars (see *Magen Abraham*, O.C. 443 §3). Others rule that it is reckoned as starting at sunrise and ending at sundown (see *Beur HaGra* to O.C. 459, s.v. ושיעור מיל, and O.C. 443:4). Ideally, one should comply with the first, more stringent, view (see O.C. 443, M.B. §8; see, however, *Igros Moshe* O.C. 1:24).

2. O.C. 666:1 and M.B. §1,2.

3. M.B. 676 §1.

4. Actually, the Torah permits these activities on the festival for festival needs (see *Exodus* 12:16) or for the needs of Shabbos that follows. But since preparing for Shabbos might lead people to think that they may even cook in preparation for a weekday, the Rabbis attached a condition to the preparation of Shabbos meals on a festival: Such preparations must be started *before* the festival (*Pesachim* 46b). Thus,

made on *Erev* Succos in order to permit cooking on Simchas Torah for the next day. Rather, a separate *eruv* should be made for Simchas Torah. However, if one forgot to make a new *eruv*, he may rely on the *eruv* made on *Erev* Succos and cook for Shabbos on Simchas Torah (provided, of course, that the *eruv*-food is still intact).[5]

4. The blessing of שֶׁהֶחֱיָנוּ is recited on Shemini Atzeres (and on Simchas Torah in the Diaspora) by women at candle-lighting and by men during *Kiddush*.[6]

5. For Shemini Atzeres one should prepare a festive meal that includes meat and wine.[7]

6. Since Shemini Atzeres is a separate festival, distinct in many ways from Succos, it requires special mention in prayer and in *Kiddush*. There are many opinions among the *poskim* as to the exact wording of this citation. *Birkei Yosef* (668 §1) garners an extensive list of *Rishonim* (*Rif, Rosh, Rashi* to *Succah* 47b, *Tosafos Yeshanim* to *Yoma* 3a, *Rambam* in his *Siddur HaTefillos, Rabbeinu Yerucham* and many others) who hold that the proper wording is יוֹם שְׁמִינִי חַג עֲצֶרֶת הַזֶּה. This is the formula codified by R' Yosef Karo in the *Shulchan Aruch* [except that he adds an additional ה — thus, הָעֲצֶרֶת rather than עֲצֶרֶת].[8]

---

when Succos or Shemini Atzeres falls on Thursday and Friday, preparations for the Shabbos meal must begin on Wednesday.

This enactment is called *eruv tavshilin*, literally, *mingling of cooked foods*. The practice symbolically combines the food prepared *before* the holiday with the foods prepared *on* the holiday, thus deeming the *eruv* as the beginning of preparations to be completed on Friday. It consists of a *challah, matzah* or a loaf of bread, along with any other cooked food (such as fish, meat or an egg), which are set aside on the day before the festival to be eaten on the Shabbos. The *eruv* foods are taken in the hand (*Orach Chaim* 527:2), a blessing is recited, and the *eruv* declaration is made. Since the person designating the *eruv* must understand its purpose, the declaration [beginning בַּהֲדֵין, *Through this*] must be said in a language he understands (see ArtScroll *Succos Machzor*, p. 2).

5. O.C. 527:14, M.B. §44-45, and *Biur Halachah* ad loc., s.v. לכתחילה.

6. O.C. 668:1. This is because Shemini Atzeres, unlike the seventh day of Pesach, is an independent festival. See Appendix. See Laws of Simchas Torah fn. 6.

7. O.C. 529:1 and M.B. §11.

8. O.C. 668:1. See M.B. §3, who cites *Pri Megadim* that עֲצֶרֶת is the correct form.

Rema objects to the usage of the term חַג with regard to Shemini Atzeres, claiming that there is no Scriptural precedent for referring to Shemini Atzeres as a חַג. *Turei Zahav* and the *Gra* (ad loc.), as well as *Bechor Shor* (*Succah* 41a), disagree[9] and follow the opinion of R' Yosef Karo.[10] *Maharshal*[11] and others suggest yet a third opinion: יוֹם שְׁמִינִי עֲצֶרֶת הֶחָג הַזֶּה. *Aruch HaShulchan* (668:1) renders this formula as "the eighth day, the assembly [or culmination] of this holiday [of Succos]." [The term *chag* is used to refer to Succos (see *I Kings* 8:2).] One should follow the custom of his Rav and community.

7. If one said אֶת יוֹם חַג הַסֻּכּוֹת הַזֶּה instead of mentioning Shemini Atzeres, there is a difference of opinion regarding whether he must repeat *Shemoneh Esrei* or *Kiddush*. *Shaarei Teshuvah*[12] quotes *Beis Yosef* that one need not repeat. *Birkei Yosef* (ad loc.) disagrees. *Chayei Adam* (28:15) writes that if one finished *Shemoneh Esrei* and took the three steps backward, he need not repeat the prayer.[13] In practice, one should consult his rabbi for a ruling.

All opinions concur that if one realized his mistake before finishing the blessing of מְקַדֵּשׁ יִשְׂרָאֵל וְהַזְּמַנִּים, he must return to וַתִּתֶּן לָנוּ and add the appropriate insertion for Shemini Atzeres.[14]

8. It is customary in Chassidic communities to make *hakafos* on the night of Shemini Atzeres besides the traditional *hakafos* on Simchas Torah.[15] In some communities this is done during the day as well.[16]

---

9. The verse וְחַגֹּתֶם אֹתוֹ חַג לַה', *And you shall celebrate it as a chag for* HASHEM (*Leviticus* 23:41), is explained in the Talmud (*Pesachim* 70b) as referring to Shemini Atzeres.

10. See M.B. 668 §3-4 and *Shaar HaTziyun* §2, who rules in accordance with this opinion.

11. Quoted in *Aruch HaShulchan* 668:1. See, however, M.B. ibid.

12. O.C. 668 §2.

13. See *Nishmas Adam* (by the author of *Chayei Adam*) ad loc. for his compelling arguments. See also *Igros Moshe* O.C. 3:93 and *Bikkurei Yaakov* 668 §2.

14. M.B. §2.

15. *Aruch HaShulchan* 668:7, *Siddur HaGraz*, R' Yaakov Emden.

16. *Likutei Maharich* writes: "In some places the custom is to make *hakafos* on the *day*

9. Many customs exist regarding eating in the *succah* on Shemini Atzeres. Due to the doubt in the Diaspora about whether Shemini Atzeres is the seventh or eighth day of Succos, a debate arose in the Talmud regarding whether those in the Diaspora should dwell in the *succah* on that day. If we dwell in the *succah* [considering the possibility that it is the seventh day of Succos], we are in effect belittling the festival of Shemini Atzeres [if it is actually the eighth day]. On the other hand, if we refrain from dwelling in the *succah* [assuming it is the eighth], we fail to fulfill the obligation to dwell in the *succah* [if it is actually the seventh].

The Talmud (*Succah* 47a) determines the halachah to be מֵיתִיב יָתְבִינָן בְּרוּכֵי לֹא מְבָרְכִין, *One must dwell in the succah, but without reciting a blessing.* While the blessing would constitute a belittling of the festival of Shemini Atzeres (*Ran* ad loc.), the act of dwelling, in and of itself, does not, since one might legitimately find dwelling in the *succah* attractive and opt to eat there even if he is not obligated to do so (*Tosafos* ad loc., s.v. מיתב).[17] Furthermore, since one does not recite a blessing over the *mitzvah* of *succah* on this day, it is clear that he dwells in the *succah* only out of doubt and not because he views the day as the seventh day of Succos, when he is truly obligated to be there. Hence, it does not constitute a belittling of the holiday of Shemini Atzeres.[18]

A difference of opinion among the *poskim* concerns the night of Shemini Atzeres. *Tur* (O.C. 568) writes, "There are those who do not dwell in the *succah* on Shemini Atzeres at

<hr />

of Shemini Atzeres as well. See the *Siddur* of R' Shabsi, who writes that the custom of *vasikin* (those scrupulous about *mitzvah* fulfillment) is to make *hakafos* by day also."

17. *Tosafos* ad loc. suggest that since this reason obviously would not apply to the taking of the four species, the sages did not obligate us to take the four species on Shemini Atzeres out of doubt that the day is in fact the seventh of Succos.

18. *Mordechai* in the name of *Ravyah*. This lack of a blessing also alleviates the problem of *bal tosif*, the prohibition against adding to the *mitzvos* — for example, by extending them beyond their prescribed time. By omitting the blessing, one clearly indicates that he does not intend to add an extra day to Succos. See *Rosh Hashanah* 28b, where Rava's conclusion is that one transgresses *bal tosif* when performing the *mitzvah* after its prescribed time only if one intends to do so as a fulfillment of the *mitzvah*.

night, but only by day. This is an improper custom." *Beis Yosef* seeks to justify the custom: Since at night one recites the *Shehecheyanu* blessing at *Kiddush* in response to the onset of the new festival of Shemini Atzeres, it would constitute an inherent contradiction to do so in the *succah*. During the day, however, no such problem exists. Nonetheless, the consensus of the *poskim* is that in the Diaspora one must eat in the *succah* both at night and during the day.[19]

In spite of this consensus, many customs have arisen regarding the matter. Some eat the morning meal and then leave the *succah*, while others make *Kiddush*, eat a bit, and then finish the meal in the house. *Aruch HaShulchan* (668:3-5) suggests a novel approach to justify the various customs. As quoted earlier, *Tosafos* states that dwelling in the *succah* does not constitute a belittlement of the holiday since "one's *succah* may be attractive to him, and he would eat in it even on Shemini Atzeres [not only because of the *mitzvah*]." If, however, he would not normally eat there and does so only because of the *mitzvah* [on the premise that the day might in fact be the seventh day of Succos, when one is *obligated* to dwell in the *succah*], it would be forbidden as a belittlement of the festival of Shemini Atzeres. Therefore, posits *Aruch HaShulchan*, in Babylonia or other places with a warm climate, one is obligated to dwell in the *succah*,[20] since it does not constitute a belittlement of the festival. However, in colder climates like ours[21] we cannot legitimately claim that sitting in the *succah* is attractive. During the festival we dwell in the *succah* in order to fulfill the *mitzvah*, but on Shemini Atzeres we are enjoined to dwell in the *succah* in a manner that does not constitute a belittlement of the holiday. In a cold climate, where the *succah* is not especially attractive, we can only accomplish

---

19. See *Ba'er Heiteiv* 668 §3 and M.B. §4.

20. The late *Rebbe* of Satmar was accustomed in Europe not to eat in the *succah* on Shemini Atzeres, yet in his years in America he did. When questioned about the change, he is reputed to have replied, "In Europe I didn't have a heated *succah*."

21. R' Yechiel Michel HaLevi Epstein, author of *Aruch HaShulchan*, lived in Novarhadok, White Russia.

this by instituting some change in the fulfillment of the *mitzvah* to indicate that today is not the seventh day of Succos. This is the reason for the various customs which have evolved. According to *Aruch HaShulchan*, the preferred custom is to eat the morning meal in the *succah* and then take leave of it. Nonetheless, each person should follow the custom of his family, community and rabbis.

10. Sleeping in the *succah* on Shemini Atzeres is forbidden by many *poskim.*[22] Their rationale is that eating is permitted since doing so without reciting the blessing לֵישֵׁב בַּסֻּכָּה indicates that one dwells in the *succah* on this day only out of doubt. But sleeping is forbidden since one never recites לֵישֵׁב בַּסֻּכָּה for sleeping in the *succah* (O.C. 639:8); thus, the lack of a blessing indicates nothing.[23] Furthermore, while the *succah* may be attractive for eating, it is not generally considered so for sleeping.[24] The *Vilna Gaon* and others (see *Shaar HaTziyun* 668 §4 for a listing) hold that one is obligated to sleep in the *succah*. The prevalent custom is to refrain from sleeping in the *succah* on Shemini Atzeres.[25]

11. Some have the custom to refrain from eating in the *succah* anything which does not require one to make the blessing לֵישֵׁב בַּסֻּכָּה. This is similar to sleep, in that the fact that one is not making a blessing is not an indication thta one is eating in the *succah* only due to the doubtful status of the day. Others permit even such foods to be eaten in the *succah*. One may therefore eat fruit, drinks or the like on Shemini Atzeres, both in the *succah* and outside of it.[26]

12. In the Diaspora, it is forbidden on Shemini Atzeres to eat the *esrog* that one used for the *mitzvah* of the four species.[27] This is true even if the *esrog* is no longer fit for use.[28] However,

---

22. See *Shaar HaTziyun* §5.
23. *Mordechai.*
24. See *Shaar HaTziyun* §6. See, however, O.C. 639:2 and M.B. §17-18.
25. M.B. O.C. 668 §6.
26. M.B. ibid.
27. O.C. 665:1.
28. Ibid., M.B. §4. See, however, *Aruch HaShulchan*, O.C. 665:2.

one may eat it on Simchas Torah.²⁹ Moreover, even if Shemini Atzeres falls out on Shabbos, one may — when necessary — eat the *esrog* on Simchas Torah.³⁰

13. In *Eretz Yisrael*, one is permitted to eat the *esrog* on Shemini Atzeres.³¹

14. It is imperative that one recite the *Shema* on Shemini Atzeres within the requisite time — the first quarter of the day. There are various opinions among the *poskim* as to how to calculate the first quarter of a day, and these are noted in many Jewish calendars. Since many congregations begin *Shacharis* late on *Yom Tov* and reach the *Shema* after the deadline, one should be careful to check a calendar for the deadline and, if necessary, recite all three passages of the *Shema* before the prayers in *shul*.³²

15. The Torah reading for Shemini Atzeres (in the Diaspora) begins with עַשֵּׂר תְּעַשֵּׂר, *You are to take tithes* (*Deuteronomy* 14:22). This portion is also read on the last days of Pesach and Shavuos, but there is a difference. If that day of Pesach or Shavuos falls on a weekday, the reading begins with כָּל הַבְּכוֹר, *Every firstborn* (*Deuteronomy* 15:19). Only when these days fall on the Sabbath, when seven people instead of five are called to the Torah and more verses are needed, do we begin from עַשֵּׂר תְּעַשֵּׂר, *You are to take tithes*. On Shemini Atzeres, however, the reading begins with the passage concerning tithes even on a weekday, because this is the time of year when people are enjoined to deliver their tithes to the needy. Since Shemini Atzeres falls during the season when crops are gathered in, it is an especially important time for all Jews to share their prosperity with the less fortunate; thus, this Torah portion is read.³³

16. Beginning with the *Mussaf* prayer on Shemini Atzeres, we insert the phrase מַשִּׁיב הָרוּחַ וּמוֹרִיד הַגֶּשֶׁם, *He makes the wind*

---

29. O.C. ibid.
30. M.B. §6 in the name of *Eliyahu Rabbah*.
31. O.C. ibid.
32. O.C. 529, M.B. §14.
33. O.C. 668:2, M.B. §12.

blow and He makes the rain descend, into the second benediction of the Shemoneh Esrei (before מְכַלְכֵּל חַיִּים).[34] This insertion continues until the Mussaf prayer of the first day of Pesach (see further). This is not an actual prayer for rain, but merely a הַזְכָּרָה, mention, of God's power to give rain. The actual request for rain (in בָּרֵךְ עָלֵינוּ, Bless on our behalf, of the weekday Shemoneh Esrei) begins on a later date.[35]

17. Just before the silent Mussaf prayer is begun, the shamash should announce: מַשִׁיב הָרוּחַ וּמוֹרִיד הַגֶּשֶׁם. If, however, no announcement is made, one should not recite this phrase in the silent Shemoneh Esrei. The chazzan, however, recites the Geshem benediction in his public repetition even in the absence of an announcement.[36] Since the public announcement of מַשִׁיב הָרוּחַ is an essential prerequisite for inserting that phrase in the silent Mussaf of Shemini Atzeres, one should be careful not to recite the Mussaf (if, for example, he is ill and is praying at home) before the congregation reaches that part of the service.[37]

18. Although מוֹרִיד הַגֶּשֶׁם is not said before the public announcement, some poskim rule that if one did recite מוֹרִיד הַגֶּשֶׁם before the proclamation, he need not repeat the Shemoneh Esrei. Moreover, even if he did so during the Maariv or Shacharis prayers of Shemini Atzeres, he need not repeat the Shemoneh Esrei.[38]

19. The essential part of the proclamation is the phrase מוֹרִיד הַגֶּשֶׁם. Thus, if the shamash said only מַשִׁיב הָרוּחַ, the proclamation is not valid, and the congregation should not include the insertion in the silent prayer.[39] If, however, one of the congregants said מוֹרִיד הַגֶּשֶׁם out loud during his silent

---

34. There is a great divergence of opinion regarding whether the word is הַגֶּשֶׁם or הַגָּשֶׁם. One should follow the custom of his family and community.

35. O.C. 114:1.

36. Rema O.C. 114:2, M.B. §4.
   See Ba'er Heiteiv 114:1, Derech Chaim, and Biur Halachah to O.C. 114:2, s.v. אסור.

37. O.C. 114:2.

38. M.B. 114 §2.

39. M.B. 114 §6.

prayers, the other congregants may also say it.[40] Nevertheless, the validity of a proclamation made by someone other than an officer of the congregation is questionable. Therefore, if someone failed to recite מוֹרִיד הַגֶּשֶׁם after such a proclamation, he need not repeat *Mussaf*.[41]

20. If one entered the synagogue and found that the congregation had already begun the silent *Mussaf*, he should recite מוֹרִיד הַגֶּשֶׁם on the assumption that the proclamation had been made in the customary manner.[42]

21. If one forgot to recite מַשִּׁיב הָרוּחַ וּמוֹרִיד הַגֶּשֶׁם, he must repeat the *Shemoneh Esrei*. This applies even to the *Mussaf* prayer of Shemini Atzeres (assuming the customary announcement was made)[43] [see details below].

22. If one recited מוֹרִיד הַטָּל, as is customary during the summer in the *Nusach Sefard* ritual and in most congregations in Israel, he need not repeat *Shemoneh Esrei*, even if he forgot מוֹרִיד הַגֶּשֶׁם. This is because he has praised God for giving dew, which is one aspect of His role as provider of the world's moisture. However, the phrase מַשִּׁיב הָרוּחַ alone — without mention of rain or dew — cannot serve as a substitute for מוֹרִיד הַגֶּשֶׁם.[44]

23. If one is not sure whether he recited מוֹרִיד הַגֶּשֶׁם in the *Mussaf* of Shemini Atzeres or in subsequent prayers, the rule is as follows: It is assumed that a person has recited whatever he has been accustomed to saying, until a different recitation becomes habitual. The Sages set down the presumption that a new formula in *Shemoneh Esrei* does not become habitual for thirty days. [Generally, one will recite *Shemoneh Esrei* ninety times in the course of thirty days.] Therefore, until thirty days after Shemini Atzeres have elapsed, one who does not remember whether he added מַשִּׁיב הָרוּחַ must

40. M.B. ibid. §4.
41. M.B. ibid.
42. O.C. 114:2.
43. O.C. 114:5 and M.B §25.
44. Ibid., M.B. §26-27.

assume that he either said nothing or that he said מוֹרִיד הַטָּל (depending on what his prior custom was).[45]

24. One is not required to repeat *Shemoneh Esrei* unless he has begun the word אַתָּה of the next benediction, אַתָּה קָדוֹשׁ. If he realizes his omission after concluding מְחַיֵּה הַמֵּתִים but he has not yet begun אַתָּה קָדוֹשׁ (or *Kedushah* of the *chazzan's Shemoneh Esrei*), he inserts the words מַשִּׁיב הָרוּחַ וּמוֹרִיד הַגֶּשֶׁם at that point and continues with אַתָּה קָדוֹשׁ. If he has not begun the concluding formula of the benediction (בָּרוּךְ . . . מְחַיֵּה הַמֵּתִים) or has at least not yet said the word *HASHEM*, he would recite מַשִּׁיב הָרוּחַ וּמוֹרִיד הַגֶּשֶׁם and then conclude the benediction.[46] [However, if he realized his error after

---

45. O.C. 114:8.

Based on R' Meir's reasoning that "behavior repeated at shorter intervals is a stronger indication of a pattern than behavior repeated at longer intervals" (*Bava Kamma* 24a), *Maharam MiRotenberg* reasoned that if the habit to recite מַשִּׁיב הָרוּחַ is formed by reciting it ninety times over thirty days, then it is certainly formed by reciting it ninety times in one day. Accordingly, every Shemini Atzeres, it was his practice to recite (not while praying) the paragraph from *Shemoneh Esrei* which contains the phrase מַשִּׁיב הָרוּחַ וּמוֹרִיד הַגֶּשֶׁם ninety times, so that he would never have to be in doubt about whether he remembered to add it during the next thirty days (see *Tur, Orach Chaim* end of §114).

Rabbeinu Peretz (cited in *Tur* there; see also *Beis Yosef* ad loc.) objects that the two cases are not comparable. In the case of מוּעָד, a habituated ox (which is the basis of R' Meir's reasoning), the three gorings serve to establish that an animal's goring is not an anomaly but is indicative of an intrinsically destructive nature. The three gorings do not *form* the animal's destructive habit; they merely *establish* that it exists. In the case of מַשִּׁיב הָרוּחַ, however, what is needed is the repetition of the phrase ninety times in order to *form* the habit of saying it. R' Meir reasons that a pattern established by three incidents over a long period is certainly established by three incidents over a shorter period, but this does not mean that a habit *formed* over a long period can be assumed to form over a shorter period. On the contrary, reason would suggest that the stronger habit is the one formed over the longer period.

Rosh, however, sides with *Maharam MiRotenberg*, and his procedure has become the one recommended in *Shulchan Aruch* (ad loc.) for all to follow. See M.B. 114 §43 and *Be'ur Halachah*, s.v. אם ביום ראשון. Some explain that *Maharam MiRotenberg* disputes *Rabbeinu Peretz's* premise that the three gorings of מוּעָד serve to *establish* the existence of rather than to *form* the animal's destructive nature. Rather, *Maharam MiRotenberg* holds that the three gorings indeed serve to form the animal's habit (R' Shimon Shkop in *Chidushei R' Shimon* §33; see also *Kehillas Yaakov, Bava Kamma* ad loc.).

46. O.C. 114:6 and *Biur Halachah*, ad loc.

saying the word וְנֶאֱמָן, he should say מַשִׁיב הָרוּחַ וּמוֹרִיד הַגֶּשֶׁם and start over from וְנֶאֱמָן.][47]

25. On Shemini Atzeres, those in the Diaspora who have the custom to eat in the *succah* should not remove from it the items needed in the house until after midday.[48] Even then, one may bring the necessary items inside but may not arrange them, since this constitutes preparation on one day of *Yom Tov* for another, which is prohibited. Nonetheless, if the items are needed in the house for use on Shemini Atzeres itself, or if one must put the items in place in order that the house not be in disarray, he may do so.[49]

26. One may not use the walls or *s'chach* decorations of the *succah* for a non-*mitzvah* purpose on Shemini Atzeres or Simchas Torah.[50] If Simchas Torah is immediately followed by Shabbos, there is a dispute among the *poskim* regarding the permissibility of such usage on this Shabbos.[51] However, one may remove curtains from the *succah* on Shemini Atzeres or Simchas Torah if he is afraid that they may be stolen or ruined by rain.[52]

27. It is forbidden to bring wine from one place to another on Shemini Atzeres for the purpose of having wine for Simchas Torah. If it will be difficult to procure wine at night, one is permitted to bring it during the day, provided: (a) it is done early enough in the day that it does not clearly appear to be in preparation for the night and might plausibly be used for consumption during the day; (b) the carrying should be done differently from the way one generally carries wine; and (c) the wine is needed on Simchas Torah for a *mitzvah* (*Kiddush* or *simchas Yom Tov*).[53]

---

47. See O.C. 114, and M.B. §29.
48. O.C. 666:1 and M.B. §1,9.
49. *Rema*, O.C. 667:1, M.B. §6.
50. O.C. 667:1.
51. Ibid. See also *Kaf HaChaim* §6.
52. Ibid., M.B. §1.
53. Ibid., M.B. §5.

28. Regarding preparing the Torah scroll on Shemini Atzeres by rolling it to the portion to be read for Simchas Torah, there are various opinions. Some *poskim*[54] forbid doing so. *Aruch HaShulchan*[55] suggests that it is permitted if one reads some verses from the scroll at the time he rolls it.

29. Some are of the opinion that one may not eat a full meal on Shemini Atzeres after nine and a half hours[56] since it is *Erev Simchas Torah* and one must enter the holiday with an appetite for the *Yom Tov* meal.[57] *Biur Halachah*[58] disagrees, because if one is hungry, it is improper to forgo עוֹנֶג יוֹם טוֹב (enjoyment of the festival) on the first day of *Yom Tov*, which is Biblically mandated, out of concern for one's appetite on the second day, which is Rabbinically mandated.

Nonetheless, one must take care not to overeat or overdrink to the extent that the meal on Simchas Torah night becomes a burden. Certainly it is forbidden to drink to such an extent that one cannot make *Kiddush* or perform other *mitzvos*.

Mishnah Berurah[59] sharply decries the practice of drinking and partying from after *Minchah* on Shemini Atzeres until well beyond nightfall. This practice is forbidden for many reasons: (a) One may not pray while drunk. (b) Once night falls, it is forbidden to eat or drink since one is obligated to make *Kiddush*. (c) Even after *Kiddush* one may not eat until he has recited the nighttime *Krias Shema*.

---

54. M.B. 667 §5, based on *Shaarei Teshuvah*.

55. O.C. 667:2.

56. See note 1 regarding the definition of "an hour" for halachic purposes.

57. *Pri Megadim* 668.

58. O.C. 529, s.v., בעיו"ט, and *Shaar HaTziun* 668 §1.

59. Introduction to O.C. 669.

Laws of Simchas Torah

1. There is a dispute among the *poskim* as to the proper time for candle-lighting on the second night of *Yom Tov*.[1] Some *poskim* maintain that one may light shortly *before* nightfall and that this is advisable in order to avoid being in the darkness during twilight.[2] Others rule that one may not light candles until *after* nightfall in order to avoid preparation from one day of *Yom Tov* to another.[3]

   One should follow the latter opinion.[4] Nonetheless, the woman of the house should try to light candles immediately *at* nightfall, so that when the men return from the synagogue they find the house well lit.[5]

2. As on all second days of *Yom Tov*, *Shehecheyanu* is recited by women at candle-lighting.[6]

3. One should not make *Kiddush* until after the *hakafos*. If it is necessary to make *Kiddush* before the *hakafos*, one must take care not to become drunk or to delay the *hakafos* unduly.[7] Certainly one may not eat before *Kiddush*.

4. It is customary to auction off the honor of reciting the introductory verses of אַתָּה הָרְאֵתָ, which are recited before the *hakafos*. In many communities the rights to other *mitzvos* over the course of the year are also auctioned off.[8] The auction should take place only after nightfall.[9]

---

1. See *Mateh Ephraim* 625 and *Elef LaMateh* ad loc. §51, and *Likkutei Maharich*, vol. 3, p. 29b, for an extensive discussion of the issue.

2. *Eliyahu Rabbah* 488 and *Shelah*.

3. *Prishah*, introduction to *Yoreh Deah*.

4. R' *Yosef Shaul Natanson*, quoted in *Ketzei HaMateh* 625 §47.

5. *Elef HaMateh* ibid.

6. O.C. 263, M.B. §23, quoting *Shaarei Teshuvah* ad loc. and *Sh'eilas Yaavetz* 107, rules that while women need not recite *Shehecheyanu* at candle-lighting (and may rely instead on the *Shehecheyanu* recited in *Kiddush*), one should not stop them from doing so where it is customary.

7. *Mishmeres Shalom* 47 §2.

8. *Maharil* (*Hilchos Succah*) writes that even though buying and selling is forbidden on *Yom Tov*, it is permitted to sell the rights to a *mitzvah*.

9. *Yosef Ometz* 1062.

5. *Hakafos* are conducted after the *Maariv* evening prayers. It is customary to remove all of the Torah scrolls from the Ark, even those that are unfit to be read from.[10] When a synagogue possesses only a few Torah scrolls, there are various opinions regarding the permissibility of bringing scrolls from another synagogue.[11] One should consult with his rabbi and adhere to his ruling.

6. The verses of אַתָּה הָרְאֵתָ are recited responsively.[12] The Ark is opened when we recite the verse that begins וַיְהִי בִּנְסֹעַ, and the Torah scrolls are removed after we recite כִּי מִצִּיּוֹן תֵּצֵא תוֹרָה.[13]

7. In olden days some communities made seven *hakafos*, while others made three.[14] Today, the almost universal custom is to make seven *hakafos*. The elders of the congregation and other honorable persons are granted the honor of carrying the Torah scrolls while making a circuit around the *bimah*.[15] These circuits are accompanied by singing and dancing.[16]

8. In some places it is customary to place a lit candle inside the empty Ark during the *hakafos*.[17] Other *poskim* object to placing a mundane object in the Ark.[18]

---

10. *Binyan Zion* 97 explains that the custom of keeping even Torah scrolls which are irreparably unfit in the Ark is based on the Talmudic statement: "Both the [second] Tablets and the broken pieces of the [first] Tablets were kept in the Ark" (*Berachos* 8b). See *Sefer HaChassidim* §934.

11. O.C. 669:1, M.B. §9.

12. *Maharil, Hilchos Simchas Torah.*

13. *Maharil* ibid.; *Eliyahu Rabbah* 669:5.

14. M.B. ibid. §10.

15. In Pressburg, Torah students were honored with *hakafos* at night, and other members of the community were honored during the daytime (*Levushei Mordechai* 4:136). *LeDavid Emes* writes that it is customary to honor young Torah students with a *hakafah* in order to encourage them to continue to spend their best years in such a noble pursuit (see *Sefer HaMataamim* §140).

Leket HaKemach makes an impassioned plea that the *hakafos* and similar honors do not become a source of dispute among people.

16. M.B. ibid. §11.

17. *Aruch HaShulchan* 660:3. This custom is based on the verse: *For a mitzvah is a candle and Torah is light* (Proverbs 6:23).

18. *Turei Zahav, O.C.* 154 §7, *Kitzur Shulchan Aruch* 137:11.

9. In many Sefardic communities it is customary that one person stands on the *bimah* with a Torah scroll, while others circle around him carrying other Torah scrolls.[19]

10. One should always hold the Torah scroll in his right hand.[20] It is customary to adorn the Torah scrolls with crowns and other adornments during the *hakafos*.[21]

11. One should make every effort to bring children, even small children, to witness the *hakafos*.[22] In addition, even in communities where women and girls generally do not attend the synagogue, it is customary that they come to the *hakafos* to witness the display of joy and honor for the Torah.[23]

12. Even if no *minyan* is present, one may conduct *hakafos*.[24]

13. The Talmud (*Kiddushin* 33b) teaches, based on a *kal vachomer* (a fortiori) argument, that if we are Biblically obligated to rise in the presence of a Torah scholar (see *Leviticus* 19:32), we must certainly stand up for a Torah scroll. Based on this, the *Shulchan Aruch* (*Yoreh Deah* 282:2) rules: "One who sees a Torah scroll being carried must rise and remain standing until the person carrying it stops and brings it to its place, or until it is out of sight." Accordingly, it seems that one would be obligated to remain standing during the *hakafos* until all the Torah scrolls are returned to

---

19. See *Mishmeres Shalom* 47 and *Chag HaAssif* 28:7, fn. 13.

20. *Rema* O.C. 134:2, M.B. ad loc. §14.

21. *Shaar HaKavannos*, based on *Zohar Pinchas* (in *Raayah Mehemna*): "And we adorn the Torah scroll with its crown." [This custom is not followed in most communities due to the fear of breakage, as well as to the fact that the crowns make the scrolls too heavy to carry for any extended period of time.]

22. *Kesser Shem Tov* 7; pg. 237; *Sefer HaMataamim* 139. It is customary that children carry flags in order to allow them to share in the festivities and develop a joy and passion for Torah study. *Sefer HaMaatamim* 142 views the symbolism of the flags as an expression that, like an army, we see the Torah as the banner around which we rally. Regarding the age at which one should be honored with a *hakafah* and the privilege of carrying a Torah Scroll, see O.C. 147, M.B. §29, and *Shaar Ephraim* 10:6. Of course, anyone who has difficulty carrying a Torah scroll should not attempt to do so, for he might risk, God forbid, dropping it. See *Kesser Shem Tov* (*Minhagim*), Vol. 1, p. 288.

23. See *Shevilei David* 669.

24. Responsa *BeTzail HaChochmah* 4:112.

the Ark or placed on the reading table. Many *poskim* decry the prevalent custom of sitting during the *hakafos.*[25]

The ruling is that, when necessary, one may sit during the dancing of the *hakafos.* However, one must stand when those bearing the Torah scroll are circling the *bimah.*[26] According to all opinions, one must also stand after the *hakafos* when the scrolls are being returned to the Ark.[27]

14. Even though dancing and clapping are forbidden on Shabbos and *Yom Tov*, it is permitted to clap or dance on Simchas Torah in order to rejoice and honor the Torah.[28] However, it is forbidden to ring bells or other sound-producing instruments. Playing musical instruments is certainly forbidden.[29]

15. Regarding one who is within the twelve months of *aveilus* (mourning) over a father or mother, or in *sheloshim* for other

---

25. *Shulchan HaTahor* 148:2, *Shoneh Halachos* 669:3.

26. *Aruch HaShulchan* (*Yoreh Deah* 282:5); see also *Responsa Yechaveh Daas* 6:42, who permits sitting only for elderly or sick persons, and only between *hakafos. Betzail HaChochmah* (5:139) suggests that only when the bearer is carrying the scroll to a destination is the viewer obligated to rise and remain standing until it is set down. When one is moving around aimlessly with the scroll, there is no obligation to rise. [A possible explanation is that when a Torah scroll is being moved, it is in a transitory state. Proper respect requires that man not feel a sense of permanence while the Torah is transitory; therefore, we stand up. When the bearer stops or the scroll arrives at its destination, it reassumes a status of permanence, thus allowing us to sit. However, if the scroll is to be used for *hakafos* and is intended to be moved around, it is not in a transitory state, and thus one may sit during that time.]

    Shemiras Shabbos KeHilchasah (Chapter 24, fn. 118) offers yet another approach to justify those who sit during *hakafos* based on *Orach Chaim* (362:5), which states that persons standing next to each other, with less than three *tefachim* (twelve inches) between them, may serve as a *mechitzah* (dividing wall) even if they are moving. This is true only if they are unaware that they are functioning in this capacity. In a crowded synagogue, therefore, the people may serve as a dividing partition between those who are seated and the Torah scrolls.

27. *BeTzail HaChochmah* ibid. §8.

28. O.C. 339:3, M.B. §8, from *Maharik* 9. These things were Rabbinically forbidden on Shabbos and *Yom Tov* out of fear that one might come to repair musical instruments on the Sabbath, which is Biblically prohibited. According to *Machatzis HaShekel* ad loc., since most laymen today are unable to fix musical instruments, the extension of this rabbinic prohibition to clapping and dancing is no longer operative. See also 669 M.B. §5 and *Shaar HaTziun* §5.

29. See O.C. 338:2 and M.B. 8.

relatives, there are diverse customs as to whether it is permissible to honor him with a *hakafah*. Some *poskim* forbid an *aveil* to be honored with a *hakafah*, based on the ruling of *Rema* that an *aveil* may not participate in the circuit around the *bimah* with the *lulav* at the time we recite *Hoshanos*.[30] Thus, these *poskim* reason that if the *aveil* is absolved of a Biblical commandment due to the *aveilus*, certainly he is absolved of the joy of the *hakafos*, which is only a custom.[31] Other authorities disagree and allow the *aveil* to hold a Torah scroll and circle the *bimah*, but not to dance. This is the accepted custom. The *aveil* may remain in the synagogue while the dancing goes on.[32]

16. In most Ashkenazic congregations (based on the Eastern European rite), the Torah is also read on the night of Simchas Torah after the *hakafos*. In olden days, there were many customs as to the readings, but in our days one custom is virtually universal: The first five sections in וְזֹאת הַבְּרָכָה (*Deuteronomy* 33:1-26) are read, and five people (in some congregations, three people) are called up to the Torah.[33] At the completion of the reading, half-*Kaddish* is recited, followed by *Aleinu*.[34]

---

30. *Rema* 660:2 and M.B. §9. The *Vilna Gaon* explains that there is an allusion to this in the Biblical commandment to rejoice in front of Hashem for seven days (*Leviticus* 23:40).

31. See *Responsa Levushei Mordechai* 4:136 and *Responsa Chelkas Yaakov* 3:75, who offer additional reasons for being at least as strict with *hakafos* as with *Hoshanos*.

32. *Kaf HaChaim* O.C. 669 §33, *Gesher HaChaim* (23:3:7). See also *Gesher HaChaim* Part II, 17:4:2. *Kaf HaChaim* O.C. 669 §33, quoting *Zachur L'Avraham* (*Yoreh Deah* prev. pp. end of §300 in *Hilchos Avel*), writes: "The mourner is permitted to sit in the synagogue on the night of Simchas Torah, during the twelve months of mourning for his father; and [the congregation] may dance and clap in front of him. And the permission also applies to the *hakafos*." *Gesher HaChaim* (23:3:7) concurs. See also *Gesher HaChaim* Part II, 17:4:2, which differentiates between *hakafos* and *Hoshanos*. *Responsa Minchas Yitzchak* (6:62) suggests that for the rabbi [or any prominent member] of the congregation to refrain from taking a *hakafah* would constitute public mourning (אֲבֵילוּת בְּפַרְהֶסְיָא), which is forbidden on *Yom Tov*.

33. See *Rema* O.C. 669:1 and M.B. §15. See also *Shaarei Ephraim* 8:57.

34. M.B. ibid. Even though *Kaddish* will be recited almost immediately (after *Aleinu*), we recite half-*Kaddish* after reading the Torah, since *Aleinu* is considered an interruption between the Torah reading and *Kaddish*.

17. According to many *poskim*, the שְׁנַיִם מִקְרָא וְאֶחָד תַּרְגוּם (personal reading of the weekly *parashah*, twice in Hebrew and once in the Aramaic Targum or with Rashi) should be read on Simchas Torah night.[35] Others disagree and offer alternatives for the appropriate time.[36]

18. In many communities it is customary that the priestly blessings (*Bircas Kohanim*) take place during *Shacharis*, rather than during *Mussaf*, as is usually the case.[37] In other communities it is recited in *Mussaf* as usual, while in some communities *Bircas Kohanim* is dispensed with altogether on Simchas Torah.[38]

19. After *Shacharis* and *hakafos*, all the Torah scrolls except three are returned to the Ark. The Torah is read as usual. The portion for the day is the last *sidrah* of the Torah — וְזֹאת הַבְּרָכָה — instead of a festival reading. We also add a passage from the beginning of *Bereishis* to demonstrate that we continually begin the Torah anew.[39] This is followed by the half-*Kaddish*, *Maftir* and *Haftarah* as usual.

---

35. M.B. 669 §4.

36. Regarding the correct time to read the *parashah*, *Sdei Chemed* writes that one should do so on the day of Simchas Torah [in the Diaspora; it is read on Shemini Atzeres in *Eretz Yisrael*] since this is the most appropriate way of reading it "along with the congregation" (see *Berachos* 8b). *Shaarei Teshuvah* (285:4) cites *Birkei Yosef*, who states in the name of the *Arizal* that the *parashah* should be read on the day of Hoshana Rabbah. This is also the ruling given by *Mishnah Berurah* (ad loc. §18). [However, in 669 §4, as mentioned above, he cites the *poskim* as ruling that one should read the *parashah* on the night of Simchas Torah. *Shoneh Halachos* follows this ruling.] *Chag HaAssif* (21:6, fn. 10-13) cites an array of opinions on the matter.

37. *Kitzur Shulchan Aruch* 138:8 rules that if *Bircas Kohanim* is recited at *Shacharis*, the introductory prayer *Vsei'areiv* is omitted. Since there is no mention of the sacrificial service in *Shacharis*, this prayer is not appropriate. *Likkutei Maharich* cites a similar ruling from *Darkei Moshe* regarding the recitation of *Vsei'areiv* when *Bircas Kohanim* is recited at *Shacharis* on Yom Kippur.

38. See M.B. 669 §17. *Likkutei Maharich* explains: In olden times the *Chassan Torah* and *Chassan Bereishis* would offer a repast (including alcoholic drinks) immediately after the Torah reading. Out of concern that the *Kohanim* might drink and become disqualified to *duchen*, the custom of moving *Bircas Kohanim* back to *Shacharis* or dispensing with it altogether evolved.

39. See *Tur* O.C. 669. See also *Shibbolei HaLeket* 372 and *Eliyahu Rabbah* 669 § 10 for other reasons.

20. The passage in וְזֹאת הַבְּרָכָה until the word מְעוֹנָה is divided into five *aliyos*. This is in fulfillment of the general law of every *Yom Tov* when five *aliyos* are obligatory. The reading from מְעוֹנָה and onward, and the beginning of *Bereishis*, are additional. The person called to read the former passage is the one who completes the year's Torah reading, and he is honored with the title חֲתַן תּוֹרָה, *Groom of the Torah*. The person called to begin the reading of *Bereishis* is honored as the חֲתַן בְּרֵאשִׁית, *Groom of Bereishis*. Both *aliyos* are considered great honors, and in most congregations they are given to people distinguished for their Torah scholarship and other attributes.[40] It is customary for the "grooms" to serve a feast (*Kiddush*) to the congregants.[41] After the *sheloshim* mourning period for one's parent has passed, he is permitted to eat at the festive meal given by the *Chassan Torah* and *Chassan Bereishis*.[42]

21. As part of the Simchas Torah celebration, the *sidrah* וְזֹאת הַבְּרָכָה is read over and over so that every male in the congregation can be called for an *aliyah*.[43] It is customary to allow Torah scrolls to be taken to anterooms of the synagogue in order to expedite this process.[44] In most congregations even young boys who are not yet *bar mitzvah* are honored with an *aliyah*, to imbue them with love for the Torah.[45]

---

40. M.B. 669 §1.

41. *Rema* 669:1.

42. *Mishnah Berurah* (669 §8), citing *Bikurei Yaakov*, who also writes (ad loc. §7) "*Responsa Maharam Mintz*, cited by *Shach* (*Yoreh Deah* §246), permits the mourner, after *sheloshim*, to eat at a *siyum* celebrating the completion of a tractate. It is true that *Bach* forbids this, but *Beis Lechem Yehudah* explains that [*Bach*] only [forbids it] when the mourner himself did not study the tractate, but simply wishes to celebrate the *siyum* along with the others. In our case, however, all Israel have completed the Torah, and the mourner has a share in the rejoicing in this *mitzvah*."

43. O.C. 669, M.B. §12.

44. Even though this practice generally is prohibited, we permit it on Simchas Torah in order not to delay the congregation unnecessarily. See *Leket HaKemach HaChadash* 137 §4.

45. See *Shaarei Ephraim* 8:57.

A mourner is permitted to be called up to the Torah on Simchas Torah.[46] However, some authorities rule that he should *not* be called up, but should step out of the synagogue during the Torah reading. If he cannot step outside — for example, if he is needed to complete the *minyan* of ten men — even these authorities rule that he is permitted to be called up to the Torah.[47]

22. Great care should be exercised to ensure that throughout these repeated readings, there will always be ten adult males who listen attentively both to the readings and the blessings.[48]

23. Even very young children who cannot recite the blessings themselves are given the honor of an *aliyah*. An adult is designated to be called for an *aliyah* עִם כָּל הַנְּעָרִים, *with all the young boys*. He is called for the last *aliyah* before the *Chassan Torah*, and his *aliyah* is aptly named *Kal HaNe'arim* (כָּל הַנְּעָרִים), literally *all the young boys*. This is considered a great honor. The designated person recites the blessings slowly and clearly so that all the children who can, are able to recite along with him. The others simply answer *Amen.*[49]

24. It is also customary to recite the verse הַמַּלְאָךְ הַגּוֹאֵל אֹתִי, *May the angel who redeems me* (Genesis 48:16), with the children. In some communities it is customary to recite the verse immediately after the Torah reading, before the blessing is recited;[50] other communities recite it after the *berachah*.

25. One of the virtually universal customs of Simchas Torah is for the congregations to crowd around the *bimah* during the

---

46. *Pischei Teshuvah* (399 §1). The same ruling is given by *Mishmeres Shalom* (subsection 5 §54), and by *Gesher HaChaim* (23:3:7). The reason is that it is an ancient custom for *everyone* in the synagogue to be called up to the Torah on Simchas Torah. If the mourner is not called up, his status would be publicized.

47. *Sdei Chemed, Aveilus* §30.

48. M.B. 669 §12.

49. See M.B. ibid. and *Shaarei Ephraim* 8:57, with *Pischei She'arim* ad loc.

50. M.B. ibid. §14.

aliyos of *Chassan Torah, Chassan Bereishis* and *Kal HaNe'arim*, holding over their heads a canopy of *taleisim.*[51]

26. In many congregations it is customary to change the usual manner of *hagbahah* [הַגְבָּהָה], *raising the Torah*, after the *Chassan Torah's aliyah.* The reason for the change is to give special honor to the Torah on this day. While the Torah is still resting on the *bimah*, the person given this honor grasps the right *eitz chaim* [literally *tree of life*, one of the two poles upon which the scroll is rolled] with his left hand, and the left *eitz chaim* with his right hand. He lifts the Torah cross-handed and then straightens out his hands, thereby turning the written side of the scroll toward the congregation. Care should be taken, however, to choose an individual who is strong or a Torah that is not heavy, in order to avoid the danger that the Torah, God forbid, may be dropped.[52]

---

51. See *Chag HaAssif* 29:32 (fn. 58) for explanations of this custom. R' Hersh Goldwurm *zt"l* suggested that perhaps it commemorates the giving of the Torah, regarding which the Sages say (*Shabbos* 88a) that God suspended Mount Sinai above the heads of the Jewish people.

52. *Shaarei Ephraim* 8:62. *Aishel Avraham* [cited in *Chag HaAssif* 29:22 (fn. 39)] offers some fascinating explanations for this custom.

Appendix: Shemini Atzeres — An Independent Festival

The day following the seventh day of Succos is called Shemini Atzeres. The Torah commands: בַּיּוֹם הַשְּׁמִינִי עֲצֶרֶת תִּהְיֶה לָכֶם, *On the eighth day, there shall be an assembly for you* (*Numbers* 29:35).

This eighth day has a dual nature; it is simultaneously an independent holiday [רֶגֶל בִּפְנֵי עַצְמוֹ] (*Succah* 47b) and a continuation of Succos.

The independent aspect of Shemini Atzeres is expressed in six areas, for which the Talmud (*Succah* ibid.) offers the acronym פַּזַ"ר קַשַׁ"ב. This stands for פ — a *payis* of its own; ז — a *z'man* of its own; ר — a *regel* of its own; ק — a *korban* of its own; ש — a *shir* of its own; ב — a *berachah* of its own. These are explained as follows:

Payis, פַּיִס

Payis literally means *lottery* and refers to the lottery conducted to determine which group of *Kohanim* would receive the lone bullock offered as a sacrifice on Shemini Atzeres.

During Temple times, there was familial watches, which took turns being responsible for the service.

The Talmud states that Moses established a system of dividing the *Kohanim* into eight watches, four each from the families of Elazar and Issamar.

The prophet Samuel and King David further subdivided the *Kohanim* into twenty-four watches. Each watch had a leader in charge of assuring that its members came up to Jerusalem for their appointed period of service. A watch would be in charge of the Temple service for one week, after which a different watch would take its place. This continued until each of the twenty-four had a turn, and then the rotation would begin anew. [Thus, generally a watch served in the Temple twice a year for one week each time] (*Rambam, Klei HaMikdash* 4:3).

The order of these shifts is listed in *I Chronicles* (Chap. 24): *The first lot came out for Yehoyariv; the second for Yedayah; the third for Charim,* etc.

On the three pilgrimage festivals of Pesach, Shavuos and Succos, *all* the watches were entitled to share in the service of the festival *mussaf* offering (*Deuteronomy* 18:7-8; *Rashi* ad loc.; *Rambam* ibid. 4). However, the regular daily service, as well as sacrifices offered by individuals, belonged to the *Kohanim* during whose watch the festival fell.

On Pesach and Shavuos it was necessary to conduct a lottery to determine which *mishmaros* would actually serve and thus be entitled to divide up the offering, since the *mussaf* on those days is not comprised of an adequate number of animals for all the *mishmaros* to receive a share.[1] On Succos, however, the *mussaf* offering always consists of enough animals to be divided among all twenty-four *mishmaros*.[2] Hence, in theory, there was no need for a lottery on Succos (see below).

The Mishnah (*Succah* 5:6) describes how the *mussaf* offering of Succos was divided. Each of the first thirteen *mishmaros* received one of the thirteen bullocks offered on the first day of Succos. The next day the apportionment of the bullocks began with the fourteenth *mishmeres*, until all twenty-four *mishmaros* had received a bullock. Then the rotation began again. Hence, since the bullocks offered over the course of the festival totaled seventy (on the first day thirteen, and on each successive day one less, culminating in seven on the seventh day), each *mishmeres* received three bulls ($3 \times 22 = 66$), with the exception of two *mishmaros* which received only two bullocks ($2 \times 2 = 4$), for a total of seventy.

The *Rishonim* disagree as to which two *mishmaros* were deprived of their third bullock. *Rashi* is of the opinion that the regular order of

---

1. On Pesach the *mussaf* of each day was the same: two bullocks, one ram, seven yearling sheep and one he-goat for a sin offering. Thus, in total, the *mussaf* was comprised of eleven animals. On Shavuos, the *mussaf* offering brought was the same.

2. The *mussaf* offering in its entirety specified by Scripture for the first day of Succos (*Numbers* 29:12-16) is as follows: *And on the fifteenth day of the seventh month … you shall offer [as] a burnt offering … thirteen bullocks, two rams, fourteen yearling sheep and one he-goat for a sin offering.*

Scripture (*Numbers* 29:13-32) requires one bullock less on each successive day of Succos: twelve for the second day, eleven for the third day, and so on, brought in conjunction with the two rams, single he-goat and fourteen yearling sheep which remain constant each day. Thus, even on the seventh day of Succos, when only seven bullocks were offered, there were a total of twenty-four animals, allowing one for each *mishmeres*.

mishmaros was followed beginning from the first day of Succos, and there was no need, therefore, to conduct a lottery to determine the order in which the *mishmaros* would serve on Succos. Accordingly, Delayahu and Maazyahu, the twenty-third and twenty-fourth *mishmaros*, did not receive a third bullock from among the seventy brought on Succos. *Meiri* and *Ritva*, among others, however, maintain that a lottery *was* held on the first day of Succos to determine the order in which the *mishmaros* would serve. According to them, it was the last two *mishmaros* picked in the lottery that did not receive the third bullock.

On Shemini Atzeres a lone bullock was offered. If Shemini Atzeres were considered a continuation of Succos, a new lottery would not be conducted and the next *mishmeres*[3] in line would receive that bullock. However, since Shemini Atzeres is an independent festival, a new lottery was held to determine which *mishmeres* was to receive that lone bullock.[4] Thus, "a *payis* of its own" refers to the lottery that was drawn on Shemini Atzeres during Temple times to determine which *mishmeres* of *Kohanim* was to receive the only bullock offered on that day.

Z'man, זְמָן

The ז in the acronym פַּזַ"ר קַשַ"ב stands for זְמָן, *time*, and refers to the *berachah* of *Shehecheyanu*. On every festival we recite the blessing שֶׁהֶחֱיָנוּ וְקִיְּמָנוּ וְהִגִּיעָנוּ לַזְּמַן הַזֶּה, *Who kept us alive, preserved us and brought us to this time.* This blessing is known as Z'man — the "Blessing of Time." In contradistinction to the seventh, and last, day of Pesach, which is merely a continuation of the previous days, Shemini Atzeres is a holiday in its own right and thus requires its own *Shehecheyanu*.

The Talmud (*Succah* 47a) suggests a textual allusion to this

---

3. According to *Rashi*, it would be the *mishmeres* of Delayahu; following *Meiri* and *Ritva*, it would be given to whichever *mishmeres* placed twenty-third in the lottery that was conducted to determine the order of service on Succos.

4. The *Chachamim*, cited in a *baraisa* (*Succah* 55a), suggest that this lottery was limited to those two *mishmaros* which had received only two bulls from among the seventy of Succos. *R' Yehudah HaNasi* disagrees and holds that all the *mishmaros* took part in the new lottery, without regard to the order in which they served on the days of Succos. *Rambam* (*Hilchos Temidim U'Mussafim* 10:13) rules like R' Yehudah HaNasi in this matter, despite the fact that his is a minority opinion.

independent quality of *Shemini Atzeres*. While the passages detailing the offerings for each successive day of Succos are linked together with the connective וּ, *and* (וּבַיּוֹם הַשֵּׁנִי, וּבַיּוֹם הַשְּׁלִישִׁי), the following passage, which details the offering of Shemini Atzeres, stands alone, without a וּ (בַּיּוֹם הַשְּׁמִינִי), indicating that this day is a festival unto itself and requires its own *Z'man*.

Regel, רֶגֶל

The ר of the acronym, which stands for רֶגֶל, *regel* (pilgrimage festival), is interpreted by the various *Rishonim* in many different ways, six of which we will elaborate on.

> 1. *Rashi* (*Succah* 48a, s.v. רגל) considers this an indication that one is not Scripturally required to dwell in the *succah* on Shemini Atzeres, since it is a separate festival and not part of the Succos holiday. Many commentators question this interpretation of Rashi on the basis that even if the eighth day were a weekday, one would be absolved from dwelling in the *succah*. Seemingly, this issue is unrelated to the holiday status of Shemini Atzeres.
>
> Why, then, would the Gemara characterize the day as *regel*?
>
> *R' S. Y. Zevin* suggests that Rashi's commentary is based on the *Targum Yonason*, who translates *On the eighth day it shall be an atzeres for you* (*Numbers* 29:35) as "On the eighth day you shall joyfully gather from your *succos* into your houses."[5] Thus, the homecoming from the *succah* is a defining characteristic of the festival. This may have been the thrust of Rashi's explanation that *regel* refers specifically to the cessation of the *mitzvah* of *succah* rather than to any other of the Succos *mitzvos* [for example, *lulav*].[6]
>
> 2. *Rashi* (*Rosh Hashanah* 4b) offers an alternative explanation as to the meaning of *regel* in the acronym פַּזַ"ר קַשַׁ"ב. When reciting prayers, *Kiddush* or *Bircas HaMazon* (Grace After

---

5. See p. 47 for the homiletic overtones of this rendering.

6. For a discussion of the obligation of Jews in the Diaspora to dwell in the *succah* on Shemini Atzeres, see pp. 115-117.

Meals), we refer to the day as Shemini Atzeres and not as Succos,[7] citing it as a distinct festival.

3. *Tosafos* (*Chagigah* 17, *Yoma* 3a and *Rosh Hashanah* 4b) quote a liturgical poem by *Rabbeinu Tam* in which the term *regel* is explained as a reference to the obligation in Temple times for a person to remain in Jerusalem until the morning after the holiday. This obligation is known as לִינָה. Even if one offered all the sacrifices of the festival before the eighth day, he must remain in Jerusalem until the morning following the Shemini Atzeres festival.

4. According to *Rabbeinu Chananel* (*Succah* 48a), the status of *Shemini Atzeres* as an independent festival affects the laws of *aveilus* (mourning). If any one of a person's seven closest relatives died within the seven-day period prior to a festival, the onset of the festival absolves him from completing the *shivah* period. Thus, if one buried his deceased relative on *Erev Yom Tov* and sat *shivah* for even an hour, the festival annuls the rest of *shivah*. After the holiday, the mourner is deemed to be in the *sheloshim* stage of *aveilus*. Thus, one who began *shivah* within seven days before Succos is absolved of fulfilling the entire *shivah* obligation due to the first day of *Yom Tov*. The seven days of *Yom Tov* and *Chol HaMoed* are reckoned as seven of the thirty *sheloshim* days. Shemini Atzeres, as an independent festival, annuls an additional seven days of the *sheloshim* period of mourning (see *Tosafos* ibid., s.v. רגל; *Shulchan Aruch Yoreh Deah* 399:11; and *Turei Zahav* ad loc.). Thus, Shemini Atzeres is imbued with the same power as other *regalim* with regard to nullifying days of mourning.

Ramban objects to this last interpretation on historical grounds. The law which teaches that Shemini Atzeres suspends seven of the days of *sheloshim* is introduced in the Talmud by Ravina (one of the later *Amoraim* — scholars of the Talmud) [see *Moed Kattan* 24b]. It is seemingly implausible to interpret the acronym פַּנְ"ר קַשַׁ"ב, stated in a

---

7. The different opinions as to the exact wording of this reference in the various prayers are discussed on pp. 113-114.

Tannaic *baraisa*, on the basis of a law promulgated many generations later. *Ritva* also offers other objections to the interpretation of *Rabbeinu Chananel*.

Ramban and *Ritva* therefore propose two other explanations of the special *regel* status of Shemini Atzeres.

5. On every pilgrimage festival one is obligated to offer two special holiday offerings. *Olas Re'iyah* is the concrete expression of the obligation for all Jewish males above *bar mitzvah* to appear in the Temple courtyard on the festivals (see *Deuteronomy* 16:16). At that time one must bring an ascent offering (*olah*). *Shalmei Chagigah*, the peace offering of the festival, is also brought at that time and provides meat for the owners so that they may celebrate the festival joyously. If one did not fulfill these obligations on the first day of the festival, he may make amends on any subsequent day of the holiday. However, if one was not obligated on the first day of the holiday [i.e., he was a minor and became *bar mitzvah* during *Chol HaMoed* (Intermediate Days)], he need not bring these offerings, even though his status changed in the interim and the reason for his being absolved is no longer relevant (see *Chagigah* 9a and *Rambam Hilchos Chagigah* 2:5).

According to *Ramban* and *Ritva*, this is not so with regard to Succos and Shemini Atzeres. Certainly if one brought the required offerings during Succos, he need not bring them again on Shemini Atzeres, since the Torah teaches explicitly that the obligations connected to the pilgrimage festivals occur *three* times a year (Pesach, Shavuos and Succos; see *Deuteronomy* ibid.), not four. However, if on the first day one was not obligated to do so for some reason and became obligated before Shemini Atzeres, he must bring the offerings on Shemini Atzeres. It is in this sense that Shemini Atzeres is considered a holiday in its own right.

6. Alternatively, *Ramban* and *Ritva* submit that *regel* refers to the Biblical prohibition of *bal te'acher* (בַּל תְּאַחֵר), delaying. One who promised to bring an offering as a vow (נֶדֶר) or as a free-will offering (נְדָבָה) must do so without unnecessary delay. If he allowed three festivals (*regalim*) to pass

successively without honoring his promise, he is in violation of *bal te'acher* (*Rambam, Hil. Maaseh HaKorbanos* 14:13). Thus, if Succos is the third *regel* to pass since one's vow was made, he is in violation of *bal te'acher* after the end of the seventh day of Succos, since Shemini Atzeres is a *regel* unto itself and not merely a continuation of Succos.

Korban, קָרְבָּן

The fourth distinctive feature of Shemini Atzeres is its *mussaf* offering, the קָרְבָּן indicated by the ק of the acronym פַּזַ"ר קָשַׁ"ב. The bulls of the *mussaf* offerings of Succos, as mentioned earlier, are offered in a descending pattern, with thirteen brought on the first day, twelve on the second day, and so on, until seven are offered on the seventh day of Succos. If Shemini Atzeres were considered a continuation of the Succos festival, it would follow that six bulls should be offered; actually, only one bull is brought. Likewise, the number of rams and sheep offered is different on Shemini Atzeres. While on all the days of Succos the *mussaf* offering includes two rams and fourteen sheep, on Shemini Atzeres only one ram and seven sheep (in addition to the single he-goat) are offered. This, too, is an indication that it is an independent festival with its own offerings.

Shir, שִׁיר

The שׁ of our acronym stands for שִׁיר, *shir* (song). Every day the Levites in the Temple would sing all or part of a chapter from the Book of *Psalms* while standing on their special platform. Regular weekdays had their specific psalms as discussed in the Talmud (*Tamid* 7:4); each holiday also had its own specific psalm. The Talmud (*Succah* 55a) delineates the psalms recited on Succos, all of which focus on the theme of helping the poor. This theme is accented on Succos as it is the time of harvest, when one must be sure to distribute the produce to which the poor are entitled. The recitation of these psalms is intended to encourage people to give magnanimously.

The psalm (song) for Shemini Atzeres (Psalm 12) is different and in no way related thematically to those designated for recitation on Succos.

[139] **SIMCHAS TORAH** — Its Significance, Laws, and Prayers

Berachah, בְּרָכָה

The last letter of the פַּז"ר קַש"ב acronym is ב, which stands for בְּרָכָה, *berachah* (blessing). According to *Rashi*, this refers to an historical incident that occurred on Shemini Atzeres. When King Solomon celebrated the dedication of the Temple, he convened the nation for a fourteen-day celebration. *On the eighth day* (Shemini Atzeres) *he sent the people away* [i.e., gave them permission to return home after the holiday], *and they blessed the king* (I Kings 8:66). The *berachah* refers to this blessing tendered by the people.

Tosafos vehemently disagrees with this interpretation of *berachah*, citing the Talmud's teaching that on the first seven days of Succos one is also obligated in *korban, shir* and *berachah*. Thus, the word *berachah* cannot be a reference to the blessing of the king, which was a one-time occurrence. Rather, *Rabbeinu Tam* proposes that *berachah* refers to the mention of Shemini Atzeres in the blessings of the *Shemoneh Esrei* prayer, *Kiddush* and *Bircas HaMazon* (Grace After Meals).[8]

Continuation of Succos

In spite of all of these features, which cast Shemini Atzeres as an independent holiday, in many ways it is similar to all other festivals and is regarded as a continuation of Succos. Of course, the same work prohibitions exist as on any *Yom Tov*. Furthermore, the Mishnah (*Succah* 4:1) equates Shemini Atzeres with the first seven days of Succos regarding the recitation of the full Hallel and the observance of *simchah* (joy) and *kavod* (honor) of *Yom Tov*.

The words וְשָׂמַחְתָּ בְּחַגֶּךָ, *You shall rejoice on your festival* (*Deuteronomy* 16:14), enjoin us to rejoice during the first seven days of Succos. [See *Rambam, Hilchos Yom Tov* 6:17-18, for the forms this rejoicing should take.] From וְהָיִיתָ אַךְ שָׂמֵחַ, *You will be purely* [lit. *only*] *joyous* (ibid. 15), the Sages derive that in Temple times there was a commandment to sacrifice peace offerings in celebration of Shemini Atzeres. Today, in place of this sacrifice, we are obligated to rejoice on this holiday. (See *Rambam* ibid.) Many question how the term אַךְ, which is generally exclusionary, can be employed to *include* Shemini

---

8. For additional homiletic interpretations of the independent festival status of *Shemini Atzeres*, see p. 29-40.

Atzeres in the obligation of שִׂמְחָה. The *Vilna Gaon* is reputed to have answered that, while all the other *mitzvos* which one was obligated to perform during Succos [*succah, lulav* and, in Temple times, *aravah* (circling the altar with the willow branches) and *nisuch hamayim* (water libations)] are no longer applicable when Shemini Atzeres arrives, the *mitzvah* of *simchah* remains. Thus, the verse teaches that "you shall be *only* happy" — that this *mitzvah* of *simchah* alone remains of all the other *mitzvos* of Succos.[9]

---

9. R' Yosef Zusmanowich (author of *Teruas Melech*) clarifies the *Vilna Gaon's* explanation. The *mitzvah* of *lulav* was a requirement in the Temple, practiced on all seven days of Succos. [Outside the Temple, the *mitzvah* of *lulav* is Biblically mandated only on the first day of Succos; for the remainder of the holiday, it is Rabbinically mandated.] This is derived from the verse: וּשְׂמַחְתֶּם לִפְנֵי ה׳ אֱלֹהֵיכֶם שִׁבְעַת יָמִים, *You shall rejoice before HASHEM, your God, for a seven-day period* (*Leviticus* 23:40). *Before HASHEM*, meaning in the Temple, one is obligated to rejoice for seven days. Thus, for the first seven days of Succos two forms of rejoicing are mandated: (a) the taking of the four species in the Temple; (b) the rejoicing in spirit by all Jews in all places. The verse אַךְ שָׂמֵחַ limits the rejoicing on the eighth day, *Shemini Atzeres*; this means that the taking of the four species ceases, and only the personal *simchah* remains. Hence, the word *only* serves to exclude one type of rejoicing while retaining the other.

[141] **SIMCHAS TORAH** — Its Significance, Laws, and Prayers

✑ Observance

Prayer for Rain / תפילת גשם

Farewell to the Succah / יציאה מן הסוכה

Hakafos / הקפות

‏תפילת גשם ‏

‏אַף־בְּרִי* אֻתַּת שֵׁם שַׂר מָטָר,‏
‏לְהַעֲבִיב וּלְהַעֲנִין לְהָרִיק לְהַמְטַר,‏
‏מַיִם אַבִּים בָּם גֵּיא לַעֲטַר, לְבַל יֵעָצְרוּ בְּנִשְׁיוֹן שְׁטָר,*‏
‏אֱמוּנִים גְּנוֹן בָּם שׁוֹאֲלֵי מָטָר.*‏

Chazzan bends his knees at ‏בָּרוּךְ‏; *bows at* ‏אַתָּה‏; *straightens up at* ‏ה׳‏.

‏בָּרוּךְ אַתָּה יהוה, מָגֵן אַבְרָהָם.‏

(.‏אָמֵן‏ — .Cong)

‏תְּפִלַּת גֶּשֶׁם‏ / **PRAYER FOR RAIN**

Since fall and winter are the rainy seasons in *Eretz Yisrael*, a country that depends on rainfall more than most, the Sages ordained that the prayer for rain be recited on Succos, the pilgrimage festival in closest proximity to the rainy season. Because the festival itself is spent primarily in the *succah*, and it is regarded as a symbol of Divine displeasure for rain to prevent people from eating and dwelling there, it would be inappropriate to pray for rain at a time when we do not want it to fall. Therefore, the prayer is recited on Shemini Atzeres, the first day that the Scriptural commandment to dwell in the *succah* is no longer in effect.

‏אַף־בְּרִי‏ — Af-Bri, the name of the angel appointed over the rainclouds (*Rashi* to *Job* 37:11), is formed from the two words ‏אַף‏, *anger*, and ‏בְּרִי‏, *health*. This name alludes to the two ways rain may fall. Sometimes it comes in harsh torrents and is a sign of Divine anger (‏אַף‏); at other times it falls in a gentler manner and brings health (‏בְּרִי‏) and prosperity in its wake (*Mateh Levi*). The responsibilities of this angel are described in the first two stanzas of this prayer.

Tosafos (*Niddah* 16b) suggests that even though the Talmud (*Taanis* 2a) teaches that rain is one of three phenomena (birth, rain and resurrection) whose accomplishment is not given into the hands of a messenger, nonetheless the angel Af-Bri is in charge of apportioning rain, according to God's instructions. Unlike other areas, where God figuratively "gives over the key" for a particular mission to angels or humans and allows them a degree of autonomy, these three areas remain the exclusive province of God, and only with His full permission may the angels act (see *Ramas Shmuel* quoted in *Anaf Yosef* on *Ein Yaakov*, *Taanis* 2a, and *Sfas Emes* ad loc.).

Maharitz Chayes (to *Niddah* ad loc.) notes that *Rashi* (to *Taanis* 25b) seems to contradict himself by suggesting that the name of the angel placed in charge of rain is Ridya. *Maharsha* (*Yoma* 21a) suggests that Af-Bri and Ridya have different functions in the process of delivering rain (see *Parashas Derachim* 21).

‏נִשְׁיוֹן שְׁטָר‏ — *Unredeemed debt* [*literally, document*]. This refers to a long list of our sins which is recorded in God's ledger. The Talmud teaches that rain does not fall unless the sins of Israel have been forgiven (*Taanis* 7b). We therefore ask that rain not be withheld because of our "unredeemed debt."

The Mishnah (*Avos* 3:20) offers the metaphor of God's ledger and His debt collectors: *And whoever wishes to borrow, let him come and borrow.* With his free choice, man can control the extent of his involvement in the pleasures of

Prayer for Rain / ‏תפילת גשם‏   [144]

אַף־בְּרִי Af-Bri* is designated as the name of the angel of rain;
    to thicken and to form clouds,
  to empty them and to cause rain.
Water with which to crown the valley's vegetation
  — may it not be withheld because of our unredeemed debt.*
In the merit of the faithful Patriarchs, protect the ones who pray for rain.*

Chazzan bends his knees at "Blessed"; bows at "You"; straightens up at "HASHEM."

Blessed are You, HASHEM, Shield of Abraham.   (Cong. – Amen.)

---

this world, and he can therefore control his debt to Heaven. The wicked foolishly overindulge themselves and are then overburdened when their payment comes due. The righteous borrow only the capital (worldly pleasures) that they need to conduct the *real* business of life (Torah study, *mitzvah* fulfillment and acts of kindness), never allowing themselves to sink into the staggering debt of iniquity (*Rav, R' Yonah, Rambam*). *The collectors make their rounds constantly, every day, and collect payment from the person* (*Avos* ibid.). "The collectors" is a figure of speech for death and other forms of punishment that are visited on man (*Rambam, Meiri*). All life's pains and difficulties are God's messengers to collect payment for one's moral debts (*Rashi, Rav*).

We implore God to have confidence that we will repent and pay back our spiritual debts, and we ask Him not to view our sins as an impediment to His granting us His blessings. As King David pleaded with God, *If You preserve iniquities, O God, my Lord, who could survive?* (*Psalms* 130:3).

Beis Avraham offers an analogy: A businessman bought a large stock of merchandise from his suppliers on credit. Due partially to negligence and partially to a turn of bad luck, he lost all the merchandise, became bankrupt, and was unable to pay his debts. Shamefacedly, he went to the supplier and told him what had happened. The supplier, an intelligent individual, realized that the only way he might possibly recoup his loss was to extend the merchant some additional credit in the hope that this time he would turn a profit.

God is called אֵל אֱמוּנָה, *a God of trust.* Even though in the past we have taken the gifts God bestows on us and used them for everything *except* His will, He nonetheless is ready to grant us more of His beneficence on credit, so to speak, in order to give us the opportunity to repent and pay up our old debts. We therefore beg of God that rain not be withheld because of our unredeemed debts.

אֱמוּנִים גְּנוֹן בָּם שׁוֹאֲלֵי מָטָר — *In the merit of the faithful Patriarchs, protect the ones who pray for rain.* The Mishnaic order *Zeraim*, which deals with the laws of agriculture, is called אֱמוּנַת, literally, faith, for planting is an act of faith (*Shabbos* 32a). *Yerushalmi* (see *Tosafos Shabbos* ad loc.) explains that one must have an abiding faith that the Master of the World will provide rain, sunlight, wind and all the other "natural" phenomena necessary to sustain growth, for without such faith, planting is an exercise in futility.

Therefore, when we ask for rain to bless our crops, we do so in the merit of the faithful Patriarchs, calling upon the storehouse of faith that is our spiritual heritage (*Imrei Moshe*).

[145] **SIMCHAS TORAH** — Its Significance, Laws, and Prayers

גבורות

אַתָּה גִבּוֹר לְעוֹלָם אֲדֹנָי, מְחַיֵּה מֵתִים אַתָּה, רַב לְהוֹשִׁיעַ.

יַטְרִיחַ לְפַלֵּג מִפֶּלֶג גֶּשֶׁם,*
לְמוֹגֵג פְּנֵי נֶשִׁי בְּצַחוֹת לֶשֶׁם,
מַיִם לְאַדִּרְךָ כְּנִיתָ בְּרֶשֶׁם,* לְהַרְגִּיעַ בְּרַעֲפָם לִנְפוּחֵי נֶשֶׁם,*
לְהַחַיּוֹת מַזְכִּירִים גְּבוּרוֹת הַגֶּשֶׁם.

[In some congregations the Ark is closed while additional prayers are recited at this point.]

אֱלֹהֵינוּ וֵאלֹהֵי אֲבוֹתֵינוּ,

זְכוֹר* אָב* נִמְשַׁךְ אַחֲרֶיךָ כַּמַּיִם,*

מִפֶּלֶג גֶּשֶׁם — *Of the segregated rain.* God separated between the heavenly waters and the earthly waters (*Genesis* 1:7). Here the "segregated rain," meaning the heavenly waters, is used as a metaphor for the spiritual flow of blessing from on high.

מַיִם לְאַדִּרְךָ כְּנִיתָ בְּרֶשֶׁם — *With water You symbolized Your might in Scripture.* The prophet (*Ezekiel* 43:2) compares God's voice to *the sound of great waters* (*Maaseh Oreg*). King David employs the same metaphor: *More than the roars of many waters, mightier than the waves of the sea — You are mighty on high, HASHEM* (*Psalms* 93:4).

לְהַרְגִּיעַ בְּרַעֲפָם לִנְפוּחֵי נֶשֶׁם — *To soothe with its drops those in whom was blown a soul. Shaar Yissaschar* and *Sfas Emes* understand our pleas for water as metaphorical. Torah knowledge is compared to water (*Bava Kamma* 17a); our request for rain, therefore, is really a plea for Torah and spiritual growth.

Accordingly, we may interpret this stanza homiletically as follows: We ask God to shower us with the heavenly waters of Torah so that our earthly existence will be suffused with spirituality. It is these waters that will soften the surface of the spiritual wasteland of our

souls and activate them to grow and reach their potential in this world.

Furthermore, Torah has a soothing effect on man, providing him with the strength to overcome life's difficulties. King David describes this balm-like quality of Torah: *Had Your Torah not been my preoccupation, I would have perished in my suffering* (*Psalms* 119:92). *Tanna d'Vei Eliyahu* (27) teaches that when a person who is threatened by affliction immerses himself in Torah study, he becomes calm and tranquil. We therefore implore God to grant rain — meaning Torah — to *soothe with its drops those in whom was blown a soul.*

זְכוֹר — *Remember.* The next six stanzas speak respectively of Abraham, Isaac, Jacob, Moses, Aaron and the twelve tribes. Each stanza is followed by a prayer that, in their merit, abundant rain should fall.

אָב — *The Patriarch.* Abraham was called אַב הֲמוֹן גּוֹיִם, *the father* [or *Patriarch*] *of a multitude of nations* (*Genesis* 17:5).

The Patriarchs [Abraham, Isaac and Jacob] are called "fathers," for they are the physical and spiritual progenitors of our nation. As our Sages taught, מַעֲשֵׂה

Prayer for Rain / תפילת גשם [146]

אַתָּה **You** are eternally mighty, my Lord, the Resuscitator of the dead are You; abundantly able to save.

יַטְרִיחַ **May** He obligate [the Angel Af-Bri]
    to give us portions of the segregated rain,*
to soften the wasteland's face when it is dry as rock.
With water You symbolized Your might in Scripture,*
    to soothe with its drops those in whom was blown a soul,*
    to keep alive the ones who recall the strengths of the rain.

[In some congregations the Ark is closed while additional prayers are recited at this point.]

Our God and the God of our forefathers:

זְכוֹר **Remember*** א the Patriarch [Abraham],*
    who was drawn behind You like water.*

אָבוֹת סִימָן לְבָּנִים, *The actions of the fathers are a sign for the children.* This constitutes an established principle of Jewish spiritual history: The actions of our forefathers portend the future of their descendants.

One aspect of this principle is that many of the forefathers' attributes were transmitted to their children as part of a spiritual genetic code. For example, the willingness of Jews throughout the ages to sacrifice their lives for the sake of God is rooted in Abraham's willingness to allow himself to be thrown into the fiery furnace, and later in his readiness to offer Isaac as a sacrifice for the sake of God. Likewise, the Jewish people's passionate love for their ancestral home was bequeathed to us spiritually through Abraham's bravery in uprooting himself from his birthplace to emigrate to the Holy Land.

A third example: By bringing famine to the Land and forcing Abraham to descend temporarily to Egypt, God conditioned us historically to exhibit unquestioning loyalty to Him and to internalize the belief that everything He brings upon us is for the good (*Ruach Chaim*).

A child is genetically endowed by his parents and in addition inherits the fortune they have succeeded in amassing by dint of their efforts. Likewise, all Jews inherit the spiritual character of the Patriarchs and are also heirs to the merit of their good deeds. We therefore invoke these merits in imploring God to grant us rain.

נִמְשַׁךְ אַחֲרֶיךָ כַּמַּיִם — *Who was drawn behind You like water.* The poet compares Abraham to water. *Yisa Berachah* offers two very beautiful perspectives on this analogy: The Midrash records that during the second day of Creation, when God created the division between the heavenly waters above the firmament and the earthly waters below (see *Genesis* 1:7), the lower waters protested that they, too, wished to be close to God. To comfort them and as compensation for distancing them from Him, God made a covenant that the water would have a share in the Temple service. Salt, which comes from the sea, would be placed on those portions of the sacrifices that go on the Altar, and spring water would be poured on the Altar every Succos (see *Rashi* to *Leviticus* 2:13).

[147] **SIMCHAS TORAH** — Its Significance, Laws, and Prayers

בֵּרַכְתּוֹ כְּעֵץ שָׁתוּל עַל פַּלְגֵי מַיִם,*
גְּנַנְתּוֹ,* הִצַּלְתּוֹ מֵאֵשׁ וּמִמַּיִם,*
דְּרַשְׁתּוֹ בְּזַרְעוֹ עַל כָּל מָיִם.*

בַּעֲבוּרוֹ אַל תִּמְנַע מָיִם. — Cong.

According to *Zohar* (1:69), this yearning of the lower waters to ascend and be close to God is reflected in the rising waves of the sea. Even though they cannot reach Heaven, God praises them for their burning desire to do so [בְּשׂוֹא גַּלָּיו אַתָּה תְשַׁבְּחֵם, *When its waves rise, You praise them (Psalms* 89:10)]. The *Zohar* concludes that, just as the sea, any person who yearns to be close to God will have his wish granted, even if his natural abilities do not allow for such an elevated relationship with God.

Abraham, our forefather, was the first person to be so magnetically drawn to God. The Midrash compares Abraham to a person who was walking through the forest when he saw from afar a magnificent castle glowing with lights. He said to himself, "It is implausible that the castle is ownerless." Immediately a voice cried out to him, "I am the owner of the castle." Likewise, Abraham saw a complex world and concluded it must have a Creator and an Owner. Because of his aspirations toward the spiritual, God revealed Himself to him, saying, "I am the Master of the World" (*Bereishis Rabbah* 39:1). When we pray for rain, we ask God to reward Abraham's thirst for Godliness by providing sustenance for his descendants.

Alternatively, we may interpret this stich based on a second analogy, which shows Abraham descending rather than rising. The Midrash (*Bereishis Rabbah* 30:10) compares Abraham to the confidant of a king. He saw the king walking along the darkened street where he himself lived, and went down to the

windows near the gloomy alley to light a lamp so that the king could see his way through. Abraham, too, saw a world of darkness, in which humanity was unenlightened to the existence of God. Abraham "went down" to the masses, like water which is drawn downwards, in order to bring to them the light of Godliness. In response to Abraham's "lowering himself" in honor of God, we ask God to come down to us, as it were, and provide for our needs, even if we are undeserving and it is, so to speak, "beneath His dignity" to do so.

בֵּרַכְתּוֹ כְּעֵץ שָׁתוּל עַל פַּלְגֵי מַיִם — *You blessed him like a tree replanted alongside streams of water.* This phrase is based on *Psalms* 1:3, where King David paints a picture of the life of the righteous. *Malbim* notes that the righteous are not considered to be *planted* in this world since, unlike the wicked, they are not enchanted by its charms. Rather, the righteous person is considered שָׁתוּל, *replanted*, meaning that he has uprooted his desire for the wordly pleasures and has replanted his soul, even while he dwells in this world, in a higher realm of existence, where it derives its vitality from spiritual sources.

Abraham, blessed with great wealth, never forgot the source of his blessings and was always careful to utilize all God gave him for heavenly purposes rather than for his own pleasures. "Replanted" firmly on the nourishing waters of Godliness, Abraham's prosperity was a true blessing. We therefore ask not only that God grant us rain, but that He enable us to appreciate this blessing

בּ *You blessed him like a tree replanted alongside streams of water.*

ג *You shielded him,* You rescued him from fire and from water.**

ד *You tested him when he sowed upon all waters.**

Cong.— *For his sake, do not hold water back!*

---

fully and utilize it — as well as all our blessings — for His service.

Alternatively, the author of this prayer alludes to the Talmud (*Taanis* 5b), which relates the story of a man who wandered in the wilderness looking for something to slake his burning thirst. Almost in a faint, he noticed a tree at a distance and collapsed under its leafy branches, where he found succulent fruit and a spring of cold, refreshing water. Before he left, he offered a figurative blessing to the tree. "Tree, O tree, how can I bless you? Your fruit is sweet, your shade is soothing, a cool spring passes under you. I only can bless you that all trees that come from you should be like you." Abraham, among the righteous, is given a similar benediction; like a tree replanted alongside streams of water, God blessed him that his descendants would inherit his good qualities, and share his material prosperity. We, the beneficiaries of this blessing, ask God that we be blessed with the prosperity, spiritual and material, that he enjoyed (*Noam Megadim*).

גְנַנְתּוֹ — *You shielded him.* It is axiomatic that God treats a person according to his merits, and that his store of merit becomes depleted if God changes the course of nature for his benefit. Abraham was apprehensive that all his merits had been depleted by the miracle of his victory over the kings. He feared that he could no longer expect Divine assistance in the future, and that he might be punished for having slain enemy soldiers in the fray (*Rashi*). Moreover, the successors to the defeated kings might collect even greater armies and launch an attack in reprisal against

him (*Ramban*). Consequently, God appeared to Abraham and reassured him that he would shield him from all enemies, danger or punishment (see *Genesis* 15:1).

We ask God for the same assurance that He shield us from all evil, and that nothing we do should prevent Him from providing us with sustenance (*Imrei Moshe*).

מֵאֵשׁ וּמִמַּיִם — *From fire and from water.* These words describe two famous occasions when Abraham's merit saved him from the elements. The Talmud (*Pesachim* 118a) and Midrash (*Bereishis Rabbah* 38) relate that Abraham allowed himself to be thrown into a fiery furnace when he refused to bow before Nimrod's idols, but God saved him. Another Midrash (*Tanchuma Vayeira* 22) describes how Satan, in the guise of a wide and deep river, attempted to drown Abraham and Isaac on their way to the *Akeidah* on Mount Moriah, but did not succeed (*Maaseh Oreg*).

דְּרַשְׁתּוֹ בְּזָרְעוֹ עַל כָּל מָיִם — *You tested him when he sowed upon all waters.* This refers to another time when God tested Abraham's faith. After following God's directive to leave his homeland, he arrived in the land of Canaan only to find himself in the midst of a famine. Though this seemed to be a direct contradiction of God's glowing promises, Abraham's faith did not waver. He turned to God as his only source of sustenance and was rewarded with ample provision. We pray that God should likewise provide for us (*Mateh Levi*).

Midrash Tanchuma (*Lech Lecha* 12) refers to Abraham as one who planted

זְכוֹר הַנּוֹלָד בִּבְשׂוֹרַת* יֻקַּח נָא מְעַט מַיִם,
וְשָׁחַתָּ לְהוֹרוֹ לְשָׁחֲטוֹ, לִשְׁפּוֹךְ דָּמוֹ כַּמַּיִם,
זָהַר גַּם הוּא לִשְׁפּוֹךְ לֵב כַּמַּיִם,
חָפַר וּמָצָא בְּאֵרוֹת מָיִם.*

— Cong. בְּצִדְקוֹ חֹן חַשְׁרַת מָיִם.

זְכוֹר טָעַן מַקְלוֹ* וְעָבַר יַרְדֵּן מַיִם,
יִחַד לֵב וְגָל אֶבֶן מִפִּי בְאֵר מָיִם,*

---

righteousness by feeding all those who passed by his tent. This echoes the Talmud (*Bava Kamma* 17a), which applies the words of the prophet — *Praiseworthy are those who sow upon all waters* (*Isaiah* 32:20) — to those who perform charitable deeds (*Maaseh Oreg*). It was the merit of this kindness that God revealed himself to Abraham on the third day after his circumcision. The word דְּרָשְׁתּוֹ might therefore be rendered as *He sought him out*, in order to reward him for his kindness (*Machzor HaMevoar*).

הַנּוֹלָד בִּבְשׂוֹרַת — *The one born with the tidings of ...* The prophecy regarding the birth of Isaac was given to Abraham after his act of hospitality toward the three angels, initiated by saying, "*Let some water be brought and wash your feet ...*" (*Genesis* 18:4).

Rashi notes that God repaid every act of kindness that Abraham performed for the angels. Those that he performed personally were repaid by God, so to speak, Himself, while those carried out through a surrogate were repaid to his children through messengers. The phrase "Let some water be brought" is in the passive form to indicate that Abraham ordered someone else to bring the water. His children were rewarded through an intermediary when Moses struck the rock and it provided the Israelites with water (see *Numbers* 20:11,

Bava Metzia 86b and *Psalms* 105:41-42). The act of hospitality is particularly potent in eliciting God's kindness towards us, for God is our shadow (see *Psalms* 121:5) Who "mimics" our every move. When we show kindness toward others, God acts kindly toward us. In our prayer for rain, we therefore evoke the merit of Abraham's hospitality.

According to *R' Chaim Vital*, water is a metaphor for pleasure which is misdirected and is employed for narcissistic rather than spiritual purposes. This is King Solomon's intention when he says in *Song of Songs* (8:7), *Many waters cannot extinguish the love and great rivers cannot inundate it.* The pursuit of pleasure can never outweigh or extinguish the intrinsic love of God which is embodied in Jewish hearts and minds, eternally and immutably.

When hosting the angels who brought the news of Isaac's imminent birth, Abraham said, "Let *a bit* of water be brought," when instructing the angels to wash themselves. This was an allusion that Isaac would serve God by minimizing his involvement with the pleasures of this world and keeping himself spiritually *clean*. It was through such service that he was able to achieve a distilled and exclusive love of God, never squandering his passion on anything besides Him. As we pray for rain, we invoke the merit of Isaac and promise

Prayer for Rain / תפילת גשם [150]

זְכוֹר Remember ה the one [Isaac] born with the tidings of,*
"Let some water be brought."
ו You told his father to slaughter him — to spill his blood like water.
ז He too was scrupulous to pour his heart like water.
ח He dug and discovered wells of water.*
Cong. — For the sake of his righteousness, grant abundant water!

זְכוֹר Remember ט the one [Jacob] who carried his staff*
and crossed the Jordan's water.
י He dedicated his heart and rolled a stone
off the mouth of a well of water,*

God that we too will not squander His blessings on anything but His service (*R' Leibele Eiger*).

בְּאֵרוֹת מָיִם — *Wells of water*. Wells symbolize the spiritual wealth that is hidden beneath layers of human smugness, materialism and laziness. Abraham, who was the spiritual father of all mankind, tried to show the world how much they could accomplish, if they chose to, through the symbolism of digging wells, which represents a quest for buried spiritual riches. The Philistines rejected his teachings, but Isaac persisted, digging no fewer than five wells (*Genesis* 26:18-22). We also ask God to provide us amply with physical sustenance so that we may also concentrate on searching for the treasure within (*R' Nosson Scherman*).

טָעַן מַקְלוֹ — *The one who carried his staff*. *Rashi* cites the Midrashic teaching that when Jacob reached the Jordan River, he placed his staff in its waters and it split for him, allowing him to pass through. Upon returning to Canaan from Aram, Jacob offered a prayer in which he declared, *For with my staff I crossed the Jordan* (*Genesis* 32:11). In this prayer Jacob pleaded to be saved from the hand of Esau even if he was undeserving of continued Divine kindness. "Even if my merits have been diminished by all the kindnesses You

have shown me in the past, still I implore that You save me once again." We, too, ask God to take care of us even if we no longer deserve His beneficence (*Imrei Moshe*).

יְחַד לֵב וְגָל אֶבֶן מִפִּי בְּאֵר מַיִם — *He dedicated his heart and rolled a stone off the mouth of a well of water*. Jacob's steadfast faith in God enabled him single-handedly to roll a huge boulder off the mouth of the well — a chore that usually required the cooperative efforts of several (many) shepherds — in order to water Laban's sheep (see *Genesis* 29:11).

Rashi (*Genesis* ad loc.) explains that Jacob's strength was so great that he was able to roll the stone off almost effortlessly. Nonetheless, this is one of the merits of Jacob that we invoke. It teaches us that even an apparently small act of kindness is of major import and can be the basis for great Heavenly reward. Likewise, man must express his appreciation to any benefactor, no matter how insignificant his act of kindness seems to be (*Alter of Slabodka*).

R' Chaim Shmulevitz views יְחַד לֵב as a type of supernatural strength which man can achieve through willpower. Only when he places limitation on his aspirations is he truly limited in what he can accomplish. The poet does not mean to celebrate the mere brute strength Jacob used to remove the boulder, for physical strength *per se* is not a merit we

כְּנֶאֱבַק לוֹ שַׂר בָּלוּל מֵאֵשׁ וּמִמַּיִם,*
לָכֵן הִבְטַחְתּוֹ הֱיוֹת עִמּוֹ בָּאֵשׁ וּבַמָּיִם.*
בַּעֲבוּרוֹ אַל תִּמְנַע מָיִם. —Cong.

זְכוֹר מָשׁוּי* בְּתֵבַת גּֽמֶא מִן הַמַּיִם,
נָמוּ* דָּלֹה דָלָה וְהִשְׁקָה צֹאן מָיִם,
סְגוּלֶיךָ עֵת צָמְאוּ לַמַּיִם,*
עַל הַסֶּֽלַע הַךְ* וַיֵּצְאוּ מָיִם.
בְּצִדְקוֹ חֹן חַשְׁרַת מָיִם. —Cong.

---

would invoke when asking God for rain. Rather, it is Jacob's purity of heart and singleness of purpose which gave him the physical strength to lift the rock. It is this that we ask God to remember. Just as he was able to transcend his own limitations in order to help the shepherds on that day at the well, so we beseech God to transcend the limitation that our own actions, so to speak, place on His ability to help us.

בָּלוּל מֵאֵשׁ וּמִמַּיִם — *Composed of fire and water.* Angels are composed of fire and water (*Yerushalmi, Rosh Hashanah* 2:5). The angel referred to specifically here is the angel who wrestled with Jacob (*Genesis* 32:25-31). This angel was the celestial captain of Esau, and he sought to dethrone Jacob from his spiritual supremacy.

Fire and water also homiletically refer to the two primary threats to Jewish existence — physical extinction and spiritual ruination.

When Esau married Basmas, daughter of Ishmael, the union resulted in a combination of the two great forces of evil — lust and anger. Ishmael, representative of lust (see *Kiddushin* 49b), and Esau, the champion of murder and bloodshed, combined to undermine the commitment of the Jew to God, an attempt which has lasted throughout the generations. Historically, we have wres-

tled with and survived the threat of fire (physical annihilation) and water (lust and the lure of the "good life") in the merit of Jacob's victory over the angel of Esau. We therefore call upon his merit to assure us continued success against these two enemies (*Shem MeShmuel*).

הִבְטַחְתּוֹ ... בָּאֵשׁ וּבַמָּיִם — *You pledged ... fire and water.* The prophet (*Isaiah* 43:1-2) proclaimed: "And now," so said HASHEM, your Creator ... "when you pass through water, I am with you ... when you go through fire, you shall not be burned ..."

God promised us that He would accompany us through all circumstances in life. He will be with us through thick and thin, in good times and in bad.

מָשׁוּי — *The one drawn forth.* When Pharaoh's daughter found a Jewish baby among the reeds, she named him מֹשֶׁה, *Moses*, because מִן הַמַּיִם מְשִׁיתִהוּ, *I have drawn him from the water* (*Exodus* 2:10).

Moses' life revolved around water. Pharaoh's astrologers pinpointed the day that the savior of the Jews would be born — either to a Jewish or an Egyptian family — and they saw that his downfall would be through water. Consequently, Pharaoh ordered that even Egyptian male babies born on that day be killed — by drowning (*Rashi*). The astrologers were not mistaken. Moses

ב *as when he was wrestled by an angel composed of fire and water.**

ל *Therefore You pledged to remain with him through fire and water.**

> Cong.— *For his sake, do not hold water back!*

זְכוֹר *Remember* מ *the one [Moses] drawn forth**
in a bulrush basket from the water.

נ *They said,* "He drew water and provided the sheep with water."*

ס *At the time Your treasured people thirsted for water,**

ע *he struck the rock* and out came water.*

> Cong.— *For the sake of his righteousness, grant abundant water!*

---

was born that day to a Jewish family and was raised in Pharaoh's own palace, and a sin involving water did cause his "downfall," preventing him from entering *Eretz Yisrael* (see *Numbers* 20:7-13). Furthermore, he was destined to lead the Jewish people through the split waters of the Reed Sea and to witness the Egyptians drowning in those same waters. Thus, the highs and lows of his life were linked to water. We, too, implore God to provide us with the water and sustenance necessary to navigate successfully all the highs and lows in our lives.

Homiletically, the idea of being "drawn forth" from water represents the need to guard oneself against the pleasures of prosperity, which are symbolized by water. King Solomon speaks of the trial of wealth when he says, *Lest I become satiated and deny God, saying, "Who is God"* (*Proverbs* 30:9). We therefore call on the merit of Moses, whose very essence was that of one "removed from the water," distanced from the lure of earthly pleasures. In his merit, we can assure God that His blessing of rain, symbolic of prosperity, will not lead to negative spiritual consequences (*Zekan Aharon*).

נָמוּ — *They said.* The daughters of Jethro reported to their father how "an Egyptian man" [Moses] had drawn water for them (see *Exodus* 2:16-19).

Moses was outraged at the injustice of the shepherds' behavior; Jethro's daugh-

ters had drawn the water, and no one had a right to take it away from them. Since that water was insufficient for their sheep, Moses drew more for them. Furthermore, he intervened on their behalf even though they were strangers to him. We pray similarly that in Moses' merit God should provide us with sustenance even when we act as "strangers" toward Him. When others attempt to take away our source of sustenance, we ask Him to intervene and provide for us.

סְגוּלֶיךָ עֵת צָמְאוּ לַמַּיִם — *At the time Your treasured people thirsted for water.* The nation of Israel enjoys a double-faceted relationship with God. We earn God's approval through our actions and good deeds, yet we also receive His love unconditionally, regardless of how we act. A Jew, no matter how deeply mired he is in sin, can never irrevocably sever his ties with God. It is this aspect of our relationship that grants us the appellation עַם סְגוּלָה, *a treasured people* (see *Exodus* 19:5). A *segulah* is something that provides help in an inexplicable way. So too, the love of God for His people is inexplicable and not directly based on their actions (*R' Avraham Greiver*). Just as God, through Moses, supplied His treasured people with water in the Wilderness, we ask Him to provide for us even if our actions do not justify such kindness.

עַל הַסֶּלַע הַךְ — *He struck the rock ...* When Israel cried for water at their

זָכוֹר פָּקִיד* שָׁתוּת* טוֹבֵל חָמֵשׁ טְבִילוֹת* בַּמַּיִם,
צוֹעֶה וּמַרְחִיץ כַּפָּיו* בְּקִדּוּשׁ מַיִם,
קוֹרֵא וּמַזֶּה טָהֲרַת מַיִם,*
רָחֵק* מֵעַם פָּחֵז כַּמָּיִם.*

‏— Cong. בַּעֲבוּרוֹ אַל תִּמְנַע מָיִם.

---

encampment in Rephidim in the Wilderness, God ordered Moses to smite a stone from which water would issue forth (see *Exodus* 17:6).

Many commentators explain these words, however, as a reference to the later incident at Mei Merivah (*Numbers* 20) when Moses was again commanded to draw water from a rock for the Jews. However, instead of speaking to it as God had instructed, he struck it. The water emerged, but not in a way that sanctified God's Name. This action was considered a sin, the result of which was that Moses and Aaron were denied the privilege of entering the Holy Land.

It appears that in our prayers for rain, we invoke the merit of the meritorious deeds of our forefathers. Why should we mention a misdeed of Moses? *R' Mendel of Vorki* explains: Had Moses carried out his charge properly, he might have infused the onlookers with faith in God and a renewed commitment to His service. Had he spoken to the rock rather than smiting it, God's Name would have been sanctified, for the nation might have drawn the intended lesson that if a dormant rock, which neither hears nor speaks, carries out God's will, surely man, who is blessed with all faculties, must do so (see *Rashi* ad loc.).

Moses, the loving shepherd of his people, was afraid that the Jews might see him speak to the rock and draw water, yet not perceive the important parallel regarding their own spiritual obligations. In such a case, Moses' success would be the cause of an indictment

against his beloved flock. Moses' love for them might have caused him to alter God's exact instructions and incur His wrath in order to save the Jews.

It is Moses' unflagging loyalty to his flock that we invoke and ask God to show us the same steadfast love and bless us with all our needs.

פָּקִיד — *The appointee.* This word refers to the holder of a high office, in this case Aaron, the first *Kohen Gadol* (*Mateh Levi*).

שָׁתוּת — *The Temple.* The Holy Temple is called the אֶבֶן שְׁתִיָּה, *Foundation Stone,* after a stone located at the center of the Holy of Holies upon which the Ark of the Covenant stood. According to the Talmud (*Yoma* 53b), this stone was the first part of the earth to be created by God, and the planet expanded and developed from it.

חָמֵשׁ טְבִילוֹת — *Five immersions.* The Mishnah (*Yoma* 3:3, based on *Leviticus* 16) teaches that the *Kohen Gadol* must immerse himself five times during the Yom Kippur Temple service. Before and after each immersion he would wash his hands and feet in a ritually prescribed manner with water that had been sanctified in a sacred vessel.

צוֹעֶה וּמַרְחִיץ כַּפָּיו — *He emptied* [*and cleansed*] *himself* [*of iniquity*] *and washed his hands through sanctification with water.* This translation of צוֹעֶה is based on *Jeremiah* 48:12 and *Isaiah* 51:14, where the term means emptying or releasing something pent up. Sin is

Prayer for Rain / תפילת גשם [154]

זְכוֹר **Remember** פ *the appointee* [Aaron] over the Temple,**
who made five immersions* in the water.

צ *He emptied [and cleansed] himself [of iniquity] and washed his hands*
through sanctification with water.*

ק *He called out and sprinkled* [blood which brought] purity as with water.**

ר *He remained apart* from a people of waterlike impetuosity.**

Cong.— *For his sake, do not hold water back!*

---

often compared in Scripture to impurity which must be purged from one's system before he can, in a spiritual sense, fully recuperate. Thus the *Kohen Gadol*, through his service on Yom Kippur, achieved Divine atonement for his own sins and those of all the people, emptying the spiritual system of the nation of the contaminating influence of sin (*Mateh Levi*).

Alternatively, צוֹעֶה might be rendered as *he goes from place to place* (see *Jeremiah* 2:20, *Metzudas David* ad loc.). The *Kohen Gadol* would enter the Holy of Holies a total of four times during the Yom Kippur service. [See *Yad Avraham* to Tractate *Yoma*, Appendix 1, pp. 164-166, for the chronological sequence of the *Kohen Gadol's* movements.]

קוֹרֵא וּמַזֶּה טָהֲרַת מַיִם — *He called out and sprinkled [blood which brought] purity as with water.* During the Yom Kippur service, the *Kohen Gadol* would sprinkle the blood of various offerings in various parts of the Temple (see *Leviticus* 16:14-18). To ensure that the proper number of sprinklings was performed, the *Kohen Gadol* would count aloud as he sprinkled the blood (see *Yoma* 5:3-4).

These sprinklings brought forgiveness for the Jewish people. The poet employs the water metaphor to express the purifying power of sprinkling based on *Ezekiel* 36:25: *I shall sprinkle pure water upon you and purify you; of all your contaminations and abominations I will purify you* (*Mateh Levi*).

Alternatively, *Machzor HaMevoar* suggests translating the phrase as *he*

read and was sprinkled with the purifying waters. The Mishnah (*Yoma* 1:3) teaches that for seven days before Yom Kippur the *Kohen Gadol*, either on his own or under the tutelage of the sages of the court, would sequester himself and study the portion of the Torah (*Leviticus* 16) dealing with the Yom Kippur service, as well as the Oral Law which elaborates upon it. Furthermore, on the third and last of the seven days, the *Kohen Gadol* underwent sprinkling with the purifying waters which were mixed with the ashes of the Red Cow. This was done in order to purify him from the *tumah*, or contamination, of a corpse which he might unknowingly have contracted (*Yoma* 8a, *Rambam, Hilchos Avodas Yom HaKippurim* 1:4).

רָחַק — *He remained apart.* This refers to Aaron's personal sanctity, which was much greater than that of anyone else in the nation. Scripture states: *And Aaron was set apart, that he be sanctified [as] holy of holies . . .* (*I Chronicles* 23:13).

Alternatively, this refers to the sequestering of the *Kohen Gadol* for seven days prior to Yom Kippur (see *Yoma* 1:1). This practice is derived from Scripture, which required that Aaron, the first *Kohen Gadol*, live in the sanctuary area for the seven days prior to the inauguration service of the Temple.

פַּחַז כַּמַּיִם — *Of waterlike impetuosity.* The nation of Israel is considered an impetuous people (see *Shabbos* 88b). The phrase פַּחַז כַּמַּיִם is borrowed from Scriptures (*Genesis* 49:4), where Jacob accused Reuben of sexual indiscretion in moving

זְכוֹר שְׁנֵים עָשָׂר שְׁבָטִים שֶׁהֶעֱבַרְתָּ בִּגְזֵרַת מַיִם,*
שֶׁהִמְתַּקְתָּ לָמוֹ מְרִירוּת מַיִם,*
תּוֹלְדוֹתָם* נִשְׁפַּךְ דָּמָם עָלֶיךָ כַּמָּיִם,
תֵּפֶן כִּי נַפְשֵׁנוּ אָפְפוּ מָיִם.

Cong.— בְּצִדְקָם חֹן חֲשַׁרַת מָיִם.

Chazzan:

שָׁאַתָּה הוּא יהוה אֱלֹהֵינוּ, מַשִּׁיב הָרוּחַ וּמוֹרִיד הַגָּשֶׁם.

Cong. then chazzan— לִבְרָכָה וְלֹא לִקְלָלָה.   (Cong.— אָמֵן.)

Cong. then chazzan— לְחַיִּים וְלֹא לַמָּוֶת.*   (Cong.— אָמֵן.)

Cong. then chazzan— לְשׂוֹבַע וְלֹא לְרָזוֹן.*   (Cong.— אָמֵן.)

---

his father's bed in Leah's tent, an example of "waterlike impetuosity." [See ArtScroll *Chumash*, Stone edition, *Genesis* 35:22, for the true meaning of the accusation.] This appellation is used in connection with the sequestering of the High Priest since one of its purposes was to prevent him from cohabiting with his wife [see *Yoma* 1:1 and *Yad Avraham* commentary]. In order to assure that he would remain chaste during this seven-day preparatory period, he was set apart from *a people of waterlike impetuosity*.

שֶׁהֶעֱבַרְתָּ בִּגְזֵרַת מַיִם — *You caused to cross through the split waters* ... This refers to the Splitting of the Sea and the Song at the Sea, which are described in *Exodus* (14:15-15:21).

Rambam (Mishnah Commentary to *Avos* 5:4) teaches that the waters formed twelve tunnels so that each tribe passed through separately on its own route. *Sfas Emes* explains that this teaches the uniqueness of every tribe. No two tribes are alike, and each has a unique role within the Jewish people. Each tribe actually deserved to have the sea split solely for its sake.

Accordingly, we might interpret this stich as a prayer to God not only to

provide rainfall, but to direct it to each tribe and person according to their individual needs (*Simchas Aharon*).

שֶׁהִמְתַּקְתָּ לָמוֹ מְרִירוּת מַיִם — *For whom You sweetened the water's bitter taste.* The story of the sweetening of the waters of Marah appears in *Exodus* (15:22-26). After traveling for three days without water, the people arrived in Marah. They found drinkable but bitter water and complained to Moses. God showed Moses a tree which he threw into the water and it became sweet.

Baal Shem Tov interprets these words homiletically as referring to the *people* themselves. It is human nature that when someone is embittered, he sees everything negatively. Because the people were bitter, they found fault with the water. This stich may therefore be interpreted as a plea that we experience no bitterness in our struggles to earn a living.

By invoking the miracle of Marah, we echo the prayer of the dove that Noah sent out after the Flood. When the dove returned, it brought back a bitter olive leaf in its mouth, symbolically saying, "Better that my food be bitter but from God's hand than sweet as honey but

***Prayer for Rain* / תפילת גשם   [156]**

זְכוֹר Remember שׁ the twelve tribes You caused
to cross through the split waters,*
שׁ for whom You sweetened the water's bitter taste.*
ת Their offspring* whose blood was spilt for You like water.
ת Turn to us — for woes engulf our souls like water.

Cong.– For the sake of their righteousness, grant abundant water!

Chazzan:

**For You are Hashem, our God,
Who makes the wind blow and makes the rain descend.**

Cong. then *chazzan* – **For blessing and not for curse.**   (Cong.– *Amen.*)

Cong. then *chazzan* – **For life and not for death.**   (Cong.– *Amen.*)

Cong. then *chazzan* – **For plenty and not for scarcity.**   (Cong.– *Amen.*)

---

from mortal man's hand." We ask God to go yet a step further and not only provide us with "water" (sustenance), so that we will not have to be dependent on anyone, but to sweeten it, just as He did for our forefathers at Marah (*Imrei Moshe*).

תּוֹלְדוֹתָם — *Their offspring.* This refers to the thousands of Jews over the generations whose blood has been spilled in sanctification of the Holy Name. Alternatively, this refers to us, the descendants of the twelve tribes, who pour out their hearts in prayer.

Ramban (*Genesis* 22:16) suggests that in reward for his readiness to sacrifice his son, God assured Abraham that even if his offspring were to sin grievously, they would never be totally destroyed, nor would they fall into the hands of their enemies permanently. This was a solemn assurance of Israel's survival and ultimate redemption. Through its spiritual legacy, the *Akeidah* also provided Jews in all later generations with the innate courage to make the ultimate sacrifice when necessary. Thus, it is because *their blood was spilt for You like water* — because of their willingness to sacrifice themselves — that Jews will always have

offspring (*Imrei Moshe*).

לְחַיִּים וְלֹא לַמָּוֶת — *For life and not for death.* Chassidic masters have noted that this text is unlike other similar grammatical formulas, such as לִבְרָכָה וְלֹא לִקְלָלָה and לְשׂוֹבַע וְלֹא לְרָזוֹן, in which both *lameds* are punctuated with a שְׁוָא. The ל of לְחַיִּים וְלֹא לַמָּוֶת, however, is punctuated with a פַּתָח. They interpret this change homiletically based on the Talmud (*Nedarim* 11a), which translates ל with a פַּתָח as *it is not*. [For example, לַחוּלִין is a form of a vow which means לֹא חוּלִין, *it is not mundane*, but rather it is consecrated.] Thus, we pray that God give us rain so that we should experience vibrant and spiritually fulfilling lives — not merely לַמָּוֶת, the absence of death.

לְשׂוֹבַע וְלֹא לְרָזוֹן — *For plenty and not for scarcity.* This redundancy might be understood in light of the Talmud (*Bava Basra* 91b), which describes a situation where the food supply is ample, and yet, due to the depressed economy, people are starving. We ask here not only for plenty, but also for the monetary means to obtain what we need, for provisions are worthless unless we can make use of them (*Torah Temimah*).

יציאה מן הסוכה ﴾

During the afternoon of Shemini Atzeres, before leaving the *succah* for the last time, it is customary to recite the following prayers:

יְהִי רָצוֹן מִלְּפָנֶיךָ, יהוה אֱלֹהֵינוּ וֵאלֹהֵי אֲבוֹתֵינוּ, כְּשֵׁם שֶׁקִּיַּמְתִּי וְיָשַׁבְתִּי בַּסֻּכָּה זוֹ, כֵּן אֶזְכֶּה לְשָׁנָה הַבָּאָה לֵישֵׁב בְּסֻכַּת עוֹרוֹ שֶׁל לִוְיָתָן.*

לְשָׁנָה הַבָּאָה בִּירוּשָׁלָיִם.*

﴾ FAREWELL TO THE SUCCAH ﴿

בְּסֻכַּת עוֹרוֹ שֶׁל לִוְיָתָן — *In the succah of the skin of the Leviathan.* According to the Aggadah of the Talmud and Midrash, the לִוְיָתָן, *Leviathan*, is a giant fish created on the fifth day of Creation and is the ruler of all the creatures of the sea.

Originally, two were created, a male and a female, as with all other species. However, God saw that if these two fish were to mate and multiply, they would destroy the entire world by dint of their great strength and numbers, for the Leviathan is so enormous that all the waters that flow from the Jordan River into the sea can scarcely quench its thirst. God, therefore, killed the female and preserved it in brine, to be eaten by the righteous at the banquet that will be prepared for them in the Time to Come. The Leviathan is also very beautiful; its fins are so radiant that they shine more powerfully than the sun, and its eyes are so bright that they sometimes illuminate the entire sea (*Bava Basra* 74b). The Talmud (*Avodah Zarah* 3b, based on *Psalms* 104:26) says that the Leviathan is, as it were, the "plaything" of God with which He "amuses" Himself.

Another huge beast whose flesh will be served to the righteous in the World to Come is the בְּהֵמוֹת, *Behemoth* (also known in Hebrew as שׁוֹר הַבָּר, and in Aramaic as תּוֹר בָּרָא, *wild ox*). The Behemoth was created on the sixth day of Creation. It is a gigantic ox and, like the Leviathan, possesses enormous strength. It, too, was created male and female, but its reproduction would have threatened the existence of the world. God therefore neutered the male and eliminated the female's desire to propagate (*Bava Basra* 74b).

The Behemoth is so monstrous that it requires the produce of a thousand hills for its daily food. Overnight, these hills are replenished with vegetation to provide the Behemoth with the next day's food (*Pirkei D'R' Eliezer*). Its need for water is so great that all the water that flows from the Jordan River for one day is only enough for one gulp. God therefore provided it with the exclusive use of the River Yubal that flows from Paradise to quench its thirst (*Vayikra Rabbah* 22:10).

When the Messiah comes, God will summon the angels to enter into battle against the Leviathan, for the amusement of the righteous. But the Leviathan will cast one glance upon them and the angels will run in fear and dismay from the field of battle. They will return to attack him with swords, but to no avail, since steel is like straw against his scales. Equally futile will be the throwing of spears and stones, as they will bounce off him with no effect (*Bava Basra* 74b). Disheartened, the angels will give up the

◆{ FAREWELL TO THE SUCCAH }◆

During the afternoon of Shemini Atzeres, before leaving the *succah* for the last time,
it is customary to recite the following prayers:

יְהִי רָצוֹן *May it be Your will, HASHEM, our God and the God of our
forefathers, that just as I have fulfilled [the mitzvah] and
dwelled in this succah, so may I merit in the coming year to dwell in the
succah of the skin of the Leviathan.**

Next year in Jerusalem.*

---

battle, and God will signal to the Leviathan and the Behemoth to fight one
another. The Leviathan will slaughter
the Behemoth with a cut from his very
sharp fins; simultaneously, the Behemoth will kill the Leviathan with a
blow from his horns (*Leviticus Rabbah*
13:3).

From the beautiful skin of the Leviathan, God will construct canopies to
shelter the righteous from the sun (*Bava
Basra* 75a). These canopies are referred
to in our prayer as סֻכַּת עוֹרוֹ שֶׁל לִוְיָתָן, *the
succah of the skin of the Leviathan.*
Under these canopies the righteous will
eat the meat of the Behemoth and the
Leviathan, amid great joy and merri-
ment, at a huge banquet (ibid. 74b).
Although the Talmud does not specify
that this banquet is a reward for fulfillment of the *mitzvah* of dwelling in the
succah, an introduction in *Pesikta D'R'
Eliezer* reads: "R' Levi taught regarding
all who fulfill the *mitzvah* of *succah* in
this world that the Holy One, Blessed is
He, will seat them in a *succah* of the skin
of the Leviathan in the World to Come."

[The above is but a very brief synopsis
of the Aggadah on the Leviathan and
the Behemoth, and the banquet at which
their flesh will be served. See ArtScroll
Akdamus, pp. 127-139, for a fuller
account, along with a complete bibliog-
raphy of Talmudic and Midrashic
sources.]

Since the Sages teach that in the
World to Come there will be no physical
eating or drinking (see *Berachos* 17a), it
is difficult to understand this banquet in
a literal sense. *Maharal (Gur Aryeh* to
Genesis 1:21) interprets the banquet as
an allegory describing a stage through
which the righteous will pass immediately before entering the World to Come.
They will not eat and drink out of
physical want; instead, this סְעוּדָה (meal)
will provide the righteous with the
spiritual sustenance (סַעַד) they need
until they enter the World to Come.

According to the *Vilna Gaon (Even
Shleimah* 11:11), the feast of the Leviathan is an allusion to the increased
knowledge of God which will characterize the Messianic era. At that time, all of
humanity will manifest a burning desire
to penetrate the great mysteries of God
and His Torah and to cleave to both.
God will rejoice in His children and they
in Him.

After spending a week in the *succah*
and living with the realization that God,
rather than our physical trappings, is our
true source of sustenance, we pray for
the advent of the Messianic age, a time
when this understanding will become an
internalized   reality   for   all   of
us.

לְשָׁנָה הַבָּאָה בִּירוּשָׁלָיִם — *The coming year
in Jerusalem.* This brief prayer is usually
understood as an expression of faith and

Some add:

רְבּוֹנָא דְעָלְמָא, יְהֵא רַעֲוָה מִן קֳדָמָךְ שֶׁאוֹתָן מַלְאָכִים הַקְּדוֹשִׁים הַשַּׁיָּכִים לְמִצְוַת סֻכָּה, וּלְמִצְוַת אַרְבָּעָה מִינִים – לוּלָב וְאֶתְרוֹג, הֲדַס וַעֲרָבָה – הַנּוֹהֲגִים בְּחַג הַסֻּכּוֹת, הֵם יִתְלַוּוּ עִמָּנוּ בְּצֵאתֵנוּ מִן הַסֻּכָּה וְיִכָּנְסוּ עִמָּנוּ לְבָתֵּינוּ לְחַיִּים וּלְשָׁלוֹם. וְלִהְיוֹת תָּמִיד עָלֵינוּ שְׁמִירָה עֶלְיוֹנָה מִמְּעוֹן קָדְשֶׁךָ, וּלְהַצִּילֵנוּ מִכָּל חֵטְא וְעָוֹן, וּמִכָּל פְּגָעִים רָעִים, וּמִכָּל שָׁעוֹת רָעוֹת הַמִּתְרַגְּשׁוֹת לָבֹא לָעוֹלָם. וְתֵעָרֶה עָלֵינוּ רוּחַ מִמָּרוֹם; וְחַדֵּשׁ כִּלְיוֹתֵינוּ לְעָבְדְךָ בֶּאֱמֶת, בְּאַהֲבָה וּבְיִרְאָה; וְנַתְמִיד מְאֹד בְּלִמּוּד תּוֹרָתְךָ הַקְּדוֹשָׁה, לִלְמוֹד וּלְלַמֵּד. וּזְכוּת אַרְבָּעָה מִינִים וּמִצְוַת סֻכָּה תַּעֲמֹד לָנוּ, שֶׁתַּאֲרִיךְ אַפְּךָ עַד שׁוּבֵנוּ אֵלֶיךָ בִּתְשׁוּבָה שְׁלֵמָה לְפָנֶיךָ; וּנְתַקֵּן כָּל אֲשֶׁר פָּגַמְנוּ; וְנִזְכֶּה לְשֶׁתֵּי שֻׁלְחָנוֹת, בְּלִי צַעַר וְיָגוֹן – אֲנִי וּבְנֵי בֵיתִי וְיוֹצְאֵי חֲלָצַי – וְנִהְיֶה כֻלָּנוּ שְׁקֵטִים וּשְׁלֵוִים, דְּשֵׁנִים וְרַעֲנַנִּים, וְעוֹבְדֵי יהוה בֶּאֱמֶת לַאֲמִתּוֹ כִּרְצוֹנְךָ הַטּוֹב, בִּכְלַל כָּל בְּנֵי יִשְׂרָאֵל, אָמֵן. יִהְיוּ לְרָצוֹן אִמְרֵי פִי, וְהֶגְיוֹן לִבִּי לְפָנֶיךָ, יהוה צוּרִי וְגוֹאֲלִי.[1]

hope that during the coming year the Messiah will arrive to redeem Israel from its exile and lead the nation back to the Holy Land, to a rebuilt Temple in Jerusalem. This interpretation, however, seems to conflict with one of the Thirteen Articles of Faith (אֲנִי מַאֲמִין) formulated by *Rambam*. The twelfth article states: "I believe with perfect faith in the advent of the Messiah, and even though he may tarry, nevertheless, I hope *each day* for his arrival." Why, then, do we pray for his arrival during the coming year and not during the present one?

Two resolutions are offered by *R' Yoel of Satmar* in his commentary to the Passover Haggadah — one grammatical, the other historical. If accented on the first syllable, the word בָּאָה means *has come*, in the past tense. If accented on the second syllable, it means *is coming*, in the present tense (see *Rashi* to *Genesis* 29:7,9). Based upon the first meaning, we

may retranslate our prayer: *The year that **has come** [הַבָּאָה* in the past tense] *in Jerusalem* — i.e., may we be in Jerusalem even during the current year, for the Messiah can come at any moment.

The historical resolution is based on a teaching of Rabbi [Yehudah HaNasi] cited in *Sifre* (*Bahaalosecha* 9:1): Originally, Israel's calendar counted time from the Exodus, as it is written: HASHEM *spoke to Moses ... in the second year of their departure from the land of Egypt* (*Numbers* 9:1). Once they entered the Land [of Israel], they began dating the years from their arrival, as it is written: *When you shall come into the Land ... [you shall count for yourselves seven shmittos of years* (*Leviticus* 25:2,8)]. When the Temple was built, they counted the years from its erection, as it is written: *And it was at the end of twenty years since Solomon had built*

רִבּוֹנָא *Master of the Universe, may it be Your will that the holy angels connected with the mitzvah of succah and the mitzvah of the Four Species — lulav, esrog, hadas, aravah — that are performed during the Festival of Succos, accompany us when we leave the succah, and may they enter our homes with us in life and in peace. May there always be upon us a heavenly protection from Your holy abode, to save us from all sin and iniquity, from evil occurrences, from malevolent periods that are stirring to come upon the world. Arouse upon us a spirit from above; rejuvenate our inner source of counsel that we may serve You in truth, in love and in awe; that we may be diligent in the study of Your holy Torah, to study and to teach. May the merit of the Four Species and the mitzvah of succah stand by us, that You act with forbearance until we have returned to You in full repentance before You; may we rectify all that we have destroyed; may we merit both tables, with neither pain nor grief — myself, my household and my offspring — may we all dwell placid and serene, vigorous and fresh, serving HASHEM in utmost truthfulness according to Your benevolent will, among all the Children of Israel; Amen. May the expression of my mouth and the thoughts of my heart find favor before You, HASHEM, my Rock and my Redeemer.*[1]

---

(1) *Psalms* 19:15.

---

the Temple of HASHEM (II Chronicles 8:1). After the destruction of Jerusalem, they began to reckon from that date, as it is written: *In the fourteenth year after the city had fallen* ... (Ezekiel 40:1) ... And just as they counted years anew, so did they count months anew [i.e., they did not wait for the year to end but immediately began the new count].

With every major change of direction in Israel's long march through history, the nation began a new count of years and months. So will it be when the Messiah arrives. No matter what year it is, no matter what part of the year it is, from that moment on we will begin a new year and a new counting. The new era will open with a new year. It is to this "coming year" that we refer when we proclaim, "The coming year in Jerusalem" (*Haggadah Mahari Tav*).

An alternate interpretation of this prayer is given by R' Eliyahu Kitov,

who suggests that it is an allusion not to the advent of the Messiah, but to the *mitzvah* we have just completed. Although we were unable to perform this *mitzvah* in the rebuilt Holy City of Jerusalem this year, we pray that we may merit to perform it there next year. Thus, at the end of the Passover *Seder* we express our desire to celebrate next year's *Seder* in the Temple in Jerusalem. Likewise, in the final minutes of Yom Kippur, the entire congregation cries out, "Next year in Jerusalem! This year we, in our local synagogue, described the *Kohen Gadol's* Yom Kippur service. May we merit that next year the actual performance of this service will take place in the Holy Temple." Similarly, upon leaving the *succah*, we pray that next year we will be able to spend the festival of Succos in Jerusalem (*Haggadah Yalkut Tov*).

Before the Ark is opened for the *Hakafos*, the following selection of verses is recited responsively:

אַתָּה הָרְאֵתָ* לָדַעַת, כִּי יהוה הוּא הָאֱלֹהִים, אֵין עוֹד מִלְבַדּוֹ.*[1]
לְעֹשֵׂה נִפְלָאוֹת גְּדֹלוֹת לְבַדּוֹ,* כִּי לְעוֹלָם חַסְדּוֹ.[2]
אֵין כָּמוֹךָ בָאֱלֹהִים,* אֲדֹנָי, וְאֵין כְּמַעֲשֶׂיךָ.[3]

⁜ הקפות לשמחת תורה / HAKAFOS FOR SIMCHAS TORAH ⁜

אַתָּה הָרְאֵתָ — *You have been shown.* Before the Torah scrolls are removed from the Ark for the *hakafos*, the congregation recites this collection of verses. Since it is the introduction to the *hakafos*, it is recited in a particularly joyous and festive manner.

In most congregations, the honor of reciting אַתָּה הָרְאֵתָ is auctioned off, with the proceeds going to the synagogue or some other charitable cause. Often, the winner of the auction will honor the rabbi or another prominent member of the congregation, or several individuals, with the privilege of chanting the verses aloud. A lovely custom has evolved among yeshivah students whereby, instead of bidding with money, the honor is auctioned off for a pledge to complete a specified number of *blatt gemara* (folios of the Talmud). This is, of course, the ultimate form of honoring the Torah — by committing oneself to study it.

Essentially, אַתָּה הָרְאֵתָ consists of all the verses that are recited when the Torah scrolls are removed from the Ark for the regular Sabbath or festival Torah readings. In honor of the *hakafos*, however, the service is augmented with many additional verses. The general themes of this selection are praise of God's greatness and prayer for the rebuilding of Zion and Jerusalem.

⧉ When God gave Israel the Torah, He revealed to them all the celestial beings and forces and He allowed them to understand the powers of nature. After all this, they could see clearly that there is only one Creator. Thus the verse states, *You have been shown [in order] to know* that God is One and that there is no other force or being like Him (*Rashi*).

אֵין עוֹד מִלְבַדּוֹ — *There is nothing beside Him.* The translation reflects the theological concept developed in both *Nefesh HaChaim* (2) and *Likkutei Amarim* that God is not only the sole Deity, He is the Source of all existence. Nothing exists without God. In the words of the *Zohar*, לֵית אַתָר דְּפָנוּי מִינֵהּ, *There is no place empty of Him.*

לְבַדּוֹ — *Alone.* Although God has delegated some of His power to intermediaries, they are not His equals or His partners; they, too, are dependent on Him. The Sages teach (*Bereishis Rabbah* 3:8) that this is the reason that there were no angels when creation began; God alone performed the *great wonders* of creating heaven, earth and the luminaries in the sky (*Rashi; Radak*).

The Sages interpret *alone* in the sense of hidden or unseen, an allusion to the fact that God performs many miracles in secrecy. The individual usually remains oblivious to the miracles of Divine Providence which preserve and protect him. For example, a person may be bitterly disappointed when a traffic jam causes him to miss a plane flight, only to learn later that the passengers were killed in a crash. Such an incident

❧ THE HAKAFAH-CIRCUITS OF SIMCHAS TORAH ❧

Before the Ark is opened for the *Hakafos*, the following selection of verses is recited responsively:

אַתָּה הָרְאֵתָ *You have been shown* [in order] to know that* H*ASHEM,*
  He is the God, there is nothing besides Him.[1]*
To Him Who alone* performs great wonders,
  for His kindness endures forever.[2]*
There is none like You among the gods,* my Lord,
  and there is nothing like Your works.[3]

---

(1) *Deuteronomy* 4:35. (2) *Psalms* 136:4. (3) 86:8.

---

is a clear manifestation of God's kindness; most of the time, however, this kindness is not as obvious. People do not realize that apparent misfortune is actually a benefit; God has acted *alone*, without revealing His purpose (*R' A. C. Feuer*).

As the Sages say: אֵין בַּעַל הַנֵּס מַכִּיר בְּנִסּוֹ, *The beneficiary of the miracle does not recognize his [own] miracle* (see *Niddah* 31a). *Noam Megadim* uses the following parable to explain why God acts in this fashion: A person had a son who turned to evil, much to his dismay. One night wild animals attacked the son while he slept in the field. Out of mercy for his son, the father chased the lion away; however, he didn't wake the son to witness what he had done for him. Had the son seen his father's action, he might never have repented and changed his ways, for he would realize that his father loves him unconditionally, no matter how he behaves.

God, our loving Father, deals with us in a similar fashion. When we abandon the path of Torah and *mitzvos*, we leave ourselves vulnerable to all kinds of pain and punishment. God, in His infinite mercy and patience, often saves us, all the while awaiting our repentance. However, in order that we feel His disappointment with us, He withholds any overt signs of His love for us as He acts on our behalf, and we remain

oblivious to His kindness. Thus, He performs great wonders *alone*.

כִּי לְעוֹלָם חַסְדּוֹ — *For His kindness endures forever.* The good works accomplished by God's intermediaries are of limited duration, because the agents themselves are finite. But God's works endure forever. *Alshich* emphasizes that only the goodness of God is genuinely altruistic, for the goodness displayed by human rulers is prompted by ulterior motives. Only of the Almighty can we say כִּי לְעוֹלָם חַסְדּוֹ, which may also be rendered: *His kindness is* לְעוֹלָם, *for the sake of the world,* rather than for Himself.

Furthermore, the fact that God always performs *great wonders in secrecy*, without the beneficiaries' awareness, demonstrates that He is truly motivated, so to speak, by His Attribute of Kindness, rather than by a "desire" for man's praise (*Shevet Mussar*).

בָּאֱלֹהִים — *Among the gods.* This refers to the seemingly godlike intermediaries, such as the angels and the planets, mentioned in the preceding verse. The idolaters who worship these forces imagine that they have independent strength. Indeed, the Almighty did invest these forces and bodies with the ability to influence events, but they are merely the agents of the Lord and have no power to act on their own (*Radak*).

[163] **SIMCHAS TORAH** — Its Significance, Laws, and Prayers

יְהִי כְבוֹד* יהוה לְעוֹלָם, יִשְׂמַח יהוה בְּמַעֲשָׂיו.*[1]
יְהִי שֵׁם* יהוה מְבֹרָךְ, מֵעַתָּה וְעַד עוֹלָם.[2]
יְהִי יהוה* אֱלֹהֵינוּ עִמָּנוּ, כַּאֲשֶׁר הָיָה עִם אֲבֹתֵינוּ,
אַל יַעַזְבֵנוּ וְאַל יִטְּשֵׁנוּ.[3]
וְאִמְרוּ, הוֹשִׁיעֵנוּ, אֱלֹהֵי יִשְׁעֵנוּ, וְקַבְּצֵנוּ וְהַצִּילֵנוּ מִן הַגּוֹיִם,*
לְהֹדוֹת לְשֵׁם קָדְשֶׁךָ, לְהִשְׁתַּבֵּחַ בִּתְהִלָּתֶךָ.[4]
יהוה מֶלֶךְ,*[5] יהוה מָלָךְ,[6] יהוה יִמְלֹךְ לְעוֹלָם וָעֶד.[7]
יהוה עֹז לְעַמּוֹ יִתֵּן,* יהוה יְבָרֵךְ אֶת עַמּוֹ בַשָּׁלוֹם.*[8]

יְהִי כְבוֹד . . . יְהִי שֵׁם . . . — *May the glory . . . Blessed be the Name . . .* Since His works endure forever, it is fitting that we glorify Him and recite His blessings at all times, and that we rejoice in His works eternally.

יִשְׂמַח ה׳ בְּמַעֲשָׂיו — *Let HASHEM rejoice in His works.* Initially God was completely satisfied with Creation, as *Genesis* 1:31 states: *And God saw all that He had made, and behold it was very good.* According to the Midrash (*Bereishis Rabbah*) this is analogous to a king who built a magnificent palace. When he completed it, he was overjoyed at how beautiful it was. He cried out, "Palace, palace, if only you would always find favor in my eyes as you do at this very moment." When God finished creating the world, He was also extremely satisfied with His Creation. "World, O world," He said, "if only you would always find favor in My eyes as you do at this moment."

This hope has not always come to fruition. Many times in the course of history, God has been profoundly saddened by His own creations. In the Messianic era and in the World to Come, His joy in His works will be completely restored.

On Shemini Atzeres, which is a portent of the World to Come, we honor God's Torah and give Him reason to rejoice in His works and in His people.

יְהִי שֵׁם ה׳ מְבֹרָךְ מֵעַתָּה וְעַד עוֹלָם — *Blessed be the Name of HASHEM, from this time and forever.* God's Name is truly blessed when His children follow His will. *Midrash Shocher Tov* observes that Israel's behavior in this world is erratic; sometimes we please God, while at other times we anger Him. In the intimate moments of Simchas Torah, as we remove the Torah scrolls from the Ark in order to honor them and to make a firm commitment to study and cherish Torah, we declare that from this time forth, the Name of God will be blessed by His loyal servants and sons (*Simchas Aharon*).

יְהִי ה׳ — *May HASHEM . . . be.* Having declared God's greatness, we pray that He not forsake us. Just as His Presence accompanied our forefathers constantly during their forty years in the Wilderness, so may He always be with us. This verse was recited by King Solomon at the dedication of the Temple, when he asked that the Divine Presence never leave the *Beis HaMikdash.*

Malbim notes that God employs two diametrically different tactics in order to arouse us to His service: By punishing us for wrongdoings and by appearing to withdraw from the stage of human affairs, God forces us to seek Him out. On the other hand, He smothers us with love and kindness, until we realize that

May the glory of HASHEM endure forever,
   let HASHEM rejoice in His works.[1]*
Blessed be the Name* of HASHEM, from this time and forever.[2]
May HASHEM, our God, be* with us, as He was with our forefathers,
   may He not forsake us nor cast us off.[3]
Say: 'Save us, O God of our salvation,
   gather us and rescue us from the nations,*
   to thank Your Holy Name and to glory in Your praise.'[4]
HASHEM reigns,[5] HASHEM has reigned,[6]
   HASHEM shall reign for all eternity.[7]
HASHEM will give might to His people,*
   HASHEM will bless His people with peace.[8]*

---

(1) *Psalms* 104:31. (2) 113:2. (3) *I Kings* 8:57. (4) *I Chronicles* 16:35.
(5) *Psalms* 10:16. (6) 93:1 et al. (7) *Exodus* 15:18. (8) *Psalms* 29:11.

---

everything good in life comes from our closeness to Him.

It was with this lovingkindness that God drew our forefathers after Him into the Wilderness in the wake of the Egyptian Exodus. The great miracles He wrought in those days and His attention to our every need during our forty-year sojourn was an effort to awaken us to His service through an outpouring of love. We pray that God will always draw us toward Him with love, rather than sending us messages through the harsh means of casting us away.

וְהַצִּילֵנוּ מִן הַגּוֹיִם — *And rescue us from the nations.* Having alluded to the *Beis HaMikdash,* we pray for our release from exile so that we may rebuild the Temple. There we will thank God and glory in His praise.

ה' מֶלֶךְ — *HASHEM reigns.* These words begin one of the most familiar verses in the entire liturgy, but surprisingly enough the verse is not found in Scripture. Rather, each phrase comes from a different part of Scripture. In combination, the three phrases express the eternity of God's reign.

ה' עֹז לְעַמּוֹ יִתֵּן — *HASHEM will give might to His people.* According to the

Talmud (*Zevachim* 116a), this refers to God's giving of the Torah, which is the source of Israel's spiritual strength and moral fortitude. *Tiferes Shlomo* offers a homiletic interpretation in the name of R' *Meir of Apt,* rendering עֹז as *obstinance* and *brazenness.* When man takes stock of himself spiritually, he sees that in actuality he is unworthy of serving God or studying His Torah. This realization might dissuade him from even attempting to pray before God or to study His holy word. It is against this spiritual apathy that God gives us עֹז, the courage to attempt what might seem impossible. We trust that God will not reject our humble attempts to serve Him, and that He will bless us with success.

בְּשָׁלוֹם — *With peace.* The last Mishnah of the Talmud states: "Rabbi Shimon ben Chalafta said, 'God could find no vessel that could contain blessings better than peace, as it says, HASHEM ... will bless His people with peace' " (*Uktzin* 3:12). This concept is so vital and precious that the word שָׁלוֹם, *peace,* is the concluding word of the Oral Torah (ibid.), the *Shemoneh Esrei* blessings, the Priestly Blessings and the *Bircas HaMazon.*

Homiletically, the verse may be referring to relief from our constant battle

וְיִהְיוּ נָא אֲמָרֵינוּ לְרָצוֹן,* לִפְנֵי אֲדוֹן כֹּל.[1]

The Ark is opened and the responsive recitation continues:

וַיְהִי בִּנְסֹעַ הָאָרֹן,* וַיֹּאמֶר מֹשֶׁה, קוּמָה יהוה, וְיָפֻצוּ אֹיְבֶיךָ,
וְיָנֻסוּ מְשַׂנְאֶיךָ מִפָּנֶיךָ.[2]
קוּמָה יהוה לִמְנוּחָתֶךָ,* אַתָּה וַאֲרוֹן עֻזֶּךָ.
כֹּהֲנֶיךָ יִלְבְּשׁוּ צֶדֶק, וַחֲסִידֶיךָ יְרַנֵּנוּ.
בַּעֲבוּר דָּוִד עַבְדֶּךָ, אַל תָּשֵׁב פְּנֵי מְשִׁיחֶךָ.[3]

---

against the force of evil. God gave us the Torah, the means to vanquish the Evil Inclination and achieve inner peace. As the Sages teach, "[God says:] I created the Evil Inclination, and I created the Torah as an antidote" (*Kiddushin* 30a). The verse might therefore be rendered, "HASHEM will give might [Torah] to His people, [and through it] HASHEM will bless His people with peace" (*Imrei Moshe*).

לְרָצוֹן — (*To*) *find favor*. Just as we conclude the *Shemoneh Esrei* blessings with the word שָׁלוֹם, *peace*, followed by a short prayer that our words find favor before God, so do our introductory verses to the *hakafos* close with שָׁלוֹם, which is also followed by a plea that God accept our words. After the individual *Shemoneh Esrei* prayer, we use the singular form (אִמְרֵי פִי, *the words of my mouth*). Here, however, where the verses are recited in unison, we use the plural (אֲמָרֵינוּ, *our words*).

וְיִהְיוּ נָא אֲמָרֵינוּ לְרָצוֹן — *May our words find favor*. *Emes LeYaakov* offers a homiletic insight: How can one rejoice on Simchas Torah when his spiritual life is such a great disappointment to the Torah? Where do we find the audacity to celebrate the finishing of the Torah and the commencement of a new cycle when we have spent the past year living in a way so incongruous with the Torah's teachings?

It is only due to our repentance on Rosh Hashanah and Yom Kippur and the resolute promises we made to honor and obey the Torah that allow us to join in its joy now. We therefore ask of God, "May our words [i.e., our promises to improve] *find favor, we pray, before the Lord of everything.*" *Toldos Yitzchak* renders the phrase as "May our words express our will that we be in front of God," always aware of His Presence and cognizant of our duties toward Him.

וַיְהִי בִּנְסֹעַ הָאָרֹן — *When the Ark would travel*. When the Holy Ark traveled through the Wilderness towards *Eretz Yisrael*, Moses prayed that God scatter the enemies who wanted to prevent us from entering the Land. Similarly, as we open the Ark in our *shul*, we pray that any impediments to our study of Torah be dispersed and scattered.

קוּמָה ה' לִמְנוּחָתֶךָ — *Arise, HASHEM, to Your resting place*. The next three verses, composed by David, were repeated by Solomon, with minor variations, when he dedicated the Temple (*II Chronicles* 6:41-42). The first verse asks that God establish His resting place among Israel. The next verse refers to the priests, who dedicate themselves to God's service, and the Levites, whose song accompanies the Temple ritual. Finally, the last verse also asks that the site chosen for the Temple — that was

Hakafos / הקפות [166]

May our words find favor,* we pray, before the Lord of everything.[1]

The Ark is opened and the responsive recitation continues:

When the Ark would travel,* Moses would say,
  'Arise, HASHEM, and let Your foes be scattered;
  let those who hate You flee from You.'[2]
Arise, HASHEM, to Your resting place,*
  You and the Ark of Your strength.
Let Your priests be clothed in righteousness,
  and Your devout ones will sing joyously.*
For the sake of David, Your servant,
  turn not away the face of Your anointed.[3]

---

(1) *Psalms* cf. 19:15. (2) *Numbers* 10:35. (2) *Psalms* 132:8-10.

---

designated by David and the prophet Nathan — not be spurned by God, but that it remain eternally holy. With this prayer God was invited, so to speak, to move from His temporary abode in the *Mishkan* to His permanent resting place in the *Beis HaMikdash*.

Our recitation of these verses indicates our desire to celebrate Simchas Torah in the rebuilt Temple. There we will recognize the Divine Presence and declare (*Isaiah* 25:9), "Behold! — this is our God ..." This also fulfills: *I shall bring Jerusalem to mind at the onset of my rejoicing* (*Psalms* 137:6).

אַתָּה וַאֲרוֹן עֻזֶּךְ — *You and the Ark of Your strength.* This alludes to the Ark's entry into the Holy of Holies at the dedication of the Temple. A glorious cloud appeared and accompanied the Ark (*II Chronicles* 5:14). This cloud embodied the essence of God's Presence and demonstrated that the *Shechinah* resided in the Temple with manifest intensity and עֹז, *strength* (*Radak*).

אַל תָּשֵׁב פְּנֵי מְשִׁיחֶךְ — *Turn not away the face of Your anointed.* These words ask God not to reject David (*Radak*) and his anointed son Solomon (*Rashi*).

The Talmud (*Shabbos* 30a) explains the deeper meaning of this verse: David

pleaded with God to demonstrate publicly that He had forgiven his impropriety with Bathsheba. Hashem replied: "During your lifetime I shall not make My forgiveness known, but during the life of Solomon, your son, I shall do so." After Solomon completed the construction of the Temple, he sought to bring the Ark into the Holy of Holies. However, the gates were fastened together and they refused to open. Solomon then pleaded before God with twenty-four רְנָנוֹת, *cries of prayer*, but still he was not answered. Other forms of entreaty also failed, until Solomon said, *O HASHEM, turn not away the face of Your anointed; remember the devout deeds of David, Your servant* (*II Chronicles* 6:42). Immediately, Solomon was answered, and the gates opened. Thus it became known to one and all that God had forgiven David's misconduct, for He had not *turned away the face of His anointed* king.

According to the Talmud (*Moed Kattan* 9a), this public vindication of King David occurred on Shemini Atzeres, as the verse teaches: *On the eighth day he released the people, and they blessed the king; they went to their tents joyous and good hearted over the good HASHEM did for His servant David and His*

[167] **SIMCHAS TORAH** — Its Significance, Laws, and Prayers

וְאָמַר בַּיּוֹם הַהוּא,* הִנֵּה אֱלֹהֵינוּ זֶה, קִוִּינוּ לוֹ וְיוֹשִׁיעֵנוּ,*
זֶה יהוה קִוִּינוּ לוֹ, נָגִילָה וְנִשְׂמְחָה בִּישׁוּעָתוֹ.¹
מַלְכוּתְךָ מַלְכוּת כָּל עֹלָמִים,* וּמֶמְשַׁלְתְּךָ בְּכָל דּוֹר וָדֹר.²
כִּי מִצִּיּוֹן תֵּצֵא תוֹרָה,* וּדְבַר יהוה מִירוּשָׁלָיִם.³

All, in unison:

אַב הָרַחֲמִים, הֵיטִיבָה בִרְצוֹנְךָ אֶת צִיּוֹן,* תִּבְנֶה חוֹמוֹת
יְרוּשָׁלָיִם.⁴ כִּי בְךָ לְבַד בָּטֶחְנוּ, מֶלֶךְ אֵל רָם וְנִשָּׂא,
אֲדוֹן עוֹלָמִים.

All the Torah scrolls are removed from the Ark and members of the congregation are given the honor of
carrying them during the procession. In some congregations, a lit candle, symbolizing the light of Torah, is
placed in the Ark while it is empty.
Some recite a kabbalistic prayer as the Torah scrolls are removed from the Ark.

FIRST *HAKAFAH*-CIRCUIT

As the Torah scrolls are carried around the *bimah*, each of the following verses is recited by the *chazzan* or
hakafah leader and is then repeated by the congregation:

אָנָּא יהוה,* הוֹשִׁיעָה נָּא.

---

people Israel (*I Kings* 8:66). "The good
Hashem did for His servant David" was
the public sign that God had accepted
his repentance (see *Shabbos* 30a).

וְאָמַר בַּיּוֹם הַהוּא — *He shall say on that
day.* The Talmud (*Taanis* 31a) teaches
that in the future God will make a circle
of all the righteous people in the Garden
of Eden, and He will sit in the middle of
the circle. Each and every person in the
circle will point toward God and declare
the words of this verse: *Behold! — this is
our God; we hoped to Him and He
saved us; this is* HASHEM *to Whom we
hoped; let us exult and be glad in His
salvation* (*Isaiah* 25:9). The meaning is
that God will reveal Himself in a significant way to the righteous, who will
perceive the revelation clearly. This is
the symbolism of the circle, in which all
points are equidistant from the center.
Likewise, all the righteous who are privileged to join this circle will be in equal
proximity to the Divine light emanating
from the center (*Pri Tzaddik*).

On Simchas Torah, the day of Jewish
unity when everyone in the nation has a
share in the joy of Torah, we make
hakafos and form circles around the
Torah, in anticipation of the ultimate
great circle in our future.

קִוִּינוּ לוֹ וְיוֹשִׁיעֵנוּ — *We hoped to Him and
He saved us.* Here Isaiah speaks of *our*
being saved, and later in the verse of *His*
salvation. What is the difference? *Yisa
Berachah* explains: On the Days of Awe
we implore God to save us by dint of our
merits. This salvation is *ours*, something
we earned on our own. However, a
salvation based on merit is limited and
may not endure for very long. (If our
actions take a turn for the worse, we
may find ourselves without sufficient
merit.) We therefore implore God to
provide us with eternal salvation — *His*
salvation — on this day of unbridled joy
so that we may exult in an eternal
assurance.

Alternatively, this verse conveys a
cardinal principle of Judaism. Since God

He shall say on that day,* 'Behold! — this is our God;
we hoped to Him and He saved us;* this is HASHEM to Whom we hoped;
let us exult and be glad in His salvation.' [1]
Your kingdom is a kingdom spanning all eternities,*
and Your dominion is throughout every generation. [2]
For from Zion the Torah will come forth,*
and the word of HASHEM from Jerusalem. [3]

All, in unison:

אַב הָרַחֲמִים *Father of compassion, do good to Zion according to Your will;* rebuild the walls of Jerusalem.* [4] *For we trust in You alone, O King, God, exalted and uplifted, Master of worlds.*

All the Torah scrolls are removed from the Ark and members of the congregation are given the honor of carrying them during the procession. In some congregations, a lit candle, symbolizing the light of Torah, is placed in the Ark while it is empty.

Some recite a kabbalistic prayer as the Torah scrolls are removed from the Ark.

FIRST HAKAFAH-CIRCUIT

As the Torah scrolls are carried around the *bimah,* each of the following verses is recited by the *chazzan* or *hakafah* leader and is then repeated by the congregation:

Please, HASHEM,* save now!

---

(1) *Isaiah* 25:9. (2) *Psalms* 145:13. (3) *Isaiah* 2:3; *Micah* 4:2. (4) *Psalms* 51:20.

---

grants man free will to act as he desires, the realization of His will in this world is not, so to speak, in His hands; He is "bound" by man's actions (see *Rashba* to *Berachos* 7a). We therefore hope for our personal salvation so that we may live according to His will, which will make us appropriate agents for the world's salvation and the fulfillment of its mission (*Simchas Aharon*).

מַלְכוּתְךָ מַלְכוּת כָּל עֹלָמִים — *Your kingdom is a kingdom spanning all eternities.* R' Hirsch notes that no royal dynasty endures forever; ultimately, the tide of history will sweep away even the most glorious imperial family. As the generations change, people's perception of leadership changes, and they demand a new order of rulers. The only Monarch who endures forever is Hashem; He leads mankind steadily towards the goal of Creation, which is known to Him alone. As we take the Torah in our

hands and pledge our loyalty to it and its Giver, we declare that our pledge is eternal, for our King is eternal (*Imrei Moshe*).

כִּי מִצִּיּוֹן תֵּצֵא תוֹרָה — *For from Zion the Torah will come forth.* Having expressed our desire for God's redemption, we explain that Jerusalem is the primary source of the Torah's most profound wisdom.

הֵיטִיבָה בִרְצוֹנְךָ אֶת צִיּוֹן — *Do good to Zion according to Your will.* Only in God's chosen Sanctuary can the study of Torah and celebration of the completion of its annual reading attain their greatest heights. Thus we pray for the rebuilding of Zion and the Temple.

אָנָּא ה' — *Please, HASHEM.* Each *hakafah* starts with three Scriptural verses, all of which begin with אָנָּא ה', *Please, HASHEM.* The first verse contains the prayer to *save,* the second to *bring*

---

[169] **SIMCHAS TORAH** — Its Significance, Laws, and Prayers

אָנָּא יהוה,* הַצְלִיחָה נָא.[1]
אָנָּא יהוה, עֲנֵנוּ בְיוֹם קָרְאֵנוּ.[2]
אֱלֹהֵי הָרוּחוֹת,* הוֹשִׁיעָה נָא.[3]
בּוֹחֵן לְבָבוֹת,* הַצְלִיחָה נָא.[4]
גּוֹאֵל חָזָק,* עֲנֵנוּ בְיוֹם קָרְאֵנוּ.[5]

In some congregations the responsive recitation continues:

שְׁמַע יִשְׂרָאֵל, יהוה אֱלֹהֵינוּ יהוה אֶחָד.[6]

---

success and the third to *answer*. These same expressions are repeated in the three verses that follow — and in each of the seven *hakafos* — where they are introduced by different titles for God, in the order of the first three letters of the *aleph-beis*, i.e., אֱלֹהֵי הָרוּחוֹת הוֹשִׁיעָה נָא, *God of the spirits, save now*, and so on.

The *piyut* was composed anonymously, probably prior to the fourteenth century, and was recited as the Torah scrolls were brought to the *bimah*. Some scholars surmise that it was originally intended as a *Hoshana* prayer. Most of its stanzas are examples of the Talmudic dictum (*Megillah* 31a): "Wherever you find God's greatness, there you find His humility." In them we find His awesome majesty contrasted with His care and protection of the lowly.

In many congregations these verses are followed by verses that declare God's Oneness, His eternality and His choice of Israel to receive His Torah and His blessings of peace.

These verses are recited loudly and responsively by the *chazzan* and congregation. Then, after each of the seven *hakafos*, many individuals recite a series of verses that allude to that *hakafah*. Each series comprises verses taken from five sources: (a) *Psalms* 18:8-11, which enumerates seven benefits of Torah

study; (b) *Psalms* 29, which contains the expression קוֹל ה', *the voice of HASHEM*, seven times; (c) *Psalms* 67, which contains seven verses (excluding the introductory verse); (d) the mystic prayer אָנָּא בְּכֹחַ, *We beg You, with the strength*, which is composed of seven stanzas; and (e) the verses recited after each of the Hoshana Rabbah *hakafos*. In most *machzorim* these verses are followed by a *piyut* which is either unique to Simchas Torah or borrowed from elsewhere in the prayers.

Each *hakafah's* liturgy concludes with a reference to the Patriarch associated with it and a kabbalistic prayer that alludes to that Patriarch and to the relevant *sefirah*-emanation.

אָנָּא ה' — *Please, HASHEM.* Ateres Yehoshua notes that אָנָּא ה' is the *gematria* equivalent of לֶחֶם (78). We recite it three times in each *hakafah* to symbolize three things in life that the Torah compares to לֶחֶם, *bread*. Torah itself is called לֶחֶם (see *Proverbs* 9:5); one's wife is allegorically called לֶחֶם (*Genesis* 39:6); and sustenance, the bread of life, is also called לֶחֶם (*Psalms* 37:25). While we all yearn to partake heartily of the bread of Torah, our obligations to family and the often spiritually debilitating pursuit of a livelihood frequently do not allow us to learn Torah to our souls' content. We therefore beseech three times, "אָנָּא ה'"

Please, HASHEM,* bring success now![1]*

Please, HASHEM, answer us on the day we call.[2]

God of the spirits,[3]* save now!*

Tester of hearts,[4]* bring success now!*

O Powerful Redeemer,[5]* answer us on the day we call!*

In some congregations the responsive recitation continues:

Hear, O Israel: HASHEM is our God, HASHEM the One and Only.[6]

---

(1) *Psalms* 118:25. (2) Cf. 20:10. (3) *Numbers* 27:16. (4) Cf. *Psalms* 7:10.
(5) Cf. *Jeremiah* 50:34. (6) *Deuteronomy* 6:4.

(which equals לֶחֶם), asking that neither domestic nor professional responsibilities stand in the way of our pursuit of Torah, the true bread of life.

אָנָּא ה׳ הַצְלִיחָה נָא — *Please, HASHEM, bring success now!* What is the greatest blessing one can give a father of children? That he be successful with his children and that they bring him much joy and *nachas.* This is our wish for our Father — that He succeed with His children, and that we give Him reason to be proud of us and our loyalty to Him and His Torah and *mitzvos* (R' Yechezkel of Kuzmir).

◆§ FIRST HAKAFAH §◆

אֱלֹהֵי הָרוּחוֹת — *God of the spirits.* When Moses asked God to appoint a leader who would replace him upon his death, he spoke of God's knowledge of the intricacies of the human mind and personality, virtues and foibles; he also mentioned that the best way to lead is to understand the needs of every follower (*Numbers* 27:16). He was implying that the sort of leader he intended was one who embodied these Godly characteristics to whatever extent possible so that he would be able to accommodate the individual needs of all the Jews (*Rashi ad loc.*).

As we ask God to save us in this *hakafah,* we must realize that ultimately it is only He Who truly knows what our needs are. We beseech the God of the spirits, Who knows intimately the nature and needs of each individual — save us!

בּוֹחֵן לְבָבוֹת הַצְלִיחָה נָא — *Tester of hearts, bring success now!* God knows each person's spirit and tests his heart to determine his innermost thoughts. Man, however, cannot judge his fellow by anything other than external actions (*R' Nosson Scherman*).

The Sages interpret the command to love God בְּכָל לְבָבְךָ as an instruction to marshal the forces of both the good and evil inclinations in God's service. [While לֵב means heart, לְבַב infers both the good and evil wills in man.] Here we ask God, Who tests and knows the strength of both our "hearts," to take into consideration our vulnerability in combating the evil within, and to grant us spiritual success (*Yisa Berachah*).

גּוֹאֵל חָזָק — *O Powerful Redeemer.* This phrase appears in the weekday *Amidah,* where we ask God to redeem us speedily *for You are a powerful Redeemer.* God is All Powerful and can dissolve even seemingly insurmountable obstacles in order to bring about Redemption. Just as He completely overturned the rules of nature in order to redeem the Jewish people miraculously from Egypt, so He can overcome all impediments which

יְהוֹה מֶלֶךְ,[1] יְהוֹה מָלָךְ,[2] יְהוֹה יִמְלֹךְ לְעֹלָם וָעֶד.[3]
יְהוֹה מֶלֶךְ, יְהוֹה מָלָךְ, יְהוֹה יִמְלֹךְ לְעֹלָם וָעֶד.
יְהוֹה עֹז לְעַמּוֹ יִתֵּן, יְהוֹה יְבָרֵךְ אֶת עַמּוֹ בַשָּׁלוֹם.[4]

Some recite all or some of the following paragraphs:

תּוֹרַת יְהוֹה תְּמִימָה,* מְשִׁיבַת נָפֶשׁ.* מִזְמוֹר לְדָוִד, הָבוּ לַיהוֹה בְּנֵי
אֵלִים,* הָבוּ לַיהוֹה כָּבוֹד וָעֹז. הָבוּ לַיהוֹה כְּבוֹד שְׁמוֹ, הִשְׁתַּחֲווּ
לַיהוֹה בְּהַדְרַת קֹדֶשׁ. קוֹל יְהוֹה עַל הַמָּיִם, אֵל הַכָּבוֹד הִרְעִים, יְהוֹה עַל
מַיִם רַבִּים.[6] לַמְנַצֵּחַ בִּנְגִינֹת* מִזְמוֹר שִׁיר. אֱלֹהִים יְחָנֵּנוּ וִיבָרְכֵנוּ,* יָאֵר
פָּנָיו אִתָּנוּ* סֶלָה.[7] אָנָּא, בְּכֹחַ גְּדֻלַּת יְמִינֶךָ, תַּתִּיר צְרוּרָה. כִּי אָמַרְתִּי,
עוֹלָם חֶסֶד יִבָּנֶה.*[8]

---

stand in the way of providing the ultimate salvation for His people (Simchas Aharon).

תּוֹרַת ה׳ תְּמִימָה — *The Torah of HASHEM is perfect.* When is the Torah of Hashem perfect? When it comes from the mouths of those who are perfect [i.e., when it is studied sincerely and unselfishly] (*Midrash Shocher Tov*).

Tosafos (*Megillah* 32a, s.v. גוללו) tells of the following custom: When the Torah is taken out of the Ark, it is customary to recite four verses in *Psalms* 19, beginning with תּוֹרַת ה׳ תְּמִימָה (*Psalms* 19:8-11) because they note the rewards of Torah study ("*It restores the soul*," "*It makes the simple one wise*," etc.). There are forty words in this section of the psalm (see gloss of the *Bach*, ibid.), which correspond to the forty days during which Moses was taught the Torah in Heaven. Then the reader says, גַּדְּלוּ לַה׳ אִתִּי וּנְרוֹמְמָה שְׁמוֹ יַחְדָּו, *Declare the greatness of HASHEM with me, and we will raise up His Name together.* This expression contains six words, corresponding to the sets of six steps at a time ascended by those who carried the Holy Ark up to Jerusalem in the time of David (*II Samuel* 6:13).

מְשִׁיבַת נָפֶשׁ — *Restoring the soul.* Torah removes the soul from the pathway leading to death and restores it to the pathway leading to life (*Rashi*).

Just as the heavenly lights sustain the earth, so does the Torah provide sustenance for the soul. Like a stranger in a foreign land who has no friends or support, so is the soul a stranger in the human body. The body has many helpers to aid it in its relentless pursuit of its desires. But the soul is a lonely, forsaken captive. Only the Torah provides guidance toward the straight path and restrains man from worldly lusts and obstacles; it redeems the soul from captivity and brings it back to its spiritual source, the place of its original glory (*R' A. C. Feuer*).

בְּנֵי אֵלִים — *Sons of the powerful.* This refers to the descendants of Abraham, Isaac and Jacob, the powerful men of spirit.

The Sages say that אֵלִים refers to the Patriarchs in three senses: They were (1) אֵלִים, *powerful in their faith.* (2) The word אֵילִים also means *rams.* The Patriarchs were willing to be slaughtered like animals for God's sake, particularly Isaac, who was prepared to allow him-

Hakafos / הקפות [172]

HASHEM reigns,[1] HASHEM has reigned,[2] HASHEM shall reign for all eternity.[3]
HASHEM reigns, HASHEM has reigned, HASHEM shall reign for all eternity.
HASHEM will give might to His people,
HASHEM will bless His people with peace.[4]

Some recite all or some of the following paragraphs:

תּוֹרַת The Torah of HASHEM is perfect,* restoring the soul.[5] A psalm of David. Render unto HASHEM, sons of the powerful,* render unto HASHEM honor and might. Render unto HASHEM honor worthy of His Name; prostrate yourselves before HASHEM in His intensely holy place. The voice of HASHEM is upon the waters, the God of Glory thunders, HASHEM is upon vast waters.[6] For the conductor, upon Neginos,* a psalm, a song. May God favor us and bless us,* may He illuminate His countenance with us,* Selah.[7] We beg you! With the strength of Your right hand's greatness, untie the bundled sins. For I have said: The world shall be built with kindness.[8]*

_____

(1) Psalms 10:16. (2) 93:1 et al. (3) Exodus 15:18. (4) Psalms 29:11. (5) 19:8. (6) 29:1-3. (7) 67:1-2. (8) 89:3.

_____

self to be offered as a sacrifice by Abraham (Midrash Shocher Tov). (3) The word can also be read as אֵילִמִים, mute ones. The Patriarchs never responded to God with audacity; they obeyed His commands in silence (Midrash Bereishis Rabbah 56:10).

לַמְנַצֵּחַ בִּנְגִינוֹת — For the conductor, upon Neginos. This psalm describes the bounteous blessings and the redemption which await the children of Israel if they dedicate themselves to the Torah. Its seven verses allude to the seven branches of the Menorah, which is symbolic of Torah, the source of intellectual illumination for Israel.

אֱלֹהִים יְחָנֵּנוּ וִיבָרְכֵנוּ — May God favor us and bless us. "Favor us" although we are undeserving; "bless us" with fertility, for the terrible persecutions of exile have decimated our numbers (Sforno). [This is an appropriate request in the hakafah of Abraham, to whom God promised a multitude of descendants.]

R' S. R. Hirsch explains that חָנַן refers to the granting of intellectual abilities, as

in the first request of the daily prayer, the Shemoneh Esrei, which begins אַתָּה חוֹנֵן לְאָדָם דַּעַת, You graciously endow man with knowledge. Even during the harshness of exile, when so many of our basic needs are unmet, Jewish education and intellectual advancement always remain the prime concern of the Jewish people (R' A. C. Feuer).

יָאֵר פָּנָיו אִתָּנוּ — May He illuminate His countenance with us. God gave us the Torah with the light of His countenance (Daily Prayers). Every time a Jew studies Torah, the Sinaitic revelation repeats itself as God again gives us the Torah along with the light of His countenance. We therefore ask that He illuminate our minds so that we may perceive the wondrous lessons of the Torah.

כִּי אָמַרְתִּי עוֹלָם חֶסֶד יִבָּנֶה — For I have said: The world shall be built with kindness. Abraham was the personification of חֶסֶד (kindness), and for this reason God chose Him to be the progenitor of His chosen people (Simchas Aharon).

[173] **SIMCHAS TORAH** — Its Significance, Laws, and Prayers

יְדִיד נֶפֶשׁ* אָב הָרַחֲמָן, מְשֹׁךְ עַבְדְּךָ* אֶל רְצוֹנֶךָ,* יָרוּץ עַבְדְּךָ כְּמוֹ אַיָּל, יִשְׁתַּחֲוֶה אֶל מוּל הֲדָרֶךָ, יֶעֱרַב לוֹ יְדִידוֹתֶיךָ, מִנֹּפֶת צוּף* וְכָל טָעַם.

הָדוּר נָאֶה זִיו הָעוֹלָם, נַפְשִׁי חוֹלַת אַהֲבָתֶךָ,* אָנָּא אֵל נָא רְפָא נָא לָהּ,* בְּהַרְאוֹת לָהּ נְעַם זִיוֶךָ, אָז תִּתְחַזֵּק וְתִתְרַפֵּא,* וְהָיְתָה לָהּ שִׂמְחַת עוֹלָם.

וָתִיק יֶהֱמוּ נָא רַחֲמֶיךָ, וְחוּסָה* נָּא עַל בֵּן אֲהוּבֶךָ,* כִּי זֶה כַּמָּה נִכְסֹף נִכְסַפְתִּי, לִרְאוֹת מְהֵרָה בְּתִפְאֶרֶת עֻזֶּךָ, אֵלֶּה חָמְדָה לִבִּי, וְחוּסָה נָּא וְאַל תִּתְעַלָּם.

יְדִיד נֶפֶשׁ — *Beloved of the soul.* The composer of this *piyut* is R' Eliezer Azikri, one of the great kabbalists and halachists of the sixteenth century. He lived in *Eretz Yisrael*, and his major work was *Sefer Charedim.* A central theme of his moral and liturgical writings is the intense love one must feel for God, a theme which is readily apparent in the *piyut.* The acrostic of the four verses forms the four-letter Divine Name.

God is both man's Beloved and Friend, and his merciful Father (אָב הָרַחֲמָן). Man can share his aspirations and dreams with God as with a close friend; he can also turn to God as a merciful Father in moments of distress, to unburden himself of pain and frustration.

מְשֹׁךְ עַבְדְּךָ — *Draw Your servant.* We plead with God to take the first step toward bringing us closer to His Will. We assure Him that if He takes the initiative, then יָרוּץ עַבְדְּךָ כְּמוֹ אַיָּל, *Your servant will hurry like a hart;* if God but helps us begin, we will continue with the alacrity of a hart. This plea and assurance are based on *Song of Songs* 1:4 as it is understood by most commentators.

אֶל רְצוֹנֶךָ — *To Your will.* It is insufficient for a Jew to be a servant of God who *does* what He wants; one must also *want* what He wants. We implore God to inspire us to change ourselves from ser-

vants who are merely obedient to loving subjects who willingly serve Him (*Imrei Moshe*).

יֶעֱרַב לוֹ יְדִידוֹתֶיךָ מִנֹּפֶת צוּף — *To him Your friendship will be sweeter than the dripping of the honeycomb.* Honey is the sweetest of delicacies. Nevertheless, its taste lingers for only a brief while, and too much can cause discomfort. God's friendship, however, is sweeter because it endures forever, becoming more beneficial the closer one draws to Him (*Radak* to *Psalms* 19:11).

[Alternatively, נֹפֶת צוּף is an allusion to the manna, which tasted like honey and yet, according to the Sages, could assume any taste according to the wishes of those who ate it. We say to God here that His friendship is even sweeter, assuming all the "tastes" appropriate for our emotional and spiritual survival.]

נַפְשִׁי חוֹלַת אַהֲבָתֶךָ — *My soul pines for Your love.* The soul that yearns for God's closeness grows lovesick, much like a person who is denied the closeness of his beloved.

Rambam (*Hilchos Teshuvah* 10:3) poetically captures the spirit of this lovesickness: "The proper love of God is a great, overwhelming and intensely passionate love, with one's soul bound up in the love of God. One should find himself blessed with this love constantly, much

יְדִיד נֶפֶשׁ *Beloved of the soul,* Compassionate Father, draw Your servant* to Your will.* Then Your servant will hurry like a hart to bow before Your majesty. To him Your friendship will be sweeter than the dripping of the honeycomb* and any taste.*

ה *Majestic, Beautiful, Radiance of the universe — my soul pines for Your love.* Please, O God, heal her now* by showing her the pleasantness of Your radiance. Then she will be strengthened and healed,* and eternal gladness will be hers.*

ו *All-worthy One — may Your mercy be aroused and please take pity* on the son of Your beloved,* because it is so very long that I have yearned intensely* to see the splendor of Your strength. Only these my heart desired, so please take pity and do not conceal Yourself.*

---

like one who is lovesick and cannot remove his attention from the love of a particular woman, constantly thinking of her, at rest or at work, [even] when he eats and drinks. The love of God in the hearts of those who love Him should be even greater than this ... This is what King Solomon said metaphorically, *For I am lovesick* (*Song of Songs* 2:5). The entire *Song of Songs* is but a parable to describe this intense love."

אָנָּא אֵל נָא רְפָא נָא לָהּ — *Please, O God, heal her now.* The wording of the plea is taken from Moses' prayer for his sister Miriam, who was stricken with leprosy in punishment for her criticism of him (*Numbers* 12:1-13). She was convinced that Moses had wronged his wife by separating himself from her, but her assessment was based on an erroneous understanding of the status and requirements imposed by her brother's continuous prophecy. Had she realized, she would not have suffered this punishing illness. Our *zemer* goes on to say that removal of the symptoms of illness is not enough — the soul must be shown God's *radiance* so that it will not sin again (*R' Avie Gold*).

אָז תִּתְחַזֵּק וְתִתְרַפֵּא — *Then she will be strengthened and healed.* Generally, a patient is healed first and later regains his strength. In this case, however, the illness came about only because the spiritual

level of the soul was weak. Once that holiness is strengthened, the healing will come naturally (*Ahavas Shalom*).

וְחוּסָה נָא עַל בֶּן אֲהוּבֶךְ — *And please take pity on the son of Your beloved.* We beseech God to take pity on Israel, the offspring of Abraham, whom God loved.

וְחוּסָה — *Take pity.* Malbim (Ezekiel 7:4,9) explains the difference between two words for *pity*: חָמַל and חוּס. The first one, חָמַל, refers to concern for the sake of another — one feels compassion for a sick child because he loves the *child*. The second, חוּס, represents the concern one feels for selfish reasons — a farmer may be reluctant to destroy a mule because he needs it to do his *own* work. Therefore, we may interpret the use of וְחוּסָה here as a plea that God take pity on Israel for His *own* sake, since His people, whatever their deficiencies, are the only ones who study His Torah, obey His commandments and teach His word (*R' Nosson Scherman*).

נִכְסֹף נִכְסַפְתִּי — *That I have yearned intensely* [literally, *yearn have I yearned*]. The double expression נִכְסֹף נִכְסַפְתִּי, *yearn have I yearned*, indicates the overpowering nature of the yearning. Laban used it to describe Jacob's strong urge to return home to his parents (see *Rashi* and *Sforno* to *Genesis* 31:30). In Jacob's case,

הַגְלֵה נָא וּפְרֹשׂ חֲבִיבִי עָלַי, אֶת סֻכַּת שְׁלוֹמֶךָ, תָּאִיר אֶרֶץ מִכְּבוֹדֶךָ,* נָגִילָה וְנִשְׂמְחָה בָּךְ. מַהֵר אֱהֹב* כִּי בָא מוֹעֵד,* וְחָנֵּנוּ כִּימֵי עוֹלָם.

שְׁכִינָה הַקְּדוֹשָׁה בְּתוֹכֵנוּ, זְכוּתֵהּ דְּאַבְרָהָם עִמָּנוּ, וְשָׁם נִשְׂמַח כֻּלָּנוּ, בְּבוֹא לְצִיּוֹן בְּרִנָּנָה. רַחֲמָנָא אִדְכַּר לָן זְכוּתֵהּ דְּאַבְרָהָם רְחִימָא.

אָנָּא יהוה, הוֹשִׁיעָה נָּא.
אָנָּא יהוה, הַצְלִיחָה נָּא.
אָנָּא יהוה, עֲנֵנוּ בְיוֹם קָרְאֵנוּ.

דּוֹבֵר צְדָקוֹת,* הוֹשִׁיעָה נָּא.
הָדוּר בִּלְבוּשׁוֹ,[1]* הַצְלִיחָה נָּא.
וָתִיק וְחָסִיד,* עֲנֵנוּ בְיוֹם קָרְאֵנוּ.

In some congregations the responsive recitation continues:

שְׁמַע יִשְׂרָאֵל, יהוה אֱלֹהֵינוּ יהוה אֶחָד.
יהוה מֶלֶךְ, יהוה מָלָךְ, יהוה יִמְלֹךְ לְעוֹלָם וָעֶד.
יהוה מֶלֶךְ, יהוה מָלָךְ, יהוה יִמְלֹךְ לְעוֹלָם וָעֶד.
יהוה עֹז לְעַמּוֹ יִתֵּן, יהוה יְבָרֵךְ אֶת עַמּוֹ בַשָּׁלוֹם.

---

he had been in a spiritual exile in Laban's household for twenty years. Understandably, he felt a powerful longing to return to the holiness of his father Isaac's proximity. The analogy describes the soul, which is trapped in a flesh-and-blood body in a material world but feels an uncontrollable yearning to see the splendor of God's strength (R' Nosson Scherman).

תָּאִיר אֶרֶץ מִכְּבוֹדֶךָ — *Illuminate the world with Your glory.* We live in a world of spiritual distortions, where our perceptions are clouded. In the Messianic age, God will cast the light of His glory upon the world so that we will once again perceive truth clearly.

מַהֵר אֱהֹב — *Hasten, show love.* That God

retains His love for Israel is unquestioned, but in the length and severity of the exile, this love is barely perceptible. Therefore, we ask God to make His love manifest.

כִּי בָא מוֹעֵד — *For the time has come.* Just as the Jewish nation would have been spiritually aborted if God had not extricated them from Egypt before they succumbed to its impurity, so we fear remaining in exile too long. We say to God that the time has come and we ask Him to act swiftly before it is too late (*Simchas Aharon*).

❧ SECOND HAKAFAH ❧

דּוֹבֵר צְדָקוֹת — *Speaker of righteousness.* The second *hakafah* is associated with

ה *Please be revealed and spread upon me, my Beloved, the shelter of Your peace. Illuminate the world with Your glory* that we may rejoice and be glad with You. Hasten, show love,* for the time has come,* and show us grace as in days of old.*

The holy Shechinah is among us, the merit of **Abraham** *is with us;*
May we all rejoice there upon arriving at Zion with glad song.
O Merciful One, remember for our sake the merit of beloved **Abraham.**

SECOND HAKAFAH-CIRCUIT

---

*Please, H*ASHEM*, save now!*
*Please, H*ASHEM*, bring success now!*
*Please, H*ASHEM*, answer us on the day we call.*

Speaker of righteousness,* save now!
Majestic One in His garb,[1]* bring success now!
Faithful and Devout One,* answer us on the day we call!

In some congregations the responsive recitation continues:

*Hear, O Israel: H*ASHEM *is our God, H*ASHEM *the One and Only.*
*H*ASHEM *reigns, H*ASHEM *has reigned, H*ASHEM *shall reign for all eternity.*
*H*ASHEM *reigns, H*ASHEM *has reigned, H*ASHEM *shall reign for all eternity.*
*H*ASHEM *will give might to His people, H*ASHEM *will bless His people with peace.*

---

(1) Cf. *Isaiah* 63:1.

Isaac. The Talmud (*Shabbos* 89b) relates that in the future God will ask each of the Patriarchs to defend the Jewish people against the charge that they have sinned. Neither Abraham nor Jacob will offer a defense: "Let them be erased to sanctify Your Name," they will reply. Only Isaac will counter with the argument, "Are they my children and not Yours?" He will then continue to defend us in front of our Maker (see ibid.). We ask of God that He mirror Isaac and serve as our advocate (*Yisa Berachah*).

הָדוּר בִּלְבוּשׁוֹ — *Majestic One in His garb.* This stanza is based on the Sages' interpretation of *Isaiah* 63:1, which says that "someone" with bloodied clothes will come from Edom. In the language of prophecy, this refers to God, Who is portrayed metaphorically as a warrior soiled by the blood of his slain foe. The Jews

will then ask, "Who is this Whose clothes are stained with blood? He has always been majestic in His garb!"

And God will reply, "It is I, the Speaker of righteousness, abundantly able to save."

When the proper time comes, God will avenge Himself on Edom for its outrages against Israel. However, as the Sages teach, no nation can be defeated on earth until its guardian angel is stripped of his power above. Consequently, when the End of Days comes, God will destroy the angel of Edom, which is also the angel of evil.

נָתִיק וְחָסִיד — *Faithful and Devout One.* God remains loyal to us even when we act unfaithfully toward Him. This is an expression of His חֶסֶד; He is kind to us even when we do not deserve it (*Imrei Moshe*).

עֵדוּת יהוה נֶאֱמָנָה,* מַחְכִּימַת פֶּתִי.*[1] קוֹל יהוה, בַּכֹּחַ.[2] לָדַעַת
בָּאָרֶץ דַּרְכֶּךָ,* בְּכָל גּוֹיִם יְשׁוּעָתֶךָ.[3] קַבֵּל רִנַּת עַמְּךָ, שַׂגְּבֵנוּ,
טַהֲרֵנוּ, נוֹרָא. לְךָ זְרוֹעַ עִם גְּבוּרָה, תָּעֹז יָדְךָ, תָּרוּם יְמִינֶךָ.[4]

אֵל מִסְתַּתֵּר* בְּשַׁפְרִיר חֶבְיוֹן,   הַשֵּׂכֶל הַנֶּעְלָם מִכָּל רַעְיוֹן,
עִלַּת הָעִלּוֹת* מֻכְתָּר בְּכֶתֶר עֶלְיוֹן,*   כֶּתֶר יִתְּנוּ לְךָ יהוה.
בְּרֵאשִׁית תּוֹרָתְךָ הַקְּדוּמָה,*   רְשׁוּמָה חָכְמָתְךָ הַסְּתוּמָה,*

נֶאֱמָנָה ה' עֵדוּת — *The testimony of HASHEM is trustworthy.* All of the mitzvos of the Torah are called עֵדוּת, testimony, because they attest to the אֱמוּנָה, faith, of those who fulfill them (*Metzudas David*).

[Furthermore, by following the word of God, Israel testifies to His existence. As the prophet (*Isaiah* 43:10) says, "*You are My witnesses*," *says* HASHEM, "*and I am God.*"]

מַחְכִּימַת פֶּתִי — *Making the simple one wise.* Torah has the power to expand one's intellectual capabilities. Even a simpleton who toils to understand it can become wise. The *Shaloh HaKadosh* asked: How can the Torah possibly *make the simple ones wise?* Does it not say, יָהֵב חָכְמְתָא לְחַכִּימִין, *He gives wisdom only to the wise* (*Daniel* 2:21)? Rather, this means that through Torah study even the unintelligent person will appreciate wisdom enough to realize that he is far from wise.

לָדַעַת בָּאָרֶץ דַּרְכֶּךָ — *To make known Your way on earth.* We ask for intellectual enlightenment so that we will be equipped to spread God's teachings throughout the world. We yearn to guide mankind toward an appreciation of *Your way*, which refers to God's beneficence (*Rashi; Sforno*).

R' S. R. Hirsch notes that God's *way* is a dual concept, for it includes both the manner in which God guides world events, and the pattern of conduct which He has directed man to follow (see *Rambam, Hil. Deios* 4:1). By shining His countenance upon the Jewish nation, God will make known both facets of His *way:* Mankind will recognize that human history is guided along designed paths towards the fulfillment of Divinely ordained goals; in addition, the blessings with which God favors the Jewish people will lead mankind to adhere to the code of human conduct prescribed by His Law and exemplified by the Jews.

אֵל מִסְתַּתֵּר — *God conceals Himself.* This mystical *piyut* was composed by Avraham Maimin, whose name is formed by the acrostic. He lived from 5282-5330 (1522-1570 C.E.) and was a student of the famed kabbalist Rabbi Moshe Cordovero. The eleven stanzas of this *zemer* are often sung during the third meal of the Sabbath. In the *hakafos*, five stanzas are recited for the second *hakafah* and six for the third.

מִסְתַּתֵּר — *Conceals Himself.* Man can have no conception of God Himself, for His true Being is beyond human intelligence. We can know Him only by the way He reveals His behavior to us: with mercy, power, judgment and so on. Since we are incapable of perceiving Him directly, these manifestations can come to us only through intermediaries. In kabbalistic literature, these intermedi-

Some recite all or some of the following paragraphs:

עֵדוּת *The testimony of* HASHEM *is trustworthy,* making the simple one wise.*[1]** The voice of* HASHEM *is in power!*[2] *To make known Your way on earth,* among all the nations Your salvation.*[3] *Accept the prayer of Your nation; strengthen us, purify us, O awesome One. Yours is the arm with strength, show us the power of Your hand, raise high Your right hand.*[4]

א *God conceals Himself* in the beauty of secrecy,*
   the wisdom hidden from all conception,
Primary Cause,* crowned with the most exalted crown* —

                    They give You a crown, O HASHEM*!*
ב *In the beginning there was Your pre-existing Torah**
   Inscribed with Your mysterious wisdom.*

---

(1) *Psalms* 19:8. (2) 29:4. (3) 67:3. (4) 89:14.

---

aries are called *Sefiros*, generally translated as *emanations*.

Although many *mitzvos* related to the *Sefiros* follow a cycle of seven [e.g., the seven *ushpizin*, guests who "visit" the *succah* on the seven days of Succos; the seven *hakafos*, circuits, of Hoshana Rabbah; the seven *hakafos* of Simchas Torah], there are actually ten *Sefiros*. However, the first three are considered to be on a higher plane than the other seven, which are often viewed independently. This *piyut* speaks of all ten *Sefiros* respectively. This introductory stanza, however, opens with the fundamental theme that God Himself chooses to conceal His essence totally from human comprehension. He is, as it were, *in the beauty of secrecy*.

עֵלַת הָעֵלוֹת — *Primary Cause* [literally, *Cause of causes*]. We are accustomed to isolating the primary cause of every event. Once we have separated it from secondary ones, we assume that we understand the development of all succeeding events. For example, a nation's need for markets will shape an overall policy that results in countless economic, military and political initiatives. The truth, however, is that God is the *Cause of all causes*; His will is the primary

determinant of all events (*R' Nosson Scherman*).

מֻכְתָּר בְּכֶתֶר עֶלְיוֹן — *Crowned with the most exalted crown.* Homiletically, *Magen Avraham* comments that God is likened to a human king. A monarch does not don his crown as a symbol of his majesty unless he is certain that the onlookers regard him with proper reverence and obedience. Similarly, God, as it were, is adorned with the crown of majesty when Israel is totally submissive to Him, accepting Him as God and King.

בְּרֵאשִׁית תּוֹרָתְךָ הַקְּדוּמָה — *In the beginning there was Your pre-existing Torah. In the beginning*, when God created heaven and earth, the Torah was already in existence [for 974 generations] (*Damasek Eliezer*). As the *Zohar* states, אִסְתַּכֵּל בְּאוֹרַיְיתָא וּבָרָא עָלְמָא, (*God*) *peered into the Torah and created the universe.* Torah was the plan from which Creation was formed.

רְשׁוּמָה חָכְמָתְךָ הַסְּתוּמָה — *Inscribed with Your mysterious wisdom.* God's wisdom is inscribed in the Torah. It is mysterious in the sense that its full extent is not stated explicitly. Rather, only God's loyal sons, those of the most

[179] **SIMCHAS TORAH** — Its Significance, Laws, and Prayers

מֵאַיִן תִּמָּצֵא* וְהִיא נֶעֶלְמָה,   רֵאשִׁית חָכְמָה יִרְאַת יהוה.*[1]
רְחוֹבוֹת הַנָּהָר נַחֲלֵי אֱמוּנָה,   מַיִם עֲמוּקִים יִדְלֶם אִישׁ תְּבוּנָה,
תּוֹצָאוֹתֶיהָ חֲמִשִּׁים שַׁעֲרֵי בִינָה,   אֱמוּנִים נֹצֵר יהוה.[2]
הָאֵל הַגָּדוֹל עֵינֵי כֹל נֶגְדֶּךָ,   רַב חֶסֶד גָּדוֹל עַל הַשָּׁמַיִם חַסְדֶּךָ,*
אֱלֹהֵי אַבְרָהָם* זְכֹר לְעַבְדֶּךָ,   חַסְדֵי יהוה אַזְכִּיר תְּהִלּוֹת יהוה.[3]
מָרוֹם נֶאְדָּר בְּכֹחַ וּגְבוּרָה,   מוֹצִיא אוֹרָה מֵאַיִן תְּמוּרָה,
פַּחַד יִצְחָק מִשְׁפָּטֵנוּ הָאִירָה,*   אַתָּה גִבּוֹר* לְעוֹלָם יהוה.

שְׁכִינָה הַקְּדוֹשָׁה בְּתוֹכֵנוּ, זְכוּתֵהּ דַּעֲקֵדַת יִצְחָק עִמָּנוּ,
וְשָׁם נִשְׂמַח כֻּלָּנוּ, בְּבוֹא לְצִיּוֹן בְּרִנָּה.
רַחֲמָנָא אִדְכַּר לָן זְכוּתֵהּ דְּיִצְחָק עֲקֵדְתָּא.

אָנָּא יהוה, הוֹשִׁיעָה נָּא
אָנָּא יהוה, הַצְלִיחָה נָּא.
אָנָּא יהוה, עֲנֵנוּ בְיוֹם קָרְאֵנוּ.
זַךְ וְיָשָׁר, הוֹשִׁיעָה נָּא.
חוֹמֵל דַּלִּים,* הַצְלִיחָה נָּא.

---

supreme spiritual standing, are granted the special ability to decipher it.

מֵאַיִן תִּמָּצֵא — *From the Invisible One it derives.* Great Chassidic masters interpreted this homiletically as meaning that Torah can only be received by one who humbly views himself as אַיִן, *nothing (of importance)*. Moses merited to bring the Torah to the Jewish people because of his humility.

רֵאשִׁית חָכְמָה יִרְאַת ה׳ — *The source* [literally, *beginning*] *of wisdom is awe of HASHEM.* The only true wisdom is the Torah, for it is God's own wisdom; and one cannot fathom the truth therein unless he is prepared to negate all his own desires and instincts. The person who feels *awe of HASHEM* recognizes his complete insignificance in relation to the Creator. He is prepared to negate himself completely to God's will — and as a result, he is fit to be a receptacle for Divine wisdom.

עַל הַשָּׁמַיִם חַסְדֶּךָ — *Higher than the heavens is Your kindness.* Vast though the heavens are, they are still part of Creation, and as such they are limited. The kindness of God is infinite, however, exceeding all limitations. This is especially so when Israel serves God לִשְׁמָהּ, *for His Name's sake*, without thought of personal reward (*Rashi* to *Psalms* 108:8). The expression is also meant to stress that the quality of God's mercy is beyond human comprehension (*Ibn Ezra*, ibid.).

חַסְדְּךָ ... אַבְרָהָם — *Your kindness ... Abraham.* Abraham was the embodi-

From the Invisible One it derives,* but it is hidden —
> The source of wisdom is awe of HASHEM!¹*

ר Like a broad flowing river, like faithful streams,
deep waters drawn by the most understanding man.
Its outflows are the fifty gates of understanding —
> Faithful ones are guarded by HASHEM²

ה O great God, all eyes look toward You,
O great One of abundant kindness,
higher than the heavens is Your kindness.*
O God of Abraham,* recall upon Your servant —
> HASHEM's kindness shall I proclaim as praises of HASHEM!³

מ The lofty One adorned with strength and power,
He draws forth light from the unequaled Torah.
O Awesome One of Isaac, illuminate our judgment —*
> You are the mightiest* forever, HASHEM!

The holy Shechinah is among us, the merit of the binding of **Isaac** is with us;
May we all rejoice there, upon arriving at Zion with glad song.
O Merciful One, remember for our sake the merit of **Isaac** who was bound
on the altar.

THIRD HAKAFAH-CIRCUIT

Please, HASHEM, save now!
Please, HASHEM, bring success now!
Please, HASHEM, answer us on the day we call.

Pure and Just One, save now!
He Who pities the poor,* bring success now!

---

(1) *Psalms* 111:10. (2) 31:24. (3) *Isaiah* 63:7.

---

ment of kindness. In his merit, we beseech God to be kind to us. חֶסֶד, *kindness*, is the fourth *Sefirah*.

פַּחַד יִצְחָק מִשְׁפָּטֵנוּ הָאִירָה — *O Awesome One of Isaac, illuminate our judgment.* Isaac represents גְּבוּרָה, *strength*, the fifth *Sefirah*. It refers to the attribute of exercising strict judgment and avoiding undeserved kindness; it also refers to the exercise of extreme caution lest one transgress God's will. Thus, it emphasizes the necessity of fear of God. We now beseech the God of Isaac to shed merciful illumination upon our judgment.

◆⟨ THIRD HAKAFAH ⟩◆

חוֹמֵל דַּלִּים — *He Who pities the poor.* The Midrash teaches that God showed Moses many storehouses of Divine reward; one for those who study Torah, one for those who do good deeds, yet another for those who perform acts of kindness, and so on. Finally God showed him the largest storehouse of all. "Who is this for?" inquired Moses. God answered, "The others are for those who have merits; this storehouse is מַתְּנַת חִנָּם, *a free gift*, for those who lack merit."

The *Avnei Nezer* explains: Those who

טוֹב וּמֵטִיב,* עֲנֵנוּ בְיוֹם קָרְאֵנוּ.

In some congregations the responsive recitation continues:

שְׁמַע יִשְׂרָאֵל, יהוה אֱלֹהֵינוּ יהוה אֶחָד.

יהוה מֶלֶךְ, יהוה מָלָךְ, יהוה יִמְלֹךְ לְעוֹלָם וָעֶד.

יהוה מֶלֶךְ, יהוה מָלָךְ, יהוה יִמְלֹךְ לְעוֹלָם וָעֶד.

יהוה עֹז לְעַמּוֹ יִתֵּן, יהוה יְבָרֵךְ אֶת עַמּוֹ בַשָּׁלוֹם.

Some individuals recite all or some of the following paragraphs:

פִּקּוּדֵי* יהוה יְשָׁרִים, מְשַׂמְּחֵי לֵב.* קוֹל יהוה, בֶּהָדָר.* יוֹדְוּךָ עַמִּים אֱלֹהִים,* יוֹדְוּךָ עַמִּים כֻּלָּם.* נָא גִבּוֹר, דּוֹרְשֵׁי יִחוּדְךָ, כְּבָבַת שָׁמְרֵם. תִּתֵּן אֱמֶת לְיַעֲקֹב, חֶסֶד לְאַבְרָהָם.

מִי אֵל כָּמוֹךָ עוֹשֵׂה גְדוֹלוֹת,   אַבִּיר יַעֲקֹב* נוֹרָא תְהִלּוֹת,* תִּפְאֶרֶת* יִשְׂרָאֵל שׁוֹמֵעַ תְּפִלּוֹת,   כִּי שֹׁמֵעַ אֶל אֶבְיוֹנִים יהוה.*

---

claim reward on the basis of their personal merits are limited in their entitlement. However, those who realize that all the good they may have done is insignificant in comparison to the endless favors God bestows upon them come to Him with תַחֲנוּנִים, *entreaties,* for מַתְּנַת חִנָּם, an undeserved gift which is not related to their merits. That storehouse is the largest, for it is not limited by what a person deserves.

The expression חוֹמֵל דַּלִּים refers here to God as pitying those who are spiritually impoverished. We invoke this attribute in asking Him to shower us with His blessings (*Imrei Moshe*).

טוֹב וּמֵטִיב — *Good and Beneficent One.* King David asks God for enlightenment in Torah with the words: *You are good and beneficent; teach me Your statutes* (Psalms 119:68).

The commentators offer many explanations for the phrase *good and beneficent* as attributes of God: *You are good* in this world *and You are beneficent* in the World to Come; *You are good* to the

forefathers *and You are beneficent* to their children after them (*Midrash Shocher Tov*); *You are good* even without a request and *You are beneficent* to those who ask for Your help (*Ibn Ezra*); *You are good,* because You have given us a good Torah and *mitzvos,* and *You are beneficent* because You enlighten us with understanding and appreciation of Your *mitzvos* (*Sforno*).

On this day when we link our destiny to the Torah, we ask God to teach us His statutes.

פִּקּוּדֵי — *The orders.* This word is derived from פְּקוּדָה, *order* or *command,* and is also related to פִּקָּדוֹן, *deposit* (*R' S. R. Hirsch*).

God has deposited into the very soul of man the capacity to appreciate the importance of these Divine commands, as well as an instinctive understanding of their significance (*Ibn Ezra; Radak*).

מְשַׂמְּחֵי לֵב — *Gladdening the heart.* The wise man will rejoice when his straight and upright intellect dominates the lowly passions of the body and steers

Good and Beneficent One,[1]* answer us on the day we call!

In some congregations the responsive recitation continues:

Hear, O Israel: HASHEM is our God, HASHEM the One and Only. ·
HASHEM reigns, HASHEM has reigned, HASHEM shall reign for all eternity.
HASHEM reigns, HASHEM has reigned, HASHEM shall reign for all eternity.
HASHEM will give might to His people, HASHEM will bless His people with peace.

Some individuals recite all or some of the following paragraphs:

פְּקוּדֵי *The orders* of HASHEM are upright, gladdening the heart.[2]* the voice of HASHEM is in majesty![3]* The nations will acknowledge You, O God,* the nations will acknowledge You, all of them.[4] Please, O strong One — those who foster Your Oneness, guard them like the pupil of an eye. Grant truth to Jacob, kindness to Abraham.[5]*

מ *What power can match You, O Doer of great deeds,*
   Champion of Jacob,* too awesome to praise,*
Splendor* of Israel Who hearkens to prayers —

For attentive to the needy is HASHEM![6]*

---

(1) Cf. *Psalms* 119:68. (2) 19:9. (3) 29:4. (4) 67:4. (5) *Micah* 7:20. (6) *Psalms* 69:34.

---

him properly (*Radak*). [Torah provides one with the joy and serenity of being in control of his own life.]

קוֹל ה׳ בֶּהָדָר — *The voice of Hashem is in majesty. Radak* comments that these words describe the deadly voice with which God will destroy our enemies in the future Messianic war of Gog and Magog, but which will leave Israel completely unharmed. Thus, the very same voice which is בַּכֹּחַ, in [*devastating*] strength for our enemies, will be בֶּהָדָר, in *majesty* and salvation for us.

יוֹדוּךְ עַמִּים אֱלֹהִים — *The nations will acknowledge You, O God.* Gradually, Israel's illuminating influence will spread God's teachings amongst the nations, until every nation will acknowledge Him and pay Him homage (*R' S. R. Hirsch*).

אֲבִיר יַעֲקֹב — *Champion of Jacob.* The term was used by Jacob himself when he conferred his blessing upon Joseph (*Genesis* 49:24). As the context there indicates, it refers to God as the Savior

Who rescues people from enmity and adversity.

נוֹרָא תְהִלּוֹת — *Too awesome to praise.* God is far too great for us to praise Him adequately. Therefore, whatever we say of Him, in a sense, contains an element of disrespect because it omits essentials; it would be as if someone were to praise the sun by saying that it is even brighter than a candle.

יַעֲקֹב ... תִּפְאֶרֶת — *Jacob ... Splendor.* Jacob represents the attribute of תִּפְאֶרֶת, splendor, which is the proper blend of חֶסֶד, kindness (Abraham's primary characteristic), and גְּבוּרָה, strength (Isaac's primary characteristic). Because Jacob was able to unify kindness and strength in the best proportion, he is described by the Sages as the "most chosen" of the Patriarchs. תִּפְאֶרֶת, splendor, is the sixth *Sefirah*.

כִּי שֹׁמֵעַ אֶל אֶבְיוֹנִים ה׳ — *For attentive to the needy is HASHEM.* God is intrinsically pure and just; He pities the poor and provides for them.

זֶה זְכוּת אָבוֹת יָגֵן עָלֵינוּ,   נֶצַח יִשְׂרָאֵל מִצָּרוֹתֵינוּ גְּאָלֵנוּ,*
וּמִבּוֹר גָּלוּת דְּלֵנוּ וְהַעֲלֵנוּ,*   לְנַצֵּחַ עַל מְלֶאכֶת בֵּית יהוה.¹
מִיָּמִין וּמִשְּׂמֹאל* יְנִיקַת הַנְּבִיאִים,*   נֶצַח וָהוֹד* מֵהֶם נִמְצָאִים,
יָכִין וּבוֹעַז בְּשֵׁם נִקְרָאִים,   וְכָל בָּנַיִךְ לְמוּדֵי יהוה.²
יְסוֹד צַדִּיק* בְּשִׁבְעָה נֶעֱלָם,   אוֹת בְּרִית הוּא לְעוֹלָם,
מֵעֵין הַבְּרָכָה צַדִּיק יְסוֹד עוֹלָם,   צַדִּיק אַתָּה יהוה.³
נָא הָקֵם מַלְכוּת דָּוִד וּשְׁלֹמֹה,*   בַּעֲטָרָה שֶׁעִטְּרָה לּוֹ אִמּוֹ,⁴
כְּנֶסֶת יִשְׂרָאֵל כַּלָּה קְרוּאָה בִנְעִימָה,*   עֲטֶרֶת תִּפְאֶרֶת בְּיַד יהוה.⁵
חָזָק מְיַחֵד כְּאֶחָד,   עֶשֶׂר סְפִירוֹת,   וּמַפְרִיד אַלּוּף* לֹא יִרְאֶה מְאוֹרוֹת,
סַפִּיר גִּזְרָתָם יַחַד מְאִירוֹת,   תִּקְרַב רִנָּתִי לְפָנֶיךָ יהוה.⁶

נֶצַח יִשְׂרָאֵל מִצָּרוֹתֵינוּ גְּאָלֵנוּ — *Eternal One of Israel, from our torments redeem us.* This plea that the merit of the Patriarchs shield us from suffering may be related to the attribute of נֶצַח, *eternity*, because their merit is eternal (*R' Nosson Scherman*).

[Just as God is an eternal God, so His people, created in His image, are also eternal. Though the exile seems to continue without end, the Nation of Israel and the ultimate triumph of its spirit are eternal.]

דְּלֵנוּ וְהַעֲלֵנוּ — *Draw us and raise us.* R' S. R. Hirsch suggests that דָּלָה connotes leaving something suspended in midair so that it doesn't fall. We ask God ultimately to raise us from the pit of exile, but in the interim at least not to let us fall.

מִיָּמִין וּמִשְּׂמֹאל — *From the right and left.* *Right* and *left* represent two different attitudes. The *right* represents warmth and friendship, while the *left* represents aloofness and displeasure, as in the Talmudic expression: שְׂמֹאל דּוֹחָה יָמִין מְקָרֵב, *The left hand repels, while the right hand draws close* (*Sotah* 47a; *Zohar* to *Korach*). Both approaches are necessary for the proper training of a child, a student or a nation, provided they are applied appropriately, according to the situation (*R' Nosson Scherman*).

יְנִיקַת הַנְּבִיאִים — *The nurture of the prophets.* The term יְנִיקָה, literally, *suckling*, refers to a mother nursing her child. The prophets are likened to a mother because they provide spiritual nourishment for the people.

נֶצַח וָהוֹד — *"Eternity"* and *"Glory."* הוֹד, *glory*, opposes — or complements — the conquering aspect of נֶצַח, *eternity*, just as גְּבוּרָה, *strength*, is the counterpoint to חֶסֶד, *kindness*. Glory represents submission to circumstances rather than an attempt to conquer them. There are situations when one's greatest *glory* is the acceptance of God's will in whatever situation he finds himself.

יְסוֹד צַדִּיק — *The foundation — the righteous one.* Rambam explains in his introduction to *Mishneh Torah* that the creation of the entire universe was worthwhile for the sake of even a single righteous person. No man, however, can function in a vacuum; he requires the context of the luminaries, the elements, the ecosystem, and the society of his fellow men. Thus, although the

י O God, may the Patriarch's merit shield us.
  Eternal One of Israel, from our torments redeem us,*
And from the pit of exile, draw us and raise us —
                To sing mightily at the service of the House of HASHEM![1]
מ From the right and left* is the nurture of the prophets,*
  "Eternity" and "Glory"* are found with them.
Yachin and Boaz are the names they are given —
                And all Your children will be students of HASHEM![2]
י The foundation — the righteous one* — is shrouded in Seven Attributes.
  He is the world's symbol of the covenant
A spring of blessing is the Tzaddik, foundation of the world —
                The ultimate Tzaddik are You, HASHEM![3]
נ Please establish the kingship of David and Solomon*
  with the crown with which his nation encrowned him.[4]
The community of Israel is fondly called a bride —*
                She is a crown of splendor in the hand of HASHEM![5]
ח O Mighty One — unite as one the Ten Emanations,
  and remove the chief* who will see no luminaries.
Those emanations hewn from sapphire, may they illuminate together —
                Bringing my glad song near You, HASHEM![6]

---

(1) Ezra 3:8; I Chronicles 23:4. (2) Isaiah 54:13. (3) Jeremiah 12:1.
(4) Song of Songs 3:11. (5) Isaiah 62:3. (6) Psalms 119:169.

---

tzaddik represents only an infinitesimal fraction of creation, he cannot accomplish his task without the support of the rest of the universe, and therefore, it exists for his sake. As a result, the tzaddik is justly called the foundation of the universe, for its continued existence rests upon him.

נָא הָקֵם מַלְכוּת דָּוִד וּשְׁלֹמֹה — Please establish the kingship of David and Solomon. Literally, these words express the hope that the Messiah will come speedily and re-establish the Davidic dynasty. In a deeper sense, they allude to the final Sefirah — מַלְכוּת, kingship — the ultimate revelation of God's sovereignty over the universe. David and Solomon, for all their greatness as rulers, are regarded as nothing more than God's surrogates on earth (see Overview to ArtScroll Ruth).

כְּנֶסֶת יִשְׂרָאֵל כַּלָּה קְרוּאָה בִּנְעִימָה — The

community of Israel is fondly called a bride [literally, is called a bride in pleasantness]. The intimate relationship between God, Israel and the Torah is frequently described allegorically as that of a bride and groom. The entire text of Song of Songs, for example, is based on this metaphor. Jeremiah describes the impulsive and passionate love of the young Israel as that of a bride. I remember for your sake the kindness of your youth, the love of your bridal days, your following Me in the Wilderness in a land not sown (Jeremiah 2:2).

וּמַפְרִיד אַלּוּף — And remove the chief. This refers to the destruction of Esau and his guardian angel, who are the chief embodiments of evil in the world. The Torah refers to Esau's most prominent offspring as chiefs (Genesis 36:15-19).

שְׁכִינָה הַקְּדוֹשָׁה בְּתוֹכֵנוּ, זְכוּתָא דִתְמִימַת יַעֲקֹב עִמָּנוּ,
וְשָׁם נִשְׂמַח כֻּלָּנוּ, בְּבוֹא לְצִיּוֹן בְּרִנָּנָה.
רַחֲמָנָא אִדְכַּר לָן זְכוּתֵהּ דְּיַעֲקֹב שְׁלֵמָתָא.

אָנָּא יהוה, הוֹשִׁיעָה נָּא.

אָנָּא יהוה, הַצְלִיחָה נָּא.

אָנָּא יהוה, עֲנֵנוּ בְיוֹם קָרְאֵנוּ.

יוֹדֵעַ מַחֲשָׁבוֹת,* הוֹשִׁיעָה נָּא.[1]

כַּבִּיר וְנָאוֹר,* הַצְלִיחָה נָּא.

לוֹבֵשׁ צְדָקוֹת, עֲנֵנוּ בְיוֹם קָרְאֵנוּ.

In some congregations the responsive recitation continues:

שְׁמַע יִשְׂרָאֵל, יהוה אֱלֹהֵינוּ יהוה אֶחָד.

יהוה מֶלֶךְ, יהוה מָלָךְ, יהוה יִמְלֹךְ לְעוֹלָם וָעֶד.

יהוה מֶלֶךְ, יהוה מָלָךְ, יהוה יִמְלֹךְ לְעוֹלָם וָעֶד.

יהוה עֹז לְעַמּוֹ יִתֵּן, יהוה יְבָרֵךְ אֶת עַמּוֹ בַשָּׁלוֹם.

Some individuals recite all or some of the following paragraphs:

מִצְוַת יהוה בָּרָה, מְאִירַת עֵינָיִם.*[2] קוֹל יהוה שֹׁבֵר אֲרָזִים, וַיְשַׁבֵּר
יהוה אֶת אַרְזֵי הַלְּבָנוֹן. וַיַּרְקִידֵם* כְּמוֹ עֵגֶל, לְבָנוֹן וְשִׂרְיוֹן

﴾ FOURTH HAKAFAH ﴿

יוֹדֵעַ מַחֲשָׁבוֹת — *Knower of Thoughts.* In explaining the incident of Judah and Tamar, the Midrash cites the verse כִּי אָנֹכִי יָדַעְתִּי אֶת הַמַּחֲשָׁבֹת, *For I know the thoughts [that I think in regard to you, says* HASHEM] (Jeremiah 29:11). The Midrash continues: "The tribes were occupied with the sale of Joseph; Joseph himself was in mourning over his fate; Reuben was in mourning over his failure to save Joseph; Jacob was mourning the loss of his beloved son; and Judah was involved with seeking a mate. And all the while God was creating the light

of the Messiah [who would issue from Judah and Tamar]." The Midrash reminds us that God's choreography of human affairs is beyond our scope. Wrapped up in our own concerns, we fail to see the larger picture and to understand that His arrangements are for our benefit. Here, we ask Him to orchestrate our redemption in this mysterious but benevolent fashion. (*Zekan Aharon*)

כַּבִּיר וְנָאוֹר — *Powerful and Enlightened One.* Elihu, in his effort to help his friend Job understand God's intimate interest in the affairs of man, says to him,

The holy Shechinah is among us, the merit of **Jacob**'s wholesomeness is with
us;
May we all rejoice there, upon arriving at Zion with glad song.
O Merciful One, remember for our sake the merit of wholesome **Jacob.**

FOURTH *HAKAFAH*-CIRCUIT

Please, HASHEM, save now!
Please, HASHEM, bring success now!
Please, HASHEM, answer us on the day we call.

Knower of Thoughts,[1]* save now!
Powerful and Enlightened One,* bring success now!
He who garbs Himself in righteousness,
answer us on the day we call!

In some congregations the responsive recitation continues:

Hear, O Israel: HASHEM is our God, HASHEM the One and Only.
HASHEM reigns, HASHEM has reigned, HASHEM shall reign for all eternity.
HASHEM reigns, HASHEM has reigned, HASHEM shall reign for all eternity.
HASHEM will give might to His people, HASHEM will bless His people with
peace.

Some individuals recite all or some of the following paragraphs:

מִצְוַת *The command of HASHEM is clear, enlightening the eyes.*[2]* *The voice
of HASHEM breaks the cedars, HASHEM shatters the cedars of
Lebanon! He makes them prance about* like a calf; Lebanon and Siryon*

---

(1) *Psalms* 94:11. (2) 19:9.

הֶן אֵל כַּבִּיר וְלֹא יִמְאָס, *See, the Almighty
is so powerful. He has no need to distance* [*the poor*] (*Job* 36:5). God possesses
wisdom and mercy in such abundance
that he has no need to distance the poor
(*Rashi* ad loc.). The Talmud (*Berachos*
8a) infers from this verse that God never
totally rejects the prayer of a Jewish
congregation (צִבּוּר). Thus, we ask God,
not as individuals but as a community,
that He cast the light of His blessing
upon us and grant us success in all our
endeavors (*Simchas Aharon*).

מְאִירַת עֵינָיִם — *Enlightening the eyes.*
Those who live without the commandments stumble in darkness, for only
God's commands light the way before
those who strive to ascend to His glory
(*Radak*). While prolonged staring at the
sun causes injury to the eyes, Torah
lights up the eyes beneficially and never
hurts them (*Metzudas David; Radak*).

וַיַּרְקִידֵם — *He makes them prance
about.* This is an allusion to the leaders
of Israel and the nations who will come
to serve God in the future. They will all
dance for joy, like lively young calves
and r'eimim. The exact translation of
r'eim is unknown, but it is an animal
with a prominent horn.

SIMCHAS TORAH — Its Significance, Laws, and Prayers

כְּמוֹ בֶן רְאֵמִים.[1] יִשְׂמְחוּ וִירַנְּנוּ לְאֻמִּים,* כִּי תִשְׁפֹּט עַמִּים מִישֹׁר,*
וּלְאֻמִּים בָּאָרֶץ תַּנְחֵם סֶלָה.[2] בָּרְכֵם, טַהֲרֵם, רַחֲמֵם, צִדְקָתְךָ תָּמִיד
גָּמְלֵם. נְעִמוֹת בִּימִינְךָ נֶצַח.[3]

אֵין בָּרוּךְ כְּבֶן עַמְרָם,	אֵין אַדִּיר* כַּיהוה,
אֵין דּוֹרְשֶׁיהָ כְּיִשְׂרָאֵל.	אֵין גְּדֻלָּה כַּתּוֹרָה,
מִפִּי אֵל, מִפִּי אֵל, יְבֹרַךְ יִשְׂרָאֵל.	

אֵין וָתִיק כְּבֶן עַמְרָם,	אֵין הָדוּר כַּיהוה,
אֵין חֲכָמֶיהָ כְּיִשְׂרָאֵל.	אֵין זַכָּיָה כַּתּוֹרָה,
מִפִּי אֵל, מִפִּי אֵל, יְבֹרַךְ יִשְׂרָאֵל.	

אֵין יָשָׁר כְּבֶן עַמְרָם,	אֵין טָהוֹר כַּיהוה,
אֵין לוֹמְדֶיהָ כְּיִשְׂרָאֵל.	אֵין כָּבוֹד כַּתּוֹרָה,
מִפִּי אֵל, מִפִּי אֵל, יְבֹרַךְ יִשְׂרָאֵל.	

אֵין נָבִיא כְּבֶן עַמְרָם,	אֵין מֶלֶךְ כַּיהוה,
אֵין עוֹסְקֶיהָ כְּיִשְׂרָאֵל.	אֵין סְגֻלָּה כַּתּוֹרָה,
מִפִּי אֵל, מִפִּי אֵל, יְבֹרַךְ יִשְׂרָאֵל.	

אֵין צַדִּיק כְּבֶן עַמְרָם,	אֵין פּוֹדֶה כַּיהוה,
אֵין רוֹמְמֶיהָ כְּיִשְׂרָאֵל.	אֵין קְדֻשָּׁה כַּתּוֹרָה,
מִפִּי אֵל, מִפִּי אֵל, יְבֹרַךְ יִשְׂרָאֵל.	

אֵין רַחוּם כְּבֶן עַמְרָם,	אֵין קָדוֹשׁ כַּיהוה,
אֵין תּוֹמְכֶיהָ כְּיִשְׂרָאֵל.	אֵין שְׁמִירָה כַּתּוֹרָה,
מִפִּי אֵל, מִפִּי אֵל, יְבֹרַךְ יִשְׂרָאֵל.	

יִשְׂמְחוּ וִירַנְּנוּ לְאֻמִּים — *Nations will be glad and sing for joy.* The words עַם and לְאֹם both mean *nation.* The word עַם means *a unified national community,* separate from all other nations. International dissension and animosity are inevitable as long as each nation seeks only its own welfare (*R' S. R. Hirsch*). לְאֹם refers to the *state* which governs a people and represents to the outside world the particular striving of that people. So long as nations are selfish and acquisitive, their nationalistic posture will reflect those traits; but ultimately, all national governments will discard this policy of selfish isolation and recognize that the welfare of mankind depends on the establishment of a harmonious community of nations joyously united in the service of God.

Kli Chemdah comments that the tolerant לְאֻמִּים, *states,* respected the exiles of Israel as their equals; they regarded them as representatives of a worthy fellow nation, rather than as despised foreigners. Since these states, with their enlightened goal of world unity and mutual respect, are compat-

like young re'eimim.[1] Nations will be glad and sing for joy,* because You will judge* the nations fairly* and guide the nations on earth, Selah.[2] Bless them, purify them, show them pity, may Your righteousness always recompense them. There is delight at Your right hand for triumph.[3]

א There is none as powerful* as HASHEM.　ב There is none as blessed as Amram's son.

ג There is no greatness like the Torah;　ד no one expounds it like Israel.
From God's mouth, from God's mouth, may Israel be blessed!

ה There is none as majestic as HASHEM.　ו There is none as worthy as Amram's son.

ז There is no merit like the Torah;　ח it has no scholars like Israel.
From God's mouth, from God's mouth, may Israel be blessed!

ט There is none as pure as HASHEM.　י There is none as straight as Amram's son.

כ There is no honor like the Torah;　ל it has no students like Israel.
From God's mouth, from God's mouth, may Israel be blessed!

מ There is no king like HASHEM.　נ There is no prophet like Amram's son.

ס There is no treasure like the Torah;　ע it has none involved with it like Israel.

From God's mouth, from God's mouth, may Israel be blessed!

פ There is none who redeems like HASHEM. צ There is none as righteous as Amram's son.

ק There is no holiness like the Torah;　ר it has none who exalt it like Israel.
From God's mouth, from God's mouth, may Israel be blessed!

ק There is none as holy as HASHEM.　ר There is none as merciful as Amram's son.

ש There is no protection like the Torah;　ת it has none who support it like Israel.
From God's mouth, from God's mouth, may Israel be blessed!

---

(1) *Pslams* 29:5-6. (2) *Psalms* 67:5. (3) 16:11.

---

ible with Israel's Messianic aspirations, they will rejoice upon the advent of the Redeemer.

כִּי תִשְׁפֹּט עַמִּים מִישֹׁר — *Because You will judge the nations fairly.* Each individual עַם, *national community*, considers itself superior and refuses to treat Israel as its equal. These nations are destined to undergo Divine judgment for their failure to ensure מִישֹׁר, *fairness, equity* (R' A. C. Feuer).

אֵין אַדִּיר — *There is none as powerful.* This *piyut* is ascribed to the Maggid of Kozhnitz, Rabbi Yisrael ben Shabsei Hapstein (1733-1814), one of the earliest Chassidic masters in Poland. It follows the order of the *aleph-beis.* Each of its six stanzas praises God, Moses (son of Amram), the Torah and its students and supporters. This *piyut* is one of the few written specifically for the Simchas Torah *hakafos.*

SIMCHAS TORAH — Its Significance, Laws, and Prayers

וִיבָרְכוּ שֵׁם כְּבוֹדֶךָ.	וְיֶאֱתָיוּ כֹל* לְעָבְדֶּךָ.
וְיִדְרְשׁוּךָ עַמִּים לֹא יְדָעוּךָ.	וִיגִּידוּ בָאִיִּים צִדְקֶךָ.
וְיֹאמְרוּ תָמִיד יִגְדַּל יְהוָה.	וִיהַלְלוּךָ כָּל אַפְסֵי אָרֶץ.
	(וְיִזְבְּחוּ לְךָ אֶת זִבְחֵיהֶם.)
וְיַחְפְּרוּ עִם פְּסִילֵיהֶם.	וְיִזְנְחוּ אֶת עֲצַבֵּיהֶם.
וְיִירָאוּךָ עִם שֶׁמֶשׁ מְבַקְשֵׁי פָּנֶיךָ.	וְיַטּוּ שְׁכֶם אֶחָד לְעָבְדֶּךָ.
וְיִלְמְדוּ תוֹעִים בִּינָה.	וִיבִירוּ כֹּחַ מַלְכוּתֶךָ.
וִינַשְּׂאוּךָ מִתְנַשֵּׂא לְכֹל לְרֹאשׁ.	וִימַלְלוּ אֶת גְּבוּרָתֶךָ.
וִיעַטְּרוּךָ נֵזֶר תִּפְאָרָה.	וִיסַלְּדוּ בְּחִילָה פָּנֶיךָ.
וְיִצְהֲלוּ אַיִים בְּמָלְכֶךָ.	וְיִפְצְחוּ הָרִים רִנָּה.
וִירוֹמְמוּךָ בִּקְהַל עָם.	וִיקַבְּלוּ עֹל מַלְכוּתְךָ עֲלֵיהֶם.
וְיִתְּנוּ לְךָ כֶּתֶר מְלוּכָה.*	וְיִשְׁמְעוּ רְחוֹקִים וְיָבֹאוּ.

שְׁכִינָה הַקְּדוֹשָׁה בְּתוֹכֵנוּ, זְכוּתֵהּ דְּ**מֹשֶׁה** רַעְיָא מְהֵימְנָא עִמָּנוּ,
וְשָׁם נִשְׂמַח כֻּלָּנוּ, בְּבוֹא לְצִיּוֹן בְּרִנָּנָה.
רַחֲמָנָא אִדְּכַּר לָן זְכוּתֵהּ דְּ**מֹשֶׁה** רַעְיָא מְהֵימְנָא.

FIFTH *HAKAFAH*-CIRCUIT

אָנָּא יהוה, הוֹשִׁיעָה נָּא.
אָנָּא יהוה, הַצְלִיחָה נָא.
אָנָּא יהוה, עֲנֵנוּ בְיוֹם קָרְאֵנוּ.
מֶלֶךְ עוֹלָמִים,*[1] הוֹשִׁיעָה נָּא.

וְיֶאֱתָיוּ כֹל — *Then all shall come.* This joyous and lyrical *piyut* describes the manner in which all people will cast off their false creeds and rally to the service of God in the Messianic era. It poetically and majestically captures the yearning of the Jewish soul for the realization of God's will in the world. Each stich in this *piyut* begins with the prefix וי, *they shall*, followed by the letters of the *aleph-beis* respectively. Of anonymous authorship, it is taken from the *Mussaf* of Rosh Hashanah and Yom Kippur.

וְיִתְּנוּ לְךָ כֶּתֶר מְלוּכָה — *And they will present You with a crown of Kingship.* The *Vilna Gaon* notes on the verses recited at the end of אָז יָשִׁיר, *Song at the Sea*, that the term מוֹשֵׁל, *ruler*, refers to one who rules by force, while a מֶלֶךְ, *king*, is willingly accepted. God is now *King* over Israel alone, because it is the only nation that acknowledges His sovereignty with love, and He *rules* the nations despite their unwillingness to accept Him. In the future, however, all nations will proclaim Him as their

וְיֶאֱתָיוּ *Then all shall come* to serve You;*
ב *they shall bless Your glorious Name*
ג *and declare Your righteousness in far-flung lands.*
ד *Peoples that knew You not will seek You out;*
ה *all ends of the earth will laud You*
ו *and always say, "May HASHEM be exalted."*
ז *They will reject their idols,*
ח *be mortified with their status,*
ט *and turn unanimously to serve You.*
י *Those who seek Your presence will revere You as long as the sun exists;*
כ *they will recognize the power of Your sovereignty,*
ל *and teach understanding to those gone astray.*
מ *They shall speak of Your strength,*
נ *they shall extol You, Who are sovereign over every leader.*
ס *In Your Presence they will pray with trepidation,*
ע *and crown You with a corona of splendor.*
פ *The mountains will burst forth with glad song,*
צ *far-flung lands will exult in Your Kingship,*
ק *they shall accept the yoke of Your Kingship upon themselves,*
ר *and exalt You among the assembled people.*
ש *Distant ones will hear and come,*
ת *and they will present You with a crown of Kingship.**

The holy Shechinah is among us, the merit of **Moses** *the faithful shepherd;*
May we all rejoice there, upon arriving at Zion with glad song.
O Merciful One, remember for our sake
the merit of **Moses** *the faithful shepherd.*

FIFTH *HAKAFAH*-CIRCUIT

Please, HASHEM, save now!
Please, HASHEM, bring success now!
Please, HASHEM, answer us on the day we call.

Eternal King,[1]** save now!*

---

(1) Cf. *Daniel* 3:33; *Psalms* 245:13.

---

sovereign and present Him with a crown of Kingship.

⊰{ FIFTH HAKAFAH }⊱

מֶלֶךְ עוֹלָמִים — *Eternal King.* While earthly kingdoms and human dynasties rise, fall, and vanish, the Kingdom of God endures forever (*Ibn Ezra* to

Psalms 145:13). Furthermore, God is the absolute King of all worlds and everything that exists in them. He is able to offer salvation that cannot be undone by any mortal being. Thus, we implore the Eternal King to save us now — and forever (*Simchas Aharon*).

[191] **SIMCHAS TORAH** — Its Significance, Laws, and Prayers

נָאוֹר וְאַדִּיר,[1]* הַצְלִיחָה נָא.
סוֹמֵךְ נוֹפְלִים,[2]* עֲנֵנוּ בְיוֹם קָרְאֵנוּ.

In some congregations the responsive recitation continues:

שְׁמַע יִשְׂרָאֵל, יהוה אֱלֹהֵינוּ יהוה אֶחָד.
יהוה מֶלֶךְ, יהוה מָלָךְ, יהוה יִמְלֹךְ לְעוֹלָם וָעֶד.
יהוה מֶלֶךְ, יהוה מָלָךְ, יהוה יִמְלֹךְ לְעוֹלָם וָעֶד.
יהוה עֹז לְעַמּוֹ יִתֵּן, יהוה יְבָרֵךְ אֶת עַמּוֹ בַשָּׁלוֹם.

Some individuals recite all or some of the following paragraphs:

יִרְאַת יהוה טְהוֹרָה,* עוֹמֶדֶת לָעַד.[3] קוֹל יהוה חֹצֵב לַהֲבוֹת אֵשׁ.[4]*
יוֹדְוּךָ עַמִּים אֱלֹהִים, יוֹדְוּךָ עַמִּים כֻּלָּם.[5] חֲסִין קָדוֹשׁ, בְּרֹב
טוּבְךָ, נַהֵל עֲדָתֶךָ. יהוה אֲדֹנֵינוּ מָה אַדִּיר שִׁמְךָ בְּכָל הָאָרֶץ, אֲשֶׁר
תְּנָה הוֹדְךָ עַל הַשָּׁמָיִם.[6]

הָאַדֶּרֶת וְהָאֱמוּנָה*	לְחֵי עוֹלָמִים.	הַבִּינָה וְהַבְּרָכָה*	לְחֵי עוֹלָמִים.
הַגַּאֲוָה וְהַגְּדֻלָּה	לְחֵי עוֹלָמִים.	הַדֵּעָה וְהַדִּבּוּר	לְחֵי עוֹלָמִים.
הַהוֹד וְהֶהָדָר	לְחֵי עוֹלָמִים.	הַוַּעַד וְהַוָּתִיקוּת*	לְחֵי עוֹלָמִים.

נָאוֹר וְאַדִּיר — *Enlightened and Mighty One.* King David teaches: *Enlightened are You, more powerful than mountains of prey* (Psalms 76:5). The illumination of God's truth will ultimately spread throughout the world, revealing His infinite might. The enemies of Israel, although they are as powerful as mountain lions, hungrily awaiting the opportunity to devour their prey, will be vanquished by God Whose strength is supreme.

Our prayer here asks that God negate the power of all the enemies of His people. Those who pose either physical or psychological threats to our success should be thwarted before causing us any harm (*Simchas Aharon*).

סוֹמֵךְ נוֹפְלִים — *Supporter of the fallen.* We all experience different types of downfalls in life. The expression *God supports all the fallen ones* (Psalms 145:14) is an implied guarantee that we can look forward to God's support even

in the face of disaster (see *Berachos* 4b). Though we may suffer reverses, they will never be complete. God will, so to speak, catch us before we fall into emotional or spiritual despair (*Maharsha* ad loc.). Another interpretation is that even after Israel, as a nation, falls to the lowest depths of degradation in exile, Hashem will raise them up through redemption (*Alshich* to *Psalms* ibid.). It is this uplifting Hand of God that we hope to experience permanently in the very near future.

יִרְאַת ה' טְהוֹרָה — *The fear of HASHEM is pure.* There are many sins against which the Torah cautions with the warning וְיָרֵאתָ מֵאֱלֹהֶיךָ, *And you shall fear your God.* These are the crimes which can be perpetrated in secrecy, such as robbery and cheating on weights and measures. The person who refrains from evil when no one is looking, controlling himself only because he recognizes God's presence,

Enlightened and Mighty One,[1]* *bring success now!*
Supporter of the fallen,[2]* *answer us on the day we call!*

In some congregations the responsive recitation continues:

Hear, O Israel: HASHEM is our God, HASHEM the One and Only.
HASHEM reigns, HASHEM has reigned, HASHEM shall reign for all eternity.
HASHEM reigns, HASHEM has reigned, HASHEM shall reign for all eternity.
HASHEM will give might to His people, HASHEM will bless His people with peace.

Some individuals recite all or some of the following paragraphs:

יִרְאַת *The fear of HASHEM is pure,* *enduring forever.*[3] *The voice of HASHEM cleaves with shafts of fire.*[4]* *The peoples will acknowledge You, O God, the peoples will acknowledge You, all of them.*[5] *Powerful Holy One, with Your abundant goodness guide Your congregation. HASHEM, our Lord, how mighty is Your Name throughout the earth; for it were fit that You place Your splendor above the heavens.*[6]

הָאַדֶּרֶת *Strength and faithfulness**	*are His Who lives eternally;**
ב *Discernment and blessing**	*are His Who lives eternally;*
ג *Grandeur and greatness*	*are His Who lives eternally;*
ד *Wisdom and speech*	*are His Who lives eternally;*
ה *Glory and majesty*	*are His Who lives eternally;*
ו *Convocation and authority**	*are His Who lives eternally;*

---

(1) Cf. *Psalms* 76:5. (2) Cf. 145:14. (3) 19:10. (4) 29:7. (5) 67:6. (6) 8:2.

---

truly deserves to be called *one with a pure fear of God* (*Radak*).

קוֹל ה׳ חֹצֵב לַהֲבוֹת אֵשׁ — *The voice of HASHEM cleaves with shafts of fire.* When God spoke at Sinai, each commandment came forth from His mouth as a flame in the shape of visible letters and words. These letters penetrated the stone tablets and engraved themselves on the stone (*Rashi*).

הָאַדֶּרֶת וְהָאֱמוּנָה — *Strength and faithfulness.* With some variations, this song is found in *Heichalos Rabbasi*, Chapter 26. It is sung by the angels when Israel recites *Baruch She'amar*; therefore, it is recited before *Baruch She'amar* on the Sabbath and festivals and, by some, every day before *Hodu*. In *Nusach Ashkenaz* it is recited on Yom Kippur, when Israel rises to the level of the

angels. It is also recited on Simchas Torah, a time of intense love between God and His children, when they offer Him most detailed and exalted praises.

הָאַדֶּרֶת . . . לְחַי עוֹלָמִים — *Strength . . . are His Who lives eternally.* The theme of all twenty-two verses is that since God is eternal, the Creator and Life-Giver of all worlds, it is to Him that all praises and attributes should be ascribed.

הַבִּינָה וְהַבְּרָכָה — *Discernment and blessing.* Because God understands the essence of every human being, He knows who is worthy of blessing.

הַוַּעַד וְהַוָּתִיקוּת — *Convocation and authority.* Human judges can die or become ill before the court convenes or pronounces its verdict, but there is no limit on God's power to convoke the Heavenly Court.

לְחַי עוֹלָמִים. הַחַיִל וְהַחֹסֶן לְחַי עוֹלָמִים. הַזָּךְ וְהַיָּשָׁר

לְחַי עוֹלָמִים. הַיִּחוּד וְהַיִּרְאָה לְחַי עוֹלָמִים. הַטֶּכֶס וְהַטֹּהַר

לְחַי עוֹלָמִים. הַלֶּקַח וְהַלִּבּוּב* לְחַי עוֹלָמִים. הַכֶּתֶר וְהַכָּבוֹד

לְחַי עוֹלָמִים. הַנּוֹי וְהַנֶּצַח לְחַי עוֹלָמִים. הַמְּלוּכָה וְהַמֶּמְשָׁלָה*

לְחַי עוֹלָמִים. הָעֹז וְהָעֲנָוָה לְחַי עוֹלָמִים. הַסִּגּוּי וְהַשֶּׂגֶב

לְחַי עוֹלָמִים. הַצְּבִי וְהַצֶּדֶק* לְחַי עוֹלָמִים. הַפְּדוּת וְהַפְּאֵר

לְחַי עוֹלָמִים. הָרֹן וְהָרוֹמֵמוּת לְחַי עוֹלָמִים. הַקְּרִיאָה וְהַקְּדֻשָׁה*

הַתְּהִלָּה וְהַתִּפְאֶרֶת לְחַי עוֹלָמִים. לְחַי עוֹלָמִים. הַשִּׁיר וְהַשֶּׁבַח

שְׁכִינָה הַקְּדוֹשָׁה בְּתוֹכֵנוּ, זְכוּתֵהּ דְּאַהֲרֹן כַּהֲנָא עִמָּנוּ,
וְשָׁם נִשְׂמַח כֻּלָּנוּ, בְּבוֹא לְצִיּוֹן בְּרִנָּנָה.
רַחֲמָנָא אִדְכַּר לָן זְכוּתֵהּ דְּאַהֲרֹן כַּהֲנָא קַדִּישָׁא.

SIXTH *HAKAFAH*-CIRCUIT

אָנָּא יהוה, הוֹשִׁיעָה נָּא.
אָנָּא יהוה, הַצְלִיחָה נָּא.
אָנָּא יהוה, עֲנֵנוּ בְיוֹם קָרְאֵנוּ.
עוֹזֵר דַּלִּים,* הוֹשִׁיעָה נָּא.
פּוֹדֶה וּמַצִּיל,* הַצְלִיחָה נָּא.

הַלֶּקַח וְהַלִּבּוּב — *Study and insight.* This refers to the study of the Torah and the ability to comprehend it fully.

הַמְּלוּכָה וְהַמֶּמְשָׁלָה — *Kingship and dominion.* A king ideally has the respect and consent of the governed, but even if people refuse to recognize God as their king, He dominates nonetheless.

הַצְּבִי וְהַצֶּדֶק — *Desire and righteousness.* Though God is beholden to no one, His "desire" is to be righteous.

הַקְּרִיאָה וְהַקְּדֻשָׁה — *Summons and sanctity.* The angels summon one another to sanctify God.

⁜ SIXTH HAKAFAH ⁜

This *hakafah* offers yet another comparison between God's eternal strength, with its cosmic implications, and His humility in redeeming and rescuing the destitute.

עוֹזֵר דַּלִּים — *Helper of the destitute.* A דַּל is one so destitute that he cannot help himself in any way. While conventional wisdom has it that God helps those who help themselves, in truth He also helps those who cannot help themselves. Whether one suffers monetary or spiritual devastation, God is always ready to raise him up no matter how wretched his situation has become.

The Bluzhever Rebbe *zt"l* would suggest that those who are childless take the *hakafah* of עוֹזֵר דַּלִּים. When God sent the angels to inform Abraham and Sarah that they would be blessed with a

ז Refinement and radiance	are His Who lives eternally;
ח Accomplishment and power	are His Who lives eternally;
ט Adornment and purity	are His Who lives eternally;
י Oneness and reverence	are His Who lives eternally;
כ Crown and honor	are His Who lives eternally;
ל Study and insight*	are His Who lives eternally;
מ Kingship and dominion*	are His Who lives eternally;
נ Beauty and triumph	are His Who lives eternally;
ס Eminence and supremacy	are His Who lives eternally;
ע Might and modesty	are His Who lives eternally;
פ Redemption and splendor	are His Who lives eternally;
צ Desire and righteousness*	are His Who lives eternally;
ק Summons and sanctity*	are His Who lives eternally;
ר Exultation and exaltation	are His Who lives eternally;
ש Song and praise	are His Who lives eternally;
ת Lauding and magnificence	are His Who lives eternally;

The holy Shechinah is among us, the merit of **Aaron** the Kohen;
May we all rejoice there,   Upon arriving at Zion with glad song.
O Merciful One, remember for our sake the merit of **Aaron** the holy Kohen.

SIXTH *HAKAFAH*- CIRCUIT

Please, HASHEM, save now!
Please, HASHEM, bring success now!
Please, HASHEM, answer us on the day we call.

Helper of the destitute,* save now!
Redeemer and Rescuer,* bring success now!

---

son, Sarah responded with disbelief: *After I have withered, shall I again have delicate skin?* (Genesis 18:12). Delicate skin is a metaphor for the rejuvenation that enables a woman to bear children. The *Rebbe* pointed out that the Hebrew word for this, עֶדְנָה, is spelled out by the first letters of the phrase עוֹזֵר דַּלִּים הוֹשִׁיעָה נָא.

Many commentators suggest that this *hakafah* is a *segulah* for wealth. In fact, in certain communities the competition for this honor is fierce. Many mistakenly think that if they beseech God as the One Who helps the destitute, He will respond by rescuing them from

their perceived poverty. The reason for the *segulah* is actually much more subtle: If one declares that he, like God, wants to aid the poor, God is more than ready to provide him with the wealth to do so. He is always looking for people to do His work and distribute charity (*Imrei Moshe*).

פּוֹדֶה וּמַצִּיל — *Redeemer and Rescuer.* According to R' Sholom of Belz, this stich refers to any travails that are related to children. Some are, God forbid, entrapped in the painful prison of childlessness and need God to redeem them; others have children, yet encounter great difficulty in raising them and

צוּר עוֹלָמִים,* עֲנֵנוּ בְּיוֹם קָרְאֵנוּ.¹

In some congregations the responsive recitation continues:

שְׁמַע יִשְׂרָאֵל, יהוה אֱלֹהֵינוּ יהוה אֶחָד.
יהוה מֶלֶךְ, יהוה מָלָךְ, יהוה יִמְלֹךְ לְעוֹלָם וָעֶד.
יהוה מֶלֶךְ, יהוה מָלָךְ, יהוה יִמְלֹךְ לְעוֹלָם וָעֶד.
יהוה עֹז לְעַמּוֹ יִתֵּן, יהוה יְבָרֵךְ אֶת עַמּוֹ בַשָּׁלוֹם.

Some individuals recite all or some of the following paragraphs:

מִשְׁפְּטֵי יהוה אֱמֶת, צָדְקוּ יַחְדָּו.* קוֹל יהוה יָחִיל מִדְבָּר,² יָחִיל יהוה
מִדְבַּר קָדֵשׁ.³ אֶרֶץ נָתְנָה יְבוּלָהּ,* יְבָרְכֵנוּ אֱלֹהִים אֱלֹהֵינוּ.⁴
יָחִיד גֵּאֶה, לְעַמְּךָ פְּנֵה, זוֹכְרֵי קְדֻשָּׁתֶךָ. צַדִּיק יהוה בְּכָל דְּרָכָיו,*
וְחָסִיד בְּכָל מַעֲשָׂיו.⁵

עַל יִשְׂרָאֵל בִּרְכָתוֹ.	עַל יִשְׂרָאֵל אֱמוּנָתוֹ.*
עַל יִשְׂרָאֵל דִּבְּרָתוֹ.*	עַל יִשְׂרָאֵל גַּאֲוָתוֹ.
עַל יִשְׂרָאֵל וְעִידָתוֹ.	עַל יִשְׂרָאֵל הֲדָרָתוֹ.
עַל יִשְׂרָאֵל חֶמְלָתוֹ	עַל יִשְׂרָאֵל זְכִירָתוֹ.*

---

deriving *nachas* from them. People in both situations are in dire need of God's help in order to succeed.

צוּר עוֹלָמִים — *Eternal Rock.* In the simple sense, this term refers to God's rocklike constancy and strength. The Sages also render the word צוּר homiletically as צָיָר, an *artisan* who fashions or molds. Thus, *God is the One Who fashioned* עוֹלָמִים, *the worlds above and below.*

We often meet great obstacles in using this world as a means to reach the World to Come. Spiritual detours abound, and we frequently lose our way. Only God, Who created both worlds, can help us get back on track and provide us with the direction to get from one world to the other (*Simchas Aharon*).

צָדְקוּ יַחְדָּו — *Altogether righteous.* There is no contradiction between one law of the Torah and another, whereas in civil

law one will very often find inconsistencies and conflicts between different statutes (*Ibn Ezra*).

אֶרֶץ נָתְנָה יְבוּלָהּ — *The earth has yielded its produce.* The political renaissance of the future will be accompanied by an agricultural rebirth, for the world's spiritual development will pervade the earth and affect the soil. The Talmud (*Sanhedrin* 98a) notes that the advent of Redemption will be heralded by agricultural changes: *You mountains of Israel shall sprout forth your branches and yield your fruit to My people Israel, for they are at hand to arrive* (Ezekiel 36:8) (*R' A. C. Feuer*).

Another interpretation is that in the future, the earth will yield its bounty effortlessly, without any cultivation or labor. Moreover, it will produce finished products, not merely the raw, unprocessed crop. The Sages (*Kesubos* 111b) state that the trees are destined to grow

Eternal Rock,*¹ answer us on the day we call!

In some congregations the responsive recitation continues:

Hear, O Israel: HASHEM is our God, HASHEM the One and Only.
HASHEM reigns, HASHEM has reigned, HASHEM shall reign for all eternity.
HASHEM reigns, HASHEM has reigned, HASHEM shall reign for all eternity.
HASHEM will give might to His people, HASHEM will bless His people with peace.

Some individuals recite all or some of the following paragraphs:

מִשְׁפְּטֵי *The judgments of HASHEM are true, altogether righteous.²* The voice of HASHEM convulses the wilderness; HASHEM convulses the wilderness of Kadesh.³ The earth has yielded its produce,* may God, our own God, bless us.⁴ One and only Exalted One, turn to Your nation which proclaims Your holiness. HASHEM is righteous in all His ways;* virtuous in all His deeds.⁵*

א *Upon Israel is His faithfulness.**   **ב** *Upon Israel is His blessing.*
ג *Upon Israel is His pride.*   **ד** *Upon Israel is His word.**
ה *Upon Israel is His majesty.*   **ו** *Upon Israel is His convocation.*
ז *Upon Israel is His remembrance.**   **ח** *Upon Israel is His compassion.*

---

(1) *Isaiah* 26:4. (2) *Psalms* 19:10. (3) 29:8. (4) 67:7. (5) 145:17.

---

baked loaves of the finest flour (*Tehillos Hashem*).

צַדִּיק ה׳ בְּכָל דְּרָכָיו — *HASHEM is righteous in all His ways.* It is easy for us, with our limited vision, to question the equity of God's distribution of sustenance. We wonder why some people are blessed with wealth and finer things, while others must subsist in poverty. The Psalmist replies that we must place our trust in God's righteousness. He made all creatures; only He knows their precise make-up and recognizes what is best for them. God may be compared to a wise doctor who prescribes sweet juices for one patient but orders bitter pills for another. The patient is incapable of comprehending the doctor's decisions (*Ibn Ezra*).

עַל יִשְׂרָאֵל אֱמוּנָתוֹ — *Upon Israel is His faithfulness.* Based upon the phrase in *Psalms* 68:35 which states that God takes special pride in the Jewish people,

this *piyut*, which follows the *aleph-beis*, depicts God's special relationship with Israel in all areas. Some verses tell what God gives to Israel (majesty, purity, pleasantness); others testify that Divinity in the world (His Kingdom, His Presence) depends upon Israel's performance of the commandments.

אֱמוּנָתוֹ — *His faithfulness.* Faith in God is found primarily among the Jewish people; in the next stich, too, the Jewish people are the ones who bless Him. By the same token, God has faith in His people and in the ultimate triumph of the good within them.

דִּבְּרָתוֹ — *His word.* God gave the gift of prophecy for the sake of Israel.

זְכִירָתוֹ — *His remembrance.* God says that despite Israel's sinfulness and disloyalty, He always remembers His people fondly and longs for the time when He will redeem them (*Jeremiah* 31:19).

[197] **SIMCHAS TORAH** — Its Significance, Laws, and Prayers

עַל יִשְׂרָאֵל יִשְׁרָתוֹ.   עַל יִשְׂרָאֵל טָהֳרָתוֹ.*

עַל יִשְׂרָאֵל לְאֻמָּתוֹ.   עַל יִשְׂרָאֵל כַּנָּתוֹ.*

עַל יִשְׂרָאֵל נְעִימָתוֹ.   עַל יִשְׂרָאֵל מַלְכוּתוֹ.

עַל יִשְׂרָאֵל עֵדָתוֹ.*   עַל יִשְׂרָאֵל סְגֻלָּתוֹ.*

עַל יִשְׂרָאֵל צִדְקָתוֹ.   עַל יִשְׂרָאֵל פְּעֻלָּתוֹ.

עַל יִשְׂרָאֵל רוֹמְמוּתוֹ.   עַל יִשְׂרָאֵל קְדֻשָּׁתוֹ.

עַל יִשְׂרָאֵל תִּפְאַרְתּוֹ.   עַל יִשְׂרָאֵל שְׁכִינָתוֹ.

שְׁכִינָה הַקְּדוֹשָׁה בְּתוֹכֵנוּ, זְכוּתֵהּ דְּיוֹסֵף צַדִּיקָא עִמָּנוּ,
וְשָׁם נִשְׂמַח כֻּלָּנוּ, בְּבוֹא לְצִיּוֹן בְּרִנָּנָה.
רַחֲמָנָא אַדְכַּר לָן זְכוּתֵהּ דְּיוֹסֵף צַדִּיקָא.

SEVENTH *HAKAFAH*-CIRCUIT

אָנָּא יהוה, הוֹשִׁיעָה נָּא.

אָנָּא יהוה, הַצְלִיחָה נָּא.

אָנָּא יהוה, עֲנֵנוּ בְיוֹם קָרְאֵנוּ.

קָדוֹשׁ וְנוֹרָא,* [1] הוֹשִׁיעָה נָּא.

רַחוּם וְחַנּוּן,* [2] הַצְלִיחָה נָּא.

טָהֳרָתוֹ — *His purity.* God purifies Israel. As R' Akiva said: Just as the *mikveh* purifies the impure, so God purifies [and accepts the repentance of] Israel (*Yoma* 85b). [Furthermore, we are blessed with His purity in the form of a נְשָׁמָה טְהוֹרָה, *a pure soul,* which God grants all Jews at birth.]

כַּנָּתוֹ — *His foundation.* God created the universe as a vehicle for spiritual growth and accomplishment. The *foundation* upon which this spiritual greatness would be built is the Jewish people (*R' S. R. Hirsch, Psalms* 80:16).

סְגֻלָּתוֹ — *His treasured status.* God says to Israel, וִהְיִיתֶם לִי סְגֻלָּה, *You shall be My treasure (Exodus* 19:5). A סְגֻלָּה is something which inexplicably brings about a desired result, even though it does noth-

ing to cause it. The Jewish people evoke God's love for them even when their actions do not justify it (*R' Avraham Greiver*).

עֵדָתוֹ — *His congregation.* Scripture says that God stands בַּעֲדַת אֵל, *in the Divine assembly* [or *congregation*] (*Psalms* 82:1). [The people of Israel are witnesses (עֵדִים) to God's existence and Presence in the world. Hence, they are called עֵדָה.]

⧫ SEVENTH HAKAFAH ⧫

Seven three-verse *hakafos* would only utilize twenty-one of the twenty-two letters of the *aleph-beis.* In order to include the twenty-second letter — ת — and at the same time maintain the three-verse stanza format, two stanzas are recited during this final *hakafah.*

ט Upon Israel is His purity.*　　　　　י Upon Israel is His uprightness.
כ Upon Israel is His foundation.*　　ל Upon Israel is His nationhood.
מ Upon Israel is His kingdom.　　　　נ Upon Israel is His pleasantness.
ס Upon Israel is His treasured status.*　ע Upon Israel is His congregation.*
פ Upon Israel is His handiwork.　　　צ Upon Israel is His righteousness.
ק Upon Israel is His holiness.　　　　ר Upon Israel is His exaltation.
ש Upon Israel is His Presence.　　　　ת Upon Israel is His splendor.

The holy Shechinah is among us, the merit of the righteous **Joseph;**
May we all rejoice there, upon arriving at Zion with glad song.
O Merciful One, remember for our sake the merit of the righteous **Joseph.**

SEVENTH *HAKAFAH*-CIRCUIT

---

*Please, H*ASHEM*, save now!*
*Please, H*ASHEM*, bring success now!*
*Please, H*ASHEM*, answer us on the day we call.*

Holy and Awesome One,[1]* save now!*
Merciful and Gracious One,[2]* bring success now!*

---

(1) *Psalms* 111:9. (2) 103:8.

The last letter (ת) is used for all three stiches of the additional stanza.

קָדוֹשׁ וְנוֹרָא — *Holy and Awesome One.* Each part of man, the physical and the spiritual, struggles to control him. Sometimes the soul seems to lose its grip and the animal force within gains ascendancy. At such times we must remember the eternal covenant that God formed to elevate Israel above all the nations: He asked holiness from us since we were created in His image, and He expects us to mirror that sanctity. *Leviticus* (11:44-45) teaches: *You shall sanctify yourselves and you shall be holy, for I am holy ... for I am H*ASHEM*, Who elevates you from the land of Egypt to be a God unto you. You shall be holy, for I am holy.* Our plea is to be able to cleave to God and reflect His sanctity, thus actualizing our own innermost, though often unacknowledged, desire.

רַחוּם וְחַנּוּן — *Merciful and Gracious One.* According to *Radak*, the term רַחוּם, *merciful*, refers to God's assurance that our captors will tolerate us and not destroy us completely, despite their hostility. Alternatively, this prayer is a plea for Divine help in avoiding the pitfalls of sin. The attribute of mercy refers to God's assistance *before* a person is engulfed in a situation beyond his control; He helps us deflect temptation which would overwhelm our normal self-control (gloss to *Tosafos, Rosh Hashanah* 17b).

The term חַנּוּן, *gracious*, refers to God's concern for our physical survival in exile; He manifests this compassion by providing wondrously for all our needs.

The term חַנּוּן is also cognate with חֵן, *charm*, which in turn is related to the word חִנָּם, *free of charge*. Since God is compassionate, He aids even those

---

שׁוֹמֵר הַבְּרִית,* עֲנֵנוּ בְיוֹם קָרְאֵנוּ.

תּוֹמֵךְ תְּמִימִים,* הוֹשִׁיעָה נָּא.

תַּקִּיף לָעַד, הַצְלִיחָה נָּא.

תָּמִים בְּמַעֲשָׂיו, עֲנֵנוּ בְיוֹם קָרְאֵנוּ.

In some congregations the responsive recitation continues:

שְׁמַע יִשְׂרָאֵל, יהוה אֱלֹהֵינוּ יהוה אֶחָד.

יהוה מֶלֶךְ, יהוה מָלָךְ, יהוה יִמְלֹךְ לְעוֹלָם וָעֶד.

יהוה מֶלֶךְ, יהוה מָלָךְ, יהוה יִמְלֹךְ לְעוֹלָם וָעֶד.

יהוה עֹז לְעַמּוֹ יִתֵּן, יהוה יְבָרֵךְ אֶת עַמּוֹ בַשָּׁלוֹם.

Some recite all or some of the following paragraphs:

הַנֶּחֱמָדִים מִזָּהָב וּמִפַּז רָב,* וּמְתוּקִים מִדְּבַשׁ וְנֹפֶת צוּפִים.[1] קוֹל
יהוה יְחוֹלֵל אַיָּלוֹת, וַיֶּחֱשֹׂף יְעָרוֹת, וּבְהֵיכָלוֹ, כֻּלוֹ
אֹמֵר כָּבוֹד. יהוה לַמַּבּוּל יָשָׁב, וַיֵּשֶׁב יהוה מֶלֶךְ לְעוֹלָם. יהוה עֹז לְעַמּוֹ
יִתֵּן,* יהוה יְבָרֵךְ אֶת עַמּוֹ בַשָּׁלוֹם.[2] יְבָרְכֵנוּ אֱלֹהִים, וְיִירְאוּ אוֹתוֹ
כָּל אַפְסֵי אָרֶץ.[3] שַׁוְעָתֵנוּ קַבֵּל, וּשְׁמַע צַעֲקָתֵנוּ, יוֹדֵעַ תַּעֲלוּמוֹת.*

---

unworthy of His kindness. Unlike the attribute of mercy, which is exercised *before* a crisis, the attribute of compassion is exercised *during* a crisis. The compassionate God responds to the pleas of a person who wants to avoid sin but whose willpower is unequal to the task. God rescues him, although he is unworthy of such aid (see introduction to ArtScroll *Tashlich*).

שׁוֹמֵר הַבְּרִית — *Keeper of the covenant.* God is described as *the faithful God, Who safeguards the covenant and the kindness for those who love Him, and for those who observe His commandments for a thousand generations* (*Deuteronomy* 7:9). There are two categories of pious people. For those who observe God's commandments only out of fear, the reward is still enormous, extending for one thousand generations (*Rashi*); for those who serve Him out of love, God extends reward for as long as

two thousand generations (see *Deuteronomy* 5:10). We ask God, Keeper of the covenant, to remember the good deeds of our forefathers and answer our call to Him on this day.

תּוֹמֵךְ תְּמִימִים — *Supporter of the wholesome.* Jews are characterized by unswerving, wholesome faith in God, following the Torah's dictate to be *wholehearted with* HASHEM *your God*. They do not need the idolatrous pursuit of fortunetelling; instead, they follow God with perfect faith (see *Deuteronomy* 18:13 and *Rashi* ad loc.). God rewards that faith by providing for our future in a most beneficent fashion. This is what we pray for here — that God support us in the merit of our wholesomeness.

Alternatively, just as we do not question our future, we beseech God, as it were, to ignore our past, to accept our repentance and focus on our resolve to improve in the future.

Keeper of the covenant, answer us on the day we call!*

Supporter of the wholesome, save now!*
Eternally strong One, bring success now!
Perfect in His deeds, answer us on the day we call!

In some congregations the responsive recitation continues:

Hear, O Israel: HASHEM is our God, HASHEM the One and Only.
HASHEM reigns, HASHEM has reigned, HASHEM shall reign for all eternity.
HASHEM reigns, HASHEM has reigned, HASHEM shall reign for all eternity.
HASHEM will give might to His people, HASHEM will bless His people with
peace.

Some individuals recite all or some of the following paragraphs:

הַנֶּחֱמָדִים *They are more desirable than gold, than even much fine gold;**
sweeter than honey and drippings from the combs.[1] The voice of
HASHEM frightens the hinds, and strips the forests bare; while in His Temple
all proclaim, "Glory!" HASHEM sat enthroned at the Deluge; HASHEM sits
enthroned as King forever. HASHEM will give might to His nation, HASHEM will*
bless His people with peace.[2] May God bless us, and may all the ends of the
*earth fear Him.[3] Accept our entreaty and hear our cry, O Knower of mysteries.**

---

(1) *Psalms* 19:11. (2) 29:9-11. (3) 67:8.

הַנֶּחֱמָדִים מִזָּהָב וּמִפַּז רָב — *They are more desirable than gold, than even much fine gold.* Men desire gold and precious stones because they are durable and of undiminishing value, but Torah surpasses them. A person cannot take gold to the grave, but Torah wisdom accompanies him in this world and in the next (*Ibn Ezra*).

Precious gems or metals only retain their high value when they are scarce. Once they are in more plentiful supply, they lose all importance, as we find in *I Kings: In the days of Solomon silver was not worth anything* (I Kings 10:21). This is not true of Torah. If the face of the earth were covered with knowledge and every man were a Torah scholar, this would only serve to make the Torah still *more* precious to man. Thus, Torah is truly dearer *than even much fine gold* (*Ohel Yaakov*).

ה' עֹז לְעַמּוֹ יִתֵּן — *HASHEM will give might to His nation.* The word עֹז also

means *audacity, stubbornness* or *toughness*, traits which are prerequisite in maintaining faith. The Talmud (*Beitzah* 25b) says: "The Torah was given to Israel only because they are עַזִּים." The *Shulchan Aruch,* the *Code of Jewish Law,* opens with the famous statement of Rabbi Yehudah ben Teima in *Avos* 5:20: "Be always עַז כַּנָּמֵר, *bold and tough as a leopard,* to do the will of your Father in heaven" (*R' A. C. Feuer*).

וּשְׁמַע צַעֲקָתֵנוּ יוֹדֵעַ תַּעֲלוּמוֹת — *And hear our cry, Knower of mysteries.* A cry is audible; why, then, do we appeal to God as the *Knower of mysteries* to heed our cry when it is not something hidden? The *Alter of Slabodka* explained: A person's deepest and most intense feelings are often the ones he finds most difficult to express. Many of his pains and frustrations simply cannot be articulated. God, Knower of mysteries, hears even the inaudible scream pent up in man's heart. [Alternatively, God knows

לְךָ יהוה הַגְּדֻלָּה וְהַגְּבוּרָה וְהַתִּפְאֶרֶת וְהַנֵּצַח וְהַהוֹד, כִּי כֹל בַּשָּׁמַיִם וּבָאָרֶץ, לְךָ יהוה הַמַּמְלָכָה, וְהַמִּתְנַשֵּׂא לְכֹל לְרֹאשׁ.[1] וְהָיָה יהוה לְמֶלֶךְ עַל כָּל הָאָרֶץ, בַּיּוֹם הַהוּא יִהְיֶה יהוה אֶחָד וּשְׁמוֹ אֶחָד.[2] וּבְתוֹרָתְךָ, כָּתוּב לֵאמֹר: שְׁמַע יִשְׂרָאֵל, יהוה אֱלֹהֵינוּ, יהוה אֶחָד.[3] בָּרוּךְ שֵׁם כְּבוֹד מַלְכוּתוֹ לְעוֹלָם וָעֶד.

אֵין כֵּאלֹהֵינוּ,* אֵין כַּאדוֹנֵינוּ, אֵין כְּמַלְכֵּנוּ, אֵין כְּמוֹשִׁיעֵנוּ.
מִי כֵאלֹהֵינוּ, מִי כַאדוֹנֵינוּ, מִי כְמַלְכֵּנוּ, מִי כְמוֹשִׁיעֵנוּ.
נוֹדֶה לֵאלֹהֵינוּ, נוֹדֶה לַאדוֹנֵינוּ, נוֹדֶה לְמַלְכֵּנוּ, נוֹדֶה לְמוֹשִׁיעֵנוּ.
בָּרוּךְ אֱלֹהֵינוּ, בָּרוּךְ אֲדוֹנֵינוּ, בָּרוּךְ מַלְכֵּנוּ, בָּרוּךְ מוֹשִׁיעֵנוּ.
אַתָּה הוּא אֱלֹהֵינוּ, אַתָּה הוּא אֲדוֹנֵינוּ,
אַתָּה הוּא מַלְכֵּנוּ, אַתָּה הוּא מוֹשִׁיעֵנוּ.

שְׁכִינָה הַקְּדוֹשָׁה בְּתוֹכֵנוּ, זְכוּתֵהּ דְּדָוִד מַלְכָּא מְשִׁיחָא עִמָּנוּ,
וְשָׁם נִשְׂמַח כֻּלָּנוּ, בְּבוֹא לְצִיּוֹן בְּרִנָּה.
רַחֲמָנָא אִדְכַּר לָן זְכוּתֵהּ דְּדָוִד מַלְכָּא מְשִׁיחָא.

The following is recited at the daytime *hakafos* only.
In the evening, continue דָּוִד מַלְכָּא מְשִׁיחָא.

יָבוֹא אַדִּיר* בִּמְהֵרָה, יָבוֹא בָּחוּר בְּיָמֵינוּ,
יָבוֹא אֵלֶיהוּ לְבַשְּׂרֵנוּ, יָבוֹא מָשִׁיחַ צִדְקֵנוּ,
בֶּן דָּוִד גֹּאֲלֵנוּ, יוֹם גִּילָה, יוֹם רִנָּה, יוֹם דִּיצָה, יוֹם חֶדְוָה, יָבוֹא אֵלֵינוּ.
יָבוֹא גָּדוֹל בִּמְהֵרָה, יָבוֹא דָּגוּל בְּיָמֵינוּ,
יָבוֹא אֵלֶיהוּ לְבַשְּׂרֵנוּ, יָבוֹא מָשִׁיחַ צִדְקֵנוּ,
בֶּן דָּוִד גֹּאֲלֵנוּ, יוֹם גִּילָה, יוֹם רִנָּה, יוֹם דִּיצָה, יוֹם חֶדְוָה, יָבוֹא אֵלֵינוּ.
יָבוֹא הָדוּר בִּמְהֵרָה, יָבוֹא וָתִיק בְּיָמֵינוּ,
יָבוֹא אֵלֶיהוּ לְבַשְּׂרֵנוּ, יָבוֹא מָשִׁיחַ צִדְקֵנוּ,
בֶּן דָּוִד גֹּאֲלֵנוּ, יוֹם גִּילָה, יוֹם רִנָּה, יוֹם דִּיצָה, יוֹם חֶדְוָה, יָבוֹא אֵלֵינוּ.
יָבוֹא זַכַּאי בִּמְהֵרָה, יָבוֹא חָסִיד בְּיָמֵינוּ,

---

(1) *I Chronicles* 29:11. (2) *Zechariah* 14:9. (3) *Deuteronomy* 6:4.

---

why we cry even when we ourselves are unaware of the reason.]

אֵין כֵּאלֹהֵינוּ — *There is none like our God.* First we must declare unequivocally our recognition that nothing and

no one compares to God. Then we may ask the rhetorical question מִי כֵאלֹקֵינוּ, *Does anyone or anything compare to Him?* The recitation of this famous hymn is particularly appropriate at the

Yours, HASHEM, is the greatness, the strength, the splendor, the triumph, and the glory, even everything in heaven and earth; Yours, HASHEM, is the kingdom and the sovereignty over every leader.[1] HASHEM will be King over all the world — on that day HASHEM will be One and His Name will be One.[2] And in Your Torah it is written: Hear O Israel, HASHEM is our God, HASHEM, the One and Only.[3] Blessed is the Name of His glorious kingdom for all eternity.

א There is none like our God;* there is none like our Master;
    there is none like our King; there is none like our Savior.
מ Who is like our God? Who is like our Master?
    Who is like our King? Who is like our Master?
נ Let us thank our God; let us thank our Master;
    let us thank our King; let us thank our Savior
Blessed is our God; blessed is our Master;
    blessed is our King; blessed is our Savior.
It is You Who is our God; it is You Who is our Master;
    it is You Who is our King; it is You Who is our Savior.

The holy Shechinah is among us, the merit of **David** the anointed king;
    May we all rejoice there, upon arriving at Zion with glad song.
O Merciful One, remember for our sake the merit of **David** the anointed king.

The following is recited at the daytime *hakafos* only.
In the evening, continue "May David the anointed king . . ."

א May the mighty one come* speedily,
ב May the excellent one come in our days,
    May Elijah come to bring us good tidings, may our righteous Messiah come,
        The offspring of David, our redeemer; may the day of mirth,
      the day of glad song, the day of pleasure, the day of delight come to us.
ג May the great one come speedily,
ד May the supreme one come in our days,
    May Elijah come to bring us good tidings, may our righteous Messiah come,
        The offspring of David, our redeemer; may the day of mirth,
      the day of glad song, the day of pleasure, the day of delight come to us.
ה May the glorious one come speedily,
ו May the faithful one come in our days,
    May Elijah come to bring us good tidings, may our righteous Messiah come,
        The offspring of David, our redeemer; may the day of mirth,
      the day of glad song, the day of pleasure, the day of delight come to us.
ז May the worthy one come speedily
ח the devout one come in our days,

---

end of the *hakafos*, for it is a declaration of our loyalty to God and to the Torah, in which we are rejoicing.

יָבוֹא אַדִּיר — *May the mighty one come.* This is a lyrical prayer for the coming of the Messiah, whose advent will be heralded by Elijah the Prophet. The Messiah is lauded with twenty-two praises, according to the order of the *aleph-beis*. At the end, the anticipated day of his arrival is described in terms of great joy.

יָבוֹא אֵלֶיהוּ לְבַשְּׂרֵנוּ, יָבוֹא מָשִׁיחַ צִדְקֵנוּ,

בֶּן דָּוִד גְּאָלֵנוּ, יוֹם גִּילָה, יוֹם רִנָּה, יוֹם דִּיצָה, יוֹם חֶדְוָה, יָבוֹא אֵלֵינוּ.

יָבוֹא **טָהוֹר** בִּמְהֵרָה, יָבוֹא **יָשָׁר** בְּיָמֵינוּ,

יָבוֹא אֵלֶיהוּ לְבַשְּׂרֵנוּ, יָבוֹא מָשִׁיחַ צִדְקֵנוּ,

בֶּן דָּוִד גְּאָלֵנוּ, יוֹם גִּילָה, יוֹם רִנָּה, יוֹם דִּיצָה, יוֹם חֶדְוָה, יָבוֹא אֵלֵינוּ.

יָבוֹא **כַּבִּיר** בִּמְהֵרָה, יָבוֹא **לָמוּד** בְּיָמֵינוּ,

יָבוֹא אֵלֶיהוּ לְבַשְּׂרֵנוּ, יָבוֹא מָשִׁיחַ צִדְקֵנוּ,

בֶּן דָּוִד גְּאָלֵנוּ, יוֹם גִּילָה, יוֹם רִנָּה, יוֹם דִּיצָה, יוֹם חֶדְוָה, יָבוֹא אֵלֵינוּ.

יָבוֹא **מוֹשִׁיעַ** בִּמְהֵרָה, יָבוֹא **נוֹרָא** בְּיָמֵינוּ,

יָבוֹא אֵלֶיהוּ לְבַשְּׂרֵנוּ, יָבוֹא מָשִׁיחַ צִדְקֵנוּ,

בֶּן דָּוִד גְּאָלֵנוּ, יוֹם גִּילָה, יוֹם רִנָּה, יוֹם דִּיצָה, יוֹם חֶדְוָה, יָבוֹא אֵלֵינוּ.

יָבוֹא **סַגִּיב** בִּמְהֵרָה, יָבוֹא **עִזּוּז** בְּיָמֵינוּ,

יָבוֹא אֵלֶיהוּ לְבַשְּׂרֵנוּ, יָבוֹא מָשִׁיחַ צִדְקֵנוּ,

בֶּן דָּוִד גְּאָלֵנוּ, יוֹם גִּילָה, יוֹם רִנָּה, יוֹם דִּיצָה, יוֹם חֶדְוָה, יָבוֹא אֵלֵינוּ.

יָבוֹא **פּוֹדֶה** בִּמְהֵרָה, יָבוֹא **צַדִּיק** בְּיָמֵינוּ,

יָבוֹא אֵלֶיהוּ לְבַשְּׂרֵנוּ, יָבוֹא מָשִׁיחַ צִדְקֵנוּ,

בֶּן דָּוִד גְּאָלֵנוּ, יוֹם גִּילָה, יוֹם רִנָּה, יוֹם דִּיצָה, יוֹם חֶדְוָה, יָבוֹא אֵלֵינוּ.

יָבוֹא **קָדוֹשׁ** בִּמְהֵרָה, יָבוֹא **רַחוּם** בְּיָמֵינוּ,

יָבוֹא אֵלֶיהוּ לְבַשְּׂרֵנוּ, יָבוֹא מָשִׁיחַ צִדְקֵנוּ,

בֶּן דָּוִד גְּאָלֵנוּ, יוֹם גִּילָה, יוֹם רִנָּה, יוֹם דִּיצָה, יוֹם חֶדְוָה, יָבוֹא אֵלֵינוּ.

יָבוֹא **שַׁדַּי** בִּמְהֵרָה, יָבוֹא **תַּקִּיף** בְּיָמֵינוּ,

יָבוֹא אֵלֶיהוּ לְבַשְּׂרֵנוּ, יָבוֹא מָשִׁיחַ צִדְקֵנוּ,

בֶּן דָּוִד גְּאָלֵנוּ, יוֹם גִּילָה, יוֹם רִנָּה, יוֹם דִּיצָה, יוֹם חֶדְוָה, יָבוֹא אֵלֵינוּ.

יְצַוֶּה צוּר חַסְדּוֹ קְהִלּוֹתָיו לְקַבֵּץ, מֵאַרְבַּע רוּחוֹת עֲדָיו לְהִקָּבֵץ,

וּבְחַר מְרוֹם הָרִים אוֹתָנוּ לְהַרְבֵּץ, וְאִתָּנוּ יָשׁוּב נִדָּחִים קוֹבֵץ.

יָשִׁיב לֹא נֶאֱמַר, כִּי אִם וְשָׁב וְקִבֵּץ.

בָּרוּךְ הוּא אֱלֹהֵינוּ אֲשֶׁר טוֹב גְּמָלָנוּ, כְּרַחֲמָיו וּכְרֹב חֲסָדָיו הִגְדִּיל לָנוּ, אֵלֶּה וְכָאֵלֶּה יוֹסֵף עִמָּנוּ, לְהַגְדִּיל שְׁמוֹ הַגָּדוֹל הַגִּבּוֹר וְהַנּוֹרָא שֶׁנִּקְרָא עָלֵינוּ.

בָּרוּךְ הוּא אֱלֹהֵינוּ שֶׁבְּרָאָנוּ לִכְבוֹדוֹ, לְהַלְּלוֹ וּלְשַׁבְּחוֹ וּלְסַפֵּר

May Elijah come to bring us good tidings, may our righteous Messiah come,
The offspring of David, our redeemer; may the day of mirth,
the day of glad song, the day of pleasure, the day of delight come to us.

ט May the pure one come speedily

י May the just one come in our days,
May Elijah come to bring us good tidings, may our righteous Messiah come,
The offspring of David, our redeemer; may the day of mirth,
the day of glad song, the day of pleasure, the day of delight come to us.

כ May the grand one come speedily

ל May the learned one come in our days,
May Elijah come to bring us good tidings, may our righteous Messiah come,
The offspring of David, our redeemer; may the day of mirth,
the day of glad song, the day of pleasure, the day of delight come to us.

מ May the savior come speedily

נ May the awesome one come in our days,
May Elijah come to bring us good tidings, may our righteous Messiah come,
The offspring of David, our redeemer; may the day of mirth,
the day of glad song, the day of pleasure, the day of delight come to us.

ס May the strong one come speedily

ע May the all-powerful come in our days,
May Elijah come to bring us good tidings, may our righteous Messiah come,
The offspring of David, our redeemer; may the day of mirth,
the day of glad song, the day of pleasure, the day of delight come to us.

פ May the redeemer come speedily

צ May the righteous one come in our days,
May Elijah come to bring us good tidings, may our righteous Messiah come,
The offspring of David, our redeemer; may the day of mirth,
the day of glad song, the day of pleasure, the day of delight come to us.

ק May the holy one come speedily

ר May the merciful one come in our days,
May Elijah come to bring us good tidings, may our righteous Messiah come,
The offspring of David, our redeemer; may the day of mirth,
the day of glad song, the day of pleasure, the day of delight come to us.

ש May the Almighty come speedily

ת May the powerful one come in our days,
May Elijah come to bring us good tidings, may our righteous Messiah come,
The offspring of David, our redeemer; may the day of mirth,
the day of glad song, the day of pleasure, the day of delight come to us.

יְצַוֶּה May the Rock command His kindness to gather in His congregations; from
the four winds to be gathered up to Him, upon the loftiest mountain to set
us down. He shall return with us, the Gatherer of outcasts — 'He shall bring back'
is not said, but "He shall return" and gather in.

Blessed is our God Who did us good. According to His mercy and His abundant
kindness He did great things for us. Both these and those may He increase with
us — to magnify His great, mighty and awesome Name Which was proclaimed
upon us.

Blessed is our God Who created us for His glory; to praise Him, laud Him and

הוֹדוּ, מִכָּל אִם גָּבַר עָלֵינוּ חַסְדּוֹ, לָכֵן בְּכָל לֵב וּבְכָל נֶפֶשׁ וּבְכָל מְאוֹדוּ, נַמְלִיכוּ וּנְיַחֲדוּ.[1]

שֶׁהַשָּׁלוֹם שֶׁלּוֹ יָשִׂים עָלֵינוּ בְּרָכָה וְשָׁלוֹם, מִשְּׂמֹאל וּמִיָּמִין עַל יִשְׂרָאֵל שָׁלוֹם, הָרַחֲמָן הוּא יְבָרֵךְ אֶת עַמּוֹ בַשָּׁלוֹם,[2] וְיִזְכּוּ לִרְאוֹת בָּנִים וּבְנֵי בָנִים עוֹסְקִים בַּתּוֹרָה וּבְמִצְוֹת, עַל יִשְׂרָאֵל שָׁלוֹם. יוֹעֵץ אֵל גִּבּוֹר אֲבִי עַד שַׂר שָׁלוֹם.[3]

דָּוִד מַלְכָּא מְשִׁיחָא יִשְׂמַח עִמָּנוּ. —Three times

לְשָׁנָה הַבָּאָה בִּירוּשָׁלָיִם. —Three times

Some congregations recite the following *piyutim* before the Torah scrolls are returned to the Ark:

אֲשֶׁר בִּגְלַל אָבוֹת* בָּנִים גִּדֵּל, וּבַעֲבוּרָם תּוֹרָה נָתַן יהוה.
בְּגַלְגַּלֵּי רְוּחַ יהוה נִגְלָה, בְּמַלְאֲכֵי צְבָאוֹת אַלְפֵי שִׁנְאָן.[4]
גִּבּוֹר עַל גֵּאִים אֱלוֹהַּ אַדִּיר, קָרָא לְמֹשֶׁה לְקַבֵּל לוּחוֹת.
דִּבְרֵי אֵל חַי שָׁמְעָה הָאָרֶץ וְעַמּוּדֶיהָ יִתְפַּלָּצוּן.[5]
הִטָּה שָׁמַיִם וַיֵּרַד, וַיִּרְכַּב עַל כְּרוּב וַיֵּדֶא עַל כַּנְפֵי רוּחַ.[6]
וַיֵּצְאוּ דְבָרִים מִתּוֹךְ הָאֵשׁ וַיִּתְחַקְּקוּ עַל לוּחוֹת הָאָבֶן.
זְמִרוֹת אָמְרוּ כָּל בְּנֵי אֱלֹהִים, שׁוֹפָר תָּקְעוּ בִּשְׁמֵי מָרוֹם.
חֲרָדָה לָבְשׁוּ כָּל בְּנֵי שֵׂעִיר, כִּי מִשֵּׂעִיר יהוה זָרַח.[7]
טָפְחוּ כֻלָּם בְּנֵי יִשְׁמָעֵאל, כִּי מִפָּארָן יהוה הוֹפִיעַ.[7]
יְמִין יהוה טְפָחִים בַּלּוּחוֹת,* וִימִין מֹשֶׁה טְפָחִים בַּלּוּחוֹת.

אֲשֶׁר בִּגְלַל אָבוֹת — *For the sake of the forefathers.* This *piyut* is of extremely early origin (possibly from Talmudic times), and its author is unknown. In some ancient communities it was recited as an enhancement to the final blessing recited by the *Chassan Torah* after the morning Torah reading on Simchas Torah. The *piyut* draws on a variety of Midrashic depictions of the giving of the Torah at Sinai; highlighting the participation of different classes of angels (*Galgalim, Cherubim, Bnei Elohim*) and Moses' role as intermediary. The *piyut* concludes with a eulogy for Moses.

יְמִין ה' טְפָחִים בַּלּוּחוֹת — *HASHEM's right hand [grasped] two handbreadths of the Tablets.* The Midrash (*Shemos Rabbah* 28:1 et al.) states that the Tablets upon which the Ten Commandments were engraved were each six handbreadths long. God held two handbreadths at one side, and Moses held the opposite two handbreadths, with the remaining two handbreadths separating their hands.

Nezer HaKodesh explains that this Midrash alludes to three planes on which the Torah may be studied: (a) תּוֹרַת ה', *the Torah of HASHEM.* This is

relate His majesty. More than any nation He strengthened His kindness over us. Therefore with complete heart, with complete soul, and with complete resources, let us proclaim Him King and proclaim Him Unique.[1]

May He to Whom peace belongs set upon us blessing and peace — from left and from right, peace upon Israel. May the Merciful One bless His people with peace;[2] and may they merit to see children and grandchildren engaging in Torah and precepts, bringing peace upon Israel. Advisor, Mighty God, Eternal Father, Prince of Peace.[3]

Three times — **May David the anointed king rejoice with us.**

Three times — **Next year in Jerusalem.**

Some congregations recite the following *piyutim* before the Torah scrolls are returned to the Ark:

א For the sake of the forefathers,* He raised the children,
    and because of them, HASHEM gave the Torah.

ב HASHEM was revealed among the spiritual Galgalim,
    among angelic legions, thousands of alacritous ones.[4]

ג Stronger than the haughty, the mighty God,
    called unto Moses, to accept the Tablets.

ד The earth heard the words of the Living God,
    and its pillars trembled.[5]

ה He bent down heavens and descended, He rode on a Cherub,
    He soared on the wings of the wind.[6]

ו Words went forth from the middle of the fire,
    and were engraved upon the stone Tablets.

ז All the Benai Elohim [i.e., angels] recited zemiros,
    they sounded the shofar from the highest heaven.

ח Trembling cloaked all the children of Seir [Esau],
    for HASHEM had shone forth from Seir.[7]

ט All the children of Ishmael clapped hands [in fright],
    for HASHEM had appeared from [Mount] Paran.[7]

י HASHEM's right hand [grasped] two handbreadths of the Tablets,*
    Moses' right hand [grasped] two handbreadths of the Tablets.

---

(1) Cf. *Deuteronomy* 6:4-5. (2) *Psalms* 29:11. (3) *Isaiah* 9:5. (4) Cf. *Psalms* 68:13 (see Tractate *Shabbos* 88b); 68:18. (5) *Job* 9:6. (6) Cf. *Psalms* 18:10-11; *II Samuel* 22:10-11. (7) Cf. *Deuteronomy* 33:2.

---

the highest level of Torah knowledge, a level to which no man has access; God, so to speak, "holds on" to this segment of the Torah and does not release it. (b) תּוֹרַת הָאָדָם, *the Torah of man*. This is the revealed Torah, which may be understood superficially, without much effort; this section is given over to all men, represented here by Moses. (c) The final portion of the Torah is that which is not readily comprehended but may be attained through diligent effort and dedication. This part lies between the other two; God neither "gave" it to Moses nor prevented him from attaining it.

כִּי אֹרֶךְ הַלּוּחוֹת שִׁשָּׁה טְפָחִים, וּטְפָחַיִם מִפְרָשׁ בֵּין יָד לְיָד.

לֵךְ מֹשֶׁה וּשְׂמַח בִּגְדֻלָּתֶךָ, כִּי אֵין כָּמוֹךָ בְּכָל הַנְּבִיאִים.[1]

מִי עָלָה שָׁמַיִם לְתוֹךְ הֶעָנָן,[2] וּמִי רָאָה תְּמוּנַת אֱלֹהֵינוּ.[3]

מֹשֶׁה עָלָה לְתוֹךְ הֶעָנָן, גַּם הוּא רָאָה תְּמוּנַת אֱלֹהֵינוּ.

נְשִׂיא נְשִׂיאִים הָיָה מֹשֶׁה רַבֵּנוּ, אָב לַחֲכָמִים וְרֹאשׁ לַנְּבִיאִים.

סָגַר הַיָּם בִּתְפִלָּתוֹ, וְעַל יַד שְׁלוּחוֹ חֲרוֹן אַף הֵשִׁיב.[4]

עָנָה יְהוָה וְאָמַר לְעַמּוֹ, אָנֹכִי יְהוָה אֱלֹהֶיךָ אֲשֶׁר הוֹצֵאתִיךָ מֵאֶרֶץ
מִצְרַיִם, וּפְדִיתִיךָ מִבֵּית עֲבָדִים.[5]

פָּתְחוּ כֻלָּם פִּיהֶם וְאָמְרוּ, יְהוָה יִמְלֹךְ לְעוֹלָם וָעֶד.[6]

צָעַק מֹשֶׁה צְעָקָה גְדוֹלָה וּמָרָה, בְּשָׁעָה שֶׁאָמַר לוֹ הַקָּדוֹשׁ בָּרוּךְ הוּא,
עֲלֵה וּמֵת בָּהָר.[7]

קָרַע בְּגָדָיו וְהֵרִים קוֹלוֹ, יְהוֹשֻׁעַ בֶּן נוּן, שְׁמָר נָא צֹאנִי.

רָאָה מֹשֶׁה מֵרֹאשׁ הַפִּסְגָּה, נַחֲלַת שְׁבָטִים[8] עוֹמְדִים לְפָנָיו.

שָׁם מֵת מֹשֶׁה עֶבֶד יְהוָה,[9] מוּל בֵּית פְּעוֹר[10] אָסְפוֹ אֱלֹהֵינוּ.

תְּפִלַּת מֹשֶׁה קָרַע רָקִיעַ, וְעָנָה צוּר לְעַמּוֹ בְּעֵת צָרוֹתָם.

תְּפִלָּתוֹ לְעוֹלָם לֹא שָׁבָה רֵיקָם, כִּי רוֹעֶה נֶאֱמָן הָיָה מֹשֶׁה
לְיִשְׂרָאֵל.   מֹשֶׁה מֵת מִי לֹא יָמוּת. עַל פִּי יְהוָה מֵת מֹשֶׁה רַבֵּנוּ.[11]

שִׂישׂוּ וְשִׂמְחוּ*[12] בְּשִׂמְחַת תּוֹרָה, וּתְנוּ כָבוֹד לַתּוֹרָה,
כִּי טוֹב סַחְרָהּ מִכָּל סְחוֹרָה,[13] מִפָּז וּמִפְּנִינִים יְקָרָה.[14]
נָגִיל וְנָשִׂישׂ בְּזֹאת הַתּוֹרָה, כִּי הִיא לָנוּ עֹז וְאוֹרָה.*

אֲהַלְלָה אֱלֹהַי וְאֶשְׂמְּחָה בוֹ, וְאָשִׂימָה תִקְוָתִי בוֹ,
אֲהוֹדֶנּוּ בְּסוֹד עַם קְרוֹבוֹ, אֱלֹהֵי צוּרִי אֶחֱסֶה בוֹ.[15]

שִׂישׂוּ וְשִׂמְחוּ — *Rejoice and be glad.* This *piyut* and those that follow were obviously written especially for Simchas Torah. Each is of unknown authorship and is apparently a fragment of a longer piece. For example, שִׂישׂוּ וְשִׂמְחוּ follows the *aleph-beis* until ה and then stops abruptly; אַשְׁרֵיכֶם, *You are praiseworthy,* is the refrain of an eleven-stanza *piyut* that appears in some *machzorim.*

כִּי הוּא לָנוּ עֹז וְאוֹרָה — *For to us it is strength and light.* A person's evil inclination employs two types of tactics to

entrap him. Sometimes, it proffers sin and does not seek to disguise it as anything less, in an attempt to overpower the person emotionally. In other instances, the Evil Inclination wraps itself in a cloak of righteousness, presenting the behavior he suggests as a *mitzvah.* The Talmud alludes to these two postures in describing the angel of Esau who fought with Jacob: "He appeared like a Torah scholar or like a thief" (see *Chullin* 91a).

The Talmud teaches that Torah is an antidote to evil, providing us with the

כ For the Tablets' length was six handbreadths,
two handbreadths separated [God's] hand from [Moses'] hand.
ל Go, O Moses, and rejoice in your greatness,
for there is none like you among the prophets.[1]
מ Who ascended the heaven into the cloud;[2]
and who perceived the image of our God?[3]
מ Moses ascended into the cloud,
and also perceived the image of our God.
נ Prince of princes was our teacher Moses,
father to the wise men, head of the prophets.
ס He [God] sealed the Sea [of Reeds] with his [Moses'] prayer,
and through His emissary [Moses] He turned aside [His] fiery wrath.[4]
ע HASHEM proclaimed and said to His people,
"I am HASHEM, your God, who delivered you from the land of Egypt;
and I redeemed you from the house of slavery."[5]
פ They all opened their mouths and said,
"HASHEM shall reign for all eternity!"[6]
צ Moses let out a great and bitter cry,
when the Holy One, Blessed is He, told him,
"Ascend ... and die upon the mountain."[7]
ק He rent his garments and called aloud,
"Joshua son of Nun, guard my flock!"
ר Moses saw from the summit of the cliff,
the heritage of the tribes[8] standing before him.
ש There Moses, servant of HASHEM died,[9]
opposite Beth Peor[10] our God gathered him in.
ת Moses' prayer rent the heavens,
[in its merit] the Rock answers His people in time of their distress.
His prayer would never return empty-handed,
for Moses was a faithful shepherd unto Israel.
If Moses died, who shall not die?
Our teacher Moses died by the mouth of HASHEM.[11]

שִׂישׂוּ Rejoice and be glad[12]* on Simchas Torah, and pay homage to the Torah
for it is better than any commerce,[13]
more precious than finest gold and gems.[14]
Let us exult and rejoice with this Torah, for to us it is strength and light.*
א I shall laud my God and be glad with Him, and place my hope in Him.
I shall praise Him in the counsel of His intimate people —
God, my Rock — I take refuge in Him.[15]

---

(1) Cf. *Deuteronomy* 34:10. (2) Cf. *Exodus* 24:15,18. (3) Cf. *Numbers* 12:8. (4) Cf. *Psalms* 106:23.
(5) Cf. *Exodus* 20:2; *Deuteronomy* 5:6. (6) *Exodus* 15:18. (7) *Deuteronomy* 32:49-50. (8) Cf. *34:1-2.*
(9) Cf. *34:5.* (10) *34:6.* (11) *34:5.* (12) Cf. *Psalms* 40:17; 70:5. (13) Cf. *Proverbs* 3:14. (14) Cf. *3:15.* (15) Cf. *II Samuel*
22:3; *Psalms* 18:3.

---

strength (עֹז) to fight off the blandish-
ment of lust and passion. In its aspect of
light (אוֹרָה), Torah opens our eyes to help
us see through the facade of our "Torah
scholar-friend," who seeks to entrap our
souls (R' Tzadok HaKohen).

נָגִיל וְנָשִׂישׂ בְּזֹאת הַתּוֹרָה, כִּי הִיא לָנוּ עֹז וְאוֹרָה.

בְּכָל לֵב אֲרַנֵּן צִדְקוֹתֶיךָ, וַאֲסַפְּרָה תְּהִלָּתֶךָ,
בְּעוֹדִי אַגִּיד נִפְלְאוֹתֶיךָ, עַל חַסְדְּךָ וְעַל אֲמִתֶּךָ.[1]

נָגִיל וְנָשִׂישׂ בְּזֹאת הַתּוֹרָה, כִּי הִיא לָנוּ עֹז וְאוֹרָה.

גּוֹאֵל תָּחִישׁ מְבַשֵּׂר טוֹב,[2] כִּי אַתָּה מִגְדַּל עֹז וְטוֹב,
גְּאוּלִים יוֹדְוּךָ בְּלֵב טוֹב, הוֹדוּ לַיהוה כִּי טוֹב.[3]

נָגִיל וְנָשִׂישׂ בְּזֹאת הַתּוֹרָה, כִּי הִיא לָנוּ עֹז וְאוֹרָה.

דָּגוּל גְּאַל נָא הֲמוֹנִי, כִּי אֵין קָדוֹשׁ כַּיהוה.[4]
דְּגוּלִים יוֹדוּךָ יהוה, מִי יְמַלֵּל גְּבוּרוֹת יהוה.[5]

נָגִיל וְנָשִׂישׂ בְּזֹאת הַתּוֹרָה, כִּי הִיא לָנוּ עֹז וְאוֹרָה.

הֲלֹא בְּאַהֲבָתוֹ בָּחַר בָּנוּ, בְּנֵי בְכוֹרִי[6] קְרָאָנוּ,
הוֹד וְהָדָר הִנְחִילָנוּ, כִּי לְעוֹלָם חַסְדּוֹ[7] עִמָּנוּ.

נָגִיל וְנָשִׂישׂ בְּזֹאת הַתּוֹרָה, כִּי הִיא לָנוּ עֹז וְאוֹרָה.

אַשְׁרֵיכֶם יִשְׂרָאֵל, אַשְׁרֵיכֶם יִשְׂרָאֵל, אַשְׁרֵיכֶם יִשְׂרָאֵל, אֲשֶׁר בָּחַר בָּכֶם אֵל, וְהִנְחִילְכֶם הַתּוֹרָה מִמִּדְבָּר מַתָּנָה.

הִתְקַבְּצוּ מַלְאָכִים* זֶה אֶל זֶה, זֶה לְקַבֵּל זֶה, וְאָמַר זֶה לָזֶה, מִי הוּא זֶה וְאֵי זֶה הוּא מְאַחֵז פְּנֵי כִסֵּא, פַּרְשֵׁז עָלָיו עֲנָנוֹ, מִי עָלָה לַמָּרוֹם, מִי עָלָה לַמָּרוֹם, וְהוֹרִיד עֹז מִבְטָחָהּ. מֹשֶׁה עָלָה לַמָּרוֹם, מֹשֶׁה עָלָה לַמָּרוֹם, מֹשֶׁה עָלָה לַמָּרוֹם, נְתַנְאֵל,* שְׁמַעְיָה, אֲבִי סוֹכוֹ, אֲבִי זָנוֹחַ, חֶבֶר, יְקוּתִיאֵל, טוֹבִיָּה, יֶרֶד, אֲבִיגְדוֹר, עָלָה לַמָּרוֹם, וְהוֹרִיד עֹז מִבְטָחָהּ.

אָגִיל וְאֶשְׂמַח[8] בְּשִׂמְחַת תּוֹרָה, בֹּא יָבֹא צֶמַח בְּשִׂמְחַת תּוֹרָה.

הִתְקַבְּצוּ מַלְאָכִים — *The angels scattered.* This *piyut* is based on the Talmudic narration of Moses' confrontation with the angels. When Moses ascended on high, the ministering angels said to the Holy One, Blessed is He, "Master of the Universe, what has one born of woman to do among us?"

He told them, "He has come to receive the Torah."

They said before Him, "The hidden treasure that You have kept concealed for 974 generations before the world was created, You wish to give to flesh and blood?"

The Talmud relates that God told Moses to respond but that he was afraid to do so until God promised to protect him by having him *hold on to the face of the Throne and spreading His cloud over him (Job 26:9).* Thereupon, Moses declared that the Torah could only be intended for man: Does the Torah not speak of God Who took you out of Egyptian slavery — were the angels ever enslaved? Do the angels require rest on

Let us exult and rejoice with this Torah, for to us it is strength and light.

ב Wholeheartedly I shall exalt Your righteousness
and I shall relate Your praise.
While I live I will relate Your wonders, tell of Your kindness and Your truth.[1]

Let us exult and rejoice with this Torah, for to us it is strength and light.

ג Redeemer, hasten the herald of good tidings,[2]
for You are a tower of strength and goodness.
The redeemed ones shall thank You in good heart:
"Give thanks to HASHEM, for He is good!"[3]

Let us exult and rejoice with this Torah, for to us it is strength and light.

ד O Bannered One, redeem now my multitude, for none is as holy as HASHEM.[4]
The bannered [tribes of Israel] shall thank You,
HASHEM. Who can express the mighty acts of HASHEM?[5]

Let us exult and rejoice with this Torah, for to us it is strength and light.

ה Has He not chosen us in His love? "My son! My firstborn!"[6] has He called us.
Majesty and splendor has He bequeathed us,
for His kindness is forever[7] with us.

אַשְׁרֵיכֶם You are praiseworthy, Israel. You are praiseworthy, Israel.
You are praiseworthy, Israel,
for God has chosen you and bequeathed you the Torah — from Sinai a gift.

הִתְקַבְּצוּ The angels gathered* to one another, opposite one another, and said
to one another, "Who is the one, which is the one, who is holding onto
the face of the throne? Upon whom He has spread His cloud?"
Who has ascended on high? Who has ascended on high?
Who has ascended on high and taken down the powerful [Torah]
from its secure spot [in heaven]?

Moses has ascended on high. Moses has ascended on high.
Nesanel,* Shemayah, Avi Socho, Avi Zanoach, Chever, Yekusiel, Toviah, Yered,
Avigdor have ascended on high and taken down the powerful [Torah] from its
secure spot [in heaven].

אָגִיל I shall rejoice and be glad[8] on Simchas Torah; may Tzemach [Messiah]

---

(1) Cf. *Psalms* 115:1. (2) Cf. *Isaiah* 52:7. (3) *Psalms* 136:1 et al. (4) *I Samuel* 2:2.
(5) *Psalms* 106:2. (6) *Exodus* 4:22. (7) *Psalms* 136:1 et al. (8) Cf. 31:8.

---

the Sabbath? Do the angels have parents whom they should honor? Do they feel jealousy that impels them to kill or lust that impels them to be immoral? Hearing this, the angels admitted that Moses was right and befriended him (see *Shabbos* 88b).

נְתַנְאֵל — *Nesanel.* Based upon the Talmudic (*Megillah* 13a) and Midrashic (*Vayikra Rabbah* 1:3) interpretations of *II Chronicles* 4:18 and 24:6, Moses was known by a total of ten names. In some congregations, the verse relating Moses' ascent is recited ten times, each time using a different name. In most congregations, however, the *piyut* is abridged, with the nine added names mentioned all together.

תּוֹרָה הִיא עֵץ חַיִּים' לְכֹלָם חַיִּים, כִּי עִמְּךָ מְקוֹר חַיִּים.² אַבְרָהָם שָׂמַח* בְּשִׂמְחַת תּוֹרָה. יִצְחָק שָׂמַח בְּשִׂמְחַת תּוֹרָה. יַעֲקֹב שָׂמַח בְּשִׂמְחַת תּוֹרָה. מֹשֶׁה וְאַהֲרֹן שָׂמְחוּ בְּשִׂמְחַת תּוֹרָה. אֵלִיָּהוּ שְׁמוּאֵל דָּוִד שְׁלֹמֹה שָׂמְחוּ בְּשִׂמְחַת תּוֹרָה. תּוֹרָה הִיא עֵץ חַיִּים, לְכֹלָם חַיִּים, כִּי עִמְּךָ מְקוֹר חַיִּים.

אַבְרָהָם שָׂמַח — *Abraham rejoiced.* This is based on the generally accepted prin-

ciple that the Patriarchs observed the Scripturally ordained *mitzvos,* the Rab-

come on Simchas Torah. The Torah is a tree of life,[1] for all of them life, for with You is the source of life.[2] Abraham rejoiced* on Simchas Torah. Isaac rejoiced on Simchas Torah. Jacob rejoiced on Simchas Torah. Moses and Aaron rejoiced on Simchas Torah. Elijah, Samuel, David and Solomon rejoiced on Simchas Torah. The Torah is a tree of life, for all of them life, for with You is the source of life.

---

(1) Cf. *Proverbs* 3:18. (2) *Psalms* 36:10.

---

binical decrees and even the customs that would later arise among their off-spring. [See, for example, the last Mishnah in *Kiddushin* 82a.]

[213] **SIMCHAS TORAH** — Its Significance, Laws, and Prayers

This volume is part of
THE ARTSCROLL SERIES®
an ongoing project of
translations, commentaries and expositions
on Scripture, Mishnah, Talmud, Halachah,
liturgy, history and the classic Rabbinic writings;
and biographies, and thought.

For a brochure of current publications
visit your local Hebrew bookseller
or contact the publisher:

Mesorah Publications, ltd

4401 Second Avenue
Brooklyn, New York 11232
(718) 921-9000